Introducing
Social Policy

Introducing Social Policy

Edited by

David C.Marsh
Professor of Applied Social Science
University of Nottingham

Routledge & Kegan Paul
London, Boston and Henley

First published in 1979
by Routledge & Kegan Paul Ltd
39 Store Street, London WC1E 7DD,
Broadway House, Newtown Road,
Henley-on-Thames, Oxon RG9 1EN and
9 Park Street, Boston, Mass. 02108, USA

Phototypeset in 10 on 12 pt. V.I.P. Times by
Western Printing Services Ltd, Bristol
and printed in Great Britain by
Whitstable Litho Ltd, Whitstable, Kent

British Library Cataloguing in Publication Data

Introducing social policy

  1. England — Social policy
  I. Marsh, David Charles
  300'.942   HN390   78—41249

  ISBN 0 7100 0132 0
  ISBN 0 7100 0133 9 Pbk

Contents

Preface   vii

1   Social Policy and Administration: The Field of Study
    Joan L.M. Eyden and David C. Marsh   1

**I   Social Policy and the Economic and
Social Environment**   25

2   Social Policy in Relation to Industry
    Mary F. Robertson   27

3   Urban Planning and Social Policy
    Meryl Aldridge   60

4   Social Policy and Housing Need
    John S. Ferris   89

**II   Policies and Services Designed to Meet
Basic Individual Needs**   113

5   Education
    Roger E. Cox   115

6   Health
    Gillian Pascall   141

7   'Social Security'
    Stewart MacPherson   165

III   Policies Designed to Deal with Social Problems   189

8   The Personal Social Services
    Joan L.M. Eyden   191

9   Social Policy in Relation to Crime
      Philip T. Bean   223
10 An Overview – Retrospect and Glimpse of the Future
      David C. Marsh   257

      Further Reading   263
      Bibliography   269
      Index   281

Preface

In the early 1960s some of my colleagues and I, who had been teaching social administration as a discipline of study for some years, were concerned at the way in which the subject was developing so rapidly, without a corresponding increase in the literature relating to it. There were of course large numbers of articles, official publications, some (though very few) research reports, and books which were mainly of historical interest. The first real textbook on the subject was *The Social Services of Modern England* written by M. Penelope Hall and published in 1952. It was an instant success and was in such demand that many revised editions were printed in succeeding years. But, excellent as Miss Hall's book was, there was still no satisfactory introductory textbook providing an outline of the subject matter of the discipline of social administration.

It was to fill this gap that we decided to write *An introduction to the study of Social Administration*, which I edited and to which my colleagues Joan Eyden, Richard Silburn and Arthur Willcocks contributed. Our aim was first to describe

> briefly the nature and scope of that study so that a potential student may see what is involved before embarking on such a course, and, secondly, for the student who has begun to study the subject a book which will act as a guide showing the framework of the discipline and point the way to specialized studies.

Whether we succeeded in achieving those modest aims is for others to judge, but one real difficulty for anyone writing in this field is the rate of change in social legislation, in methods of organization and administration, and in the discovery or rediscovery of social problems. Hence substantial parts of our book, which was published in 1965, are by now of historical interest.

The 'knowledge explosion' of recent years has of course affected all disciplines of study, and in our particular field there are by now very many publications on social policy and administration as is shown in the references and suggestions for further reading at the end of each of the chapters in this book. Because of the considerable growth in knowledge, we have therefore adopted a different approach from that of 1965. We do not now attempt, even briefly, to elaborate on the historical background, but concentrate essentially on the major developments which have occurred in the past few years. We have not of course completely eliminated an historical approach because all too often, in trying to unravel the complex nature of social policy, an understanding of the past is essential to an understanding of the present and may even be a guide to the future.

Apart from the considerable increase in the output of academic writers, there has been an explosion in the number and variety of official publications. These include the reports of committees of inquiry, research sponsored by government departments or research councils, annual and occasional reports of government departments, and far more statistical information relating to social policy than was available even ten years ago. In our previous book I complained that 'all too often in the past social policies have been formulated, social services created and methods of administration devised without any clear expression of aims or tests of their effectiveness' and the hope was expressed that 'as the study of social administration becomes more refined and mature that its students will contribute through research to more systematic analyses of the aims, purposes, methods and effectiveness of social policy and social action, which in a Welfare State affects us all as citizens'. There is no doubt that far more research has been carried out since 1965 than was contemplated in the past, and that far more of our contemporary social policies are based on knowledge rather than on ignorance, or hunch. This is not to say that we have now reached the stage where all policies are based on knowledge and sound judgment or that we can relax our search for the facts on which to base them.

Social conditions and human needs are continually changing, probably more rapidly than ever before in a society like ours, and therefore the response to those changes as expressed through social policy must be dynamic. It may well be that the rate of change in the future will be less rapid than it has been since the 1950s so that, for example, the system of social security, established under the Social Security Act, 1975, will remain in force relatively unchanged for many more years than the system introduced in the late 1940s, which has been subjected to an enormous number of modifications in its thirty years of existence. How far all the other major services described by my colleagues in this book will have been transformed by the end of the century is anybody's guess and it would be unwise to speculate.

Ideally the study of social policy and its implementation in Britain (and that means basically England and Wales because Scotland differs in some respects in its methods of provision of some social services) should be accompanied by the study of the principles, policies and practices in other countries. There is now a rapidly growing body of literature available for the study of comparative social administration, but regretfully we cannot be concerned with this wider field in an introductory text.

To my colleagues who have given of their time in contributing to this book my thanks are willingly given, but as editor I accept responsibility for any errors or omissions in the book as a whole.

David C. Marsh

1

Social Policy and Administration: The Field of Study

Joan L. M. Eyden and David C. Marsh

In recent years there has been a remarkable growth in the number of organizations designed to encourage the study of social policy and its implementation. For example, in 1967 the Centre for Environmental Studies was established with funds provided by the government and the Ford Foundation as an independent body for the furtherance and dissemination of research into problems and processes of urban, regional and national planning. (Environmental Studies, Centre for, 1976). In the first ten years of its activities it organized conferences and seminars, sponsored research at the CES and other institutions in Britain and elsewhere and by now has published a very large number of reports (see the list in the Annual Reports). Then in 1970 the Centre for Studies in Social Policy was formed as a result of a generous benefaction by the Joseph Rowntree Memorial Trust and it has become 'one of the main independent and non-partisan policy studies institutions in the U.K., specialising as a resource and forum for realistic analysis and discussion of the social factors relevant to public policy of all kinds' (Social Policy, Centre for Studies in, 1977). In seven years its members of staff and associates had published more than 180 papers on a wide variety of topics ranging from social policy in general to specific topics such as race relations, health care, housing, education, social security, employment and industrial relations, the personal social services and a particularly important study on demographic change and social policy (CES, 1976). These two independent bodies reflect the growing interest since the end of the Second World War in the development and evaluation of social policy in what we have become accustomed to call 'the welfare state'. But the recognition of the need for social policies to deal with the myriad variety of individual and social problems in a complex industrialized society such as ours goes back much further either than the last war or this century.

For many centuries past the State has attempted, often in a muddled manner, to provide help to the poor, and the history of the Poor Laws from the sixteenth century onwards (which has been well documented) exemplifies the base from which our complex modern system of social policy and administration has been developed. But poverty was not the only social problem for which solutions or, at the very least, palliatives had to be found through action by the State and/or voluntary organizations. Poverty was of course a major problem but many social reformers, especially in the nineteenth century, exposed a variety of other evils which called for action. The appalling living conditions under which a large proportion of the rapidly increasing population in the first half of the nineteenth century existed, especially in the towns, where bad housing, overcrowding, insanitary conditions, the lack of decent water supplies and the like required urgent reform. Inhuman working conditions for men, women and children abounded in coal mines, factories and other forms of employment which accompanied the growing industrialization of the early nineteenth century and were later alleviated by the collective action of workers and the State or of idealistic employers such as Robert Owen. The illiteracy of the great majority of the population, for formal education was restricted to the few and not available to the many, and the scourge of diseases of many kinds, which killed children and adults alike at a very high rate, were gradually recognized and in due course attempts were made to conquer them and many other forms of 'social evils' through legislation and voluntary action.

By the latter part of the nineteenth century, attempts – sometimes only tentative – had been made to deal with many of the basic problems: lack of education; environmental hygiene; disease; conditions of employment; and, to a limited extent, poverty. But despite the progress made in what Maurice Bruce has called *The Coming of the Welfare State* (Bruce, 1961) even at the end of that century there were still many serious problems to be conquered.

The social surveys of Booth and Rowntree in London and York had revealed that even in the then richest country in the world poverty existed on a massive scale (Booth, 1892; Rowntree, 1901), and it was probably revelations of this kind that led to the development of the study of social policy and administration in the universities.

> For example, in 1901 the London School of Sociology and Economics was established after experimental courses for voluntary social workers had been provided in the previous four years by a joint committee of representatives of the Women's University Settlement, the Charity Organisation Society and the National Union of Women Workers, and in 1912 this school became the Social Science Department of the London School of Economics and Political Science which had been founded essentially by Sidney and Beatrice Webb (Marsh, 1965).[1]

In the first decades of the twentieth century there was almost a revolution in the attack made on the problems of poverty caused by old age, ill-health and unemployment, in the provision of medical services, in housing, conditions of employment and to a lesser extent in the provision of educational facilities, which was brought about by a spate of legislation which made the whole field of social policy more complex than it had ever been in the past.[2] But during and especially after the Second World War, the complexity of earlier years seemed to pale into insignificance compared with the mass of legislation and the creation of new policies and methods of administration which came into being after 1944. Succeeding chapters in this book deal with the major developments which have occurred, especially in the years from 1944 to 1974 when probably more legislation relating to social policy and its implementation was placed on the statute books of this country than in the whole of the previous two thousand years of our history. It is therefore not surprising that the study of social administration should become even more necessary than it was in the past, and that in recent years determined efforts should have been made by a number of academic writers to define its subject matter.[3]

Even now there is probably no definition of the term 'social administration' which would be universally agreed upon by all those concerned with studying it in this country, and certainly there would be varied interpretations in other countries. But one suspects that a majority view would regard the field of social administration as being concerned with the human problems which arise in developed societies and the ways in which they are tackled through the provision of, for example, social services provided by voluntary and statutory organizations.

In the same way it is doubtful if the term 'social policy' can be defined in a universally acceptable phrase, and indeed one leading writer on the subject has stated, 'Social Policy is not a technical term with an exact meaning' (Marshall, 1965). On the other hand as early as 1950, R. M. Titmuss called his official history of the social services during the war, *Problems of Social Policy*, and in his later writings he expands and elaborates on his views of social policy (Titmuss, 1950, 1968, 1974). Numerous other writers have given their views on social policy, for example François Lafitte (1962), who argued that in

> our kind of society social policy is not essentially interested in economic relations, but is very much concerned with the extent to which economic relations and aspirations should be allowed to dominate other aspects of life; more specifically that social policy addresses itself to a whole range of needs – material, cultural, emotional – outside the wide realm of satisfactions which can conveniently be left to the market. There is attraction too in Professor Myrdal's description of 'social policy in its broadest sense' simply as a convenient way of referring to 'the continuous growth in the volume of public, quasi-public and private interventions in social life' – interventions which are no longer sporadic but more and more take the form of continuing activity, steered to influence and control a social process in a certain direction

In more recent years many younger academics have pursued the study of social policy and administration in great detail,[4] and no doubt the debate will continue as to the nature of this field of study. But one fact would be agreed by all and that is that social policies cannot be static because they must respond to changing human and social needs and be influenced by the ideologies of political and other pressure groups in democratic societies.

Social Administration and Ideology

Just as social administration as an academic study has its roots in many different branches of learning – economic, philosophical, political, legal – so social policy and its implementation have been affected by many factors and the social services have been shaped by diverse influences and in their turn have widespread effect. There is considerable disagreement among scholars as to the determinants of social policy and to the relative importance of the various factors which have led to the emergence of the modern complex of collective provision and the concept of the welfare state. In this introduction to the study of social administration, it is possible to comment only on some of the major differences of definition, interpretation and opinion. A particular difficulty is to estimate the importance of basic ideologies to the actual shaping of social policy decisions as well as to the stance of academic commentators. Some of the difficulty lies in the recognizing and making explicit of the values and aims which are implicit in many social policy decisions. Indeed many of those who are engaged practically in making and implementing policy pride themselves on their pragmatism. Thus the Conservative Party has, until recently, regarded their pragmatism and lack of ideology as a major asset at the polls. It was not until 1974 that the Conservative Centre for Policy Studies was created to provide 'a corrective to the collectivist and dirigiste ideas which have dominated British political and economic thought during the twentieth century and to the constant drift leftwards of the "middle ground" of political and public opinion' (Bradley, 1978). This commentator concludes 'The Centre has not yet managed to wean the British electorate from its deep distrust of all ideology. Until it does so, a Conservative Party with an intellectual face is unlikely to be much of a vote catcher.' This widespread pragmatism may be one important factor in explaining the anomalies and inconsistencies with which one is confronted in any examination of social policy in Britain.

Nevertheless, there are persistent attempts among writers on social policy to relate these anomalies and inconsistencies to underlying beliefs, and implicit as well as explicit assumptions and attitudes, attempts which have been given a new urgency by the growing disillusion with the realities of our so-called welfare state. George and Wilding (1976) suggest that it is possible to distinguish four groups of writers on social policy according to their basic political beliefs and values. They list these as the anticollectivists, the reluctance collectivists, the Fabian socialists and the Marxists.

Most of those whose views they examine have been in a position to influence the formation of social and economic policy and not merely to write about it. W. H. Beveridge, J. M. Keynes and C. A. R. Crosland, for instance, directly contributed to shaping the government policies of the past three decades, and others have had considerable if more indirect influence. The discussion of the connection between social, economic and political values and social welfare policies is of course not new. It is the basic theme of much of the writing, for instance, of R. H. Tawney (Tawney, 1921, 1926). G. D. H. Cole (Bourdillon, 1945), writing of the attitudes of social reformers and philanthropists, suggested that

> the problem of poverty . . . has presented itself to a sequence of generations animated by widely different social philosophies. . . . It has made, for example, a vast difference whether the philanthropists have believed that there were too many people or too few; whether they have been readier to attribute the sufferings of the poor to vice, or to misfortune; whether they have been in the main 'other worldly' or 'this worldly' in their attitude to the problems of mankind; and whether they have, or have not believed in the 'invisible hand' or in the sovereign virtues of an economic system of laissez-faire.

Similarly, the view one takes of the social policies of the last thirty years depends to a considerable degree on one's view of the role of the State, of the virtues of the capitalist system or of a 'mixed economy', of the importance of social justice or the interpretation of and emphasis one puts upon such concepts as equality, liberty and fraternity. Is expenditure on collectively provided services a burden – an impediment to growth and economic development, the 'Public Burden Model of Welfare' (Titmuss, 1968)? Are the social services an essential and integral part of modern industrial societies concerned with the insecurities and diswelfares that social and economic progress brings (Titmuss, 1968)? Is the welfare state a milestone on the road to the transformation of capitalism into a socialist state (Crosland, 1956, 1974)? Does it belong more to a democracy than to socialism and do we now have a democratic-welfare-capitalist society which may modify the most blatant disservices of an aggressive capitalist society but leaves its essential values unaltered (Marshall 1965, 1972)? Is the welfare state the twentieth-century version of the Victorian ideal of self-help (Saville, 1958) or 'the opiate of the people'? Has the thrust of welfare policy been 'hopelessly weakened because of the absence of a set of values which support and legitimate welfare policy'? Have 'social policies been grafted on to an economic system intrinsically hostile to the welfare ethic' (George and Wilding, 1976)?

Questions such as these must inevitably concern any serious student of social administration. They are important not only in considering the making of social policy but in its implementation. The beliefs, attitudes and assumptions of those responsible for administering the social services will affect the way in which they are provided and the feelings of the recipients, and will largely determine whether or not the stated aims of policy are in fact achieved. In this introduction to the study of social administration, it is possible to describe and analyse only briefly the main areas of social policy and to comment on some of the major differences of definition, interpretation and opinion.

The Development of Social Policy

The scope of modern social services is very wide and many of them are used extensively by most citizens. However, the problem of poverty has been traditionally the basic social problem with which the social services were originally concerned to meet, for 'the condition of having little or no wealth or material possessions; of indigence, destitution, want' (Shorter OED) entails that none of one's material needs are adequately met and probably few non-material ones either.

The social aspects of poverty were perhaps first emphasized in the sixteenth century. The transition from an age of status to one of contract was gathering pace. The agricultural, commercial, social and religious changes all tended to greater insecurity for the many and to unemployment and destitution for a growing few, and unemployment and destitution were a political threat to which successive Tudor statesmen as well as their modern counterparts were increasingly sensitive. Thus it was in the sixteenth century that poverty was first systematically attacked. As a national economy superseded town and local economies, the central government began to interfere more effectively in economic matters. The Statute of Artificers (1563), by the enforcement of apprenticeship and wage-fixing, was primarily an economic measure to reduce unemployment and thus a potential threat to political stability, but it had important social and educational aims as well. At the same time the central government found itself compelled to take step after step to provide for the destitute not only or mainly by traditional repressive measures against the vagrant and beggar, but by trying to develop a comprehensive system of relief. The 1531 Act, Concerning Punishment of Beggars and Vagabonds, attempted to distinguish between the deserving and undeserving poor and gave JPs the power of granting licences to beg to 'all aged poor and impotent persons'. This may seem little enough in comparison with our modern idea of a welfare state, but for the first time there was statutory recognition that some people were unable to support themselves and that, in the absence of relatives able to care, society might have a responsibility for their support.

A series of Acts made each parish responsible for its own destitute (1536); introduced a compulsory poor rate (1572); authorized JPs to put the genuinely unemployed to work on materials supplied at the expense of the parish, and to erect bridlewells or houses of correction for the 'idle rogue or vagabond' (1576); and defined those relatives who could be legally made to support a destitute person if they were able. These provisions were re-enacted with some amendments in the famous Act, For the Relief of the Poor (1601). This is famous because it firmly established a nationwide system of relief for the destitute, children, the disabled and infirm, the unemployed and the work-shy, based on the parish as the responsible unit of administration. It is famous also because it remained the basis for the statutory provision for destitution until the National Assistance Act (1948). The year 1601 was also important for another reason. The personal and religious charities typical of the Middle Ages had tended to be replaced by more secular concerns. The same century which saw the development of the Poor Law also saw a great number of charitable bequests and endowments designed to ameliorate or eradicate the causes of poverty by a variety of undertakings including the extension of educational opportunities. The Statute of Charitable Uses, enacted in 1601, was a recognition of these massive endowments and endeavoured to protect them. It secured the enforcement of charitable uses by instructing the Chancellor to appoint commissioners to inquire into abuses, to take evidence, to impanel juries and to hand down decisions subject only to his own review. Although by the eighteenth century the Act had largely fallen into disuse, the nineteenth century witnessed a new attack on the maladministration of charitable trusts, and it remained unrepealed until 1888, but the famous preamble to the Act, listing those uses properly considered as charitable, was retained as a working definition until the Charities Act (1960).

Philanthropy and the Poor Law continued to be the main methods of helping the destitute for the next three centuries, but the objects of the former and the way the latter was administered both reflected changing attitudes towards the problem of the poor. The factors at work effecting these changes are the subject of some controversy. Tawney suggested that the effect of Puritanism in the seventeenth century was to usher in a period in which the poor were condemned as idle and irresponsible. By a fortunate dispensation, the virtues enjoined on Christians – diligence, moderation, sobriety, thrift – were the very qualities most conducive to commercial success. The Puritan (Tawney, 1926)

> convinced that character is all and circumstances nothing,
> sees in the poverty of those who fall by the way, not a
> misfortune to be pitied and relieved, but a moral failing to be
> condemned, and in riches, not an object of suspicion –
> though like other gifts they may be abused – but the blessing
> which rewards the triumph of energy and will.

The wage-earners of the seventeenth and eighteenth centuries were considered to be self-indulgent and idle, 'everyone but an idiot knows that the lower classes must be kept poor or they will never be industrious'. Tawney (1926) comments,

> The most curious feature in the whole discussion and that
> which is most sharply in contrast with the long debate on
> pauperism carried on in the sixteenth century was the
> resolute refusal to admit that society had any responsibility
> for the causes of distress. Tudor divines and statesmen had
> little mercy for idle rogues. But the former always and the
> latter ultimately regarded pauperism primarily as a social
> phenomenon produced by economic dislocation.

The political upheavals of the seventeenth century meant that central control of the Poor Law through the Privy Council was considerably relaxed and until the beginning of the nineteenth century there was much local variation in the way it was administered. The notion that the poor could be turned into a source of profit appealed to the growing commercialism of the age; the workhouse movement of the eighteenth century was an attempt to be both deterrent and economic. 'There were two motives behind it: the business motive of assembling the poor under one roof and coping with them as a single problem, replacing as it were domestic by factory relief, and the ethical motive of punishing idleness by compulsory work' (Fay, 1962). Bruce has pointed out that 'it was the blurring in practice of the distinction between the genuinely unemployed and the merely idle, between the workhouse, the poor house and the house of correction, that was largely to characterize poor relief during the next two centuries and a half' (Bruce, 1961).

At the same time, in both the seventeenth and eighteenth centuries, philanthropic activities continued to flourish. The growing spirit of inquiry and interest in things scientific, which was to help in the transformation of the economic organization of the country within a comparatively few years, had a profound effect upon the development of philanthropy particularly in the eighteenth century, as seen, for example, in John Howard's inquiries into the conditions of prisons, the foundation of the Retreat at York, and Jonas Hanway's concern for pauper children. The medical profession was moving out of the dark ages of traditional superstition and some of the most popular objects of philanthropy were hospitals and dispensaries. The middle of the century saw the beginnings of a new humanitarianism and a new interest in contemporary living and working conditions reflected in, for instance, Fielding's novels and Hogarth's engravings. These conditions were beginning to change with ever-increasing rapidity so that within the next hundred years England was to develop from a predominantly rural society, based on ancient village communities, into a bustling industrial urban society.

The social effects of the industrial revolution, coupled as it was with a rapid increase in the population, have been described, analysed and debated by many writers. Suffice it to say here that the development of large urban areas, the spread of the factory system, the much greater division of labour and the mass production of many goods led to an unprecedented rise in the standard of living, a bewildering choice of occupations, much greater mobility – both physical and social – and ease of communication. But they also led to urban slum areas, to the 'discipline of the factory whistle', to greater social and economic insecurity – even for the prosperous working classes – and to a degree of mass squalor and poverty which became more and more intolerable. The traditional methods of meeting the need, the Poor Law and philanthropy, fought a losing battle against the social problems thrown up by the economic and social dislocation resulting from these changes.

Towards the end of the eighteenth century reform was in the air, reform of the law, of Parliament, of prisons, and the freeing of trade and industry, but the French Revolution, although at first welcomed in this country, soon roused so much concern and insecurity among the ruling classes that reform was postponed until the third decade of the nineteenth century. Instead, a combination of economic and political circumstances led on the one hand to repressive measures such as the Combination Act (1800) born of the fear of rebellion and subversion, and on the other to attempts to stem the rising tide of rural destitution through the Poor Law by such devices as the Speenhamland system of allowances in support of wages, the Labour Rate and the roundsman system. Philanthropy became more than ever tangled up with preaching to the poor the virtues of submission to Church and State, and 'of demeaning themselves in all humility towards their betters' (Bourdillon, 1945). Even Hannah More, with a genuine concern for the education of the poor, and who was instrumental in starting charity schools and women's clubs in the villages, was fearful lest the poor should be contaminated by revolutionary ideas (More, 1925).

By the 1820s and the 1830s there was growing interest in the teaching of such philosophers and political economists as: Bentham, who advocated the testing of all social institutions by the criterion of utility and whose essay 'A Fragment on Government' (1770) was to have such an effect on that single-minded advocate of sanitary reform, Edwin Chadwick; Adam Smith whose *The Wealth of Nations* (1776) was to dominate economic thought for a century and who stressed the beneficent working of the economic laws; and Malthus, who was concerned with the pressure of the rising population (1798) helped to earn for economics the soubriquet of the 'gloomy science'. Although reform, when it came, gradually transformed the organization of government, freed industry and trade from outgrown restrictions, and liberalized the legal system, it was accompanied by a doctrinaire opposition to State intervention in economic affairs, an acceptance of the principles of 'deterrence' and 'less eligibility' enshrined in the Poor Law Amendment Act (1834) and an attitude towards the poor fully as harsh as that which had characterized the earlier part of the eighteenth century.

The part which religious thought played in moulding economic and social developments in the nineteenth century is difficult to estimate. The religious toleration of the eighteenth century was ruffled by a religious revival which affected both the established Church and Nonconformity, but as Briggs (1964) has pointed out, it is difficult to determine the role of organized religion in the industrial growth of the nineteenth century, or to evaluate the interaction between religion and capitalism. He suggests that Nonconformity, which according to Tawney and Weber had moulded capitalism, became in part an agency for its destruction – or at least its modification. Yet in spite of many Christian rebels, the most general impression of the nineteenth century is of a commonly held belief in a divinely appointed, harmonious order producing a sense of tranquillity and of firm confidence in the future which tended to bring a feeling of optimism and complacency only occasionally punctured by the distress of the 'other nation'.

Throughout the nineteenth century the Poor Law remained the only statutory provision for the relief of poverty, and the principles of the 1834 Poor law Amendment Act ensured that such poverty had to amount to destitution before it could be relieved. The mixed workhouses, the hated 'Bastilles of the poor', continued to be a symbol of social failure and degradation for a century; even the receipt of outdoor relief carried with it a social and political stigma which has still not been eradicated in many people's minds and colours the attitude, of the older generations particularly, even today towards the acceptance of assistance from public funds.

It is perhaps not surprising that, in an era when economic freedom and opportunity were so greatly stressed, it seemed most natural that private enterprise in welfare would be considered the proper means of meeting the needs of those who fell by the wayside in the economic race. As the middle classes became richer and more politically powerful, so some at least recognized a responsibility towards their less fortunate brethren. There developed an outpouring of private charity, much of it ephemeral in character, some providing constructively for the needs of the day. Soup kitchens, hospitals, reformatories, ragged schools, cripples guilds, orphanages and many other institutions all witnessed to a growing concern for the victims of the violent social and economic upheaval of the nineteenth century. Contributing to charitable causes might be to many an insurance against revolution, a sop to an uneasy conscience, or an opportunity of participating at a small cost in praiseworthy and increasingly fashionable 'good works', but there were some who were genuinely concerned for the needs of others and were activated by humanitarian and religious motives. Inevitably their concern tended to find its expression in ways acceptable to the prevailing philosophies of the time, but the organizations set up by these charitably minded pioneers were the forerunners of many of the voluntary societies and institutions of the twentieth century. Because these associations grew up spontaneously and were shaped by the interests – and indeed the whims of their founders – they were infinitely varied in purpose and method, but all were designed, at least overtly, 'to compensate for inequalities and to supplement the needs of the underprivileged' (Bourdillon, 1945). They were primarily concerned with those existing in the slums of the great industrial areas, who were apathetic and destitute to such a degree that they were unable to help themselves or their neighbours.

Other voluntary organizations of a quite different character also developed in the nineteenth century. The mutual aid or self-help movements, the trade unions, the friendly societies, the co-operative societies, were also attempts at meeting the social and economic insecurity felt even by the more prosperous of the working classes. It was only those who had a margin of time, money and energy, as a result of rising standards of living, who could afford to make their weekly contributions to these associations and thus contribute through mutual aid to the fashioning of some defence for themselves and their families against the uncertainties of an ever-changing industrial economy. The attitude of the governing classes to the development of these movements was mixed. They welcomed the evidence of hard work, thrift and self-reliance among the labouring classes, but were concerned at their political and social implications. The experience members of the working class gained through these movements was to have profound effects on the political situation, especially after the Acts of 1867 and 1884 brought about adult male suffrage. Moreover these movements were the pioneers in social insurance, which was later taken over and generalized by the State. The Co-operative movement, besides providing for the investment of small savings, was a means of protecting the working-class consumer against over-priced and adulterated goods and thus contributed to the subsequent development of legislation designed to safeguard health such as the Food and Drugs Acts of a later period. Similarly, early building societies, run on democratic lines, paved the way not only for the Small Dwellings Acquisition Act (1899) but also for municipal action in the housing field.

But even at a period when the doctrine of laissez-faire and individualism was apparently at its most influential the government was forced by events to take an ever-increasing part in social and economic affairs. Indeed, ideas of individualism did not necessarily imply opposition to all forms of State interference. On the contrary, Bentham, for instance, might be described as a precursor to the Fabians in his advocacy of State action to promote the greatest happiness of the greatest number, the principle of utility. As Chambers (1961) put it.

> For this supreme end he proposed, in effect, a revolution
> in the machinery of justice, health and education: and when
> he found that the existing ruling class were primarily
> interested in promoting the happiness, not of the greatest
> number, but of themselves, he became an advocate of a
> radical widening of the franchise.

One of the most notable legislative achievements of the nineteenth century was the control of the environmental conditions developed to safeguard the health of the public. But the battle for sanitary reform associated with the names of Edwin Chadwick, Dr James Kay, Dr Southwood Smith and others, was a hard one. A long series of investigations and reports from the *Moral and Physical Condition of the Working Class* (1832) and the *Sanitary Condition of the Labouring Population* (1842) to the *Royal Commission on the Housing of the Working Classes* (1885) revealed the connection between impure water supplies, inadequate sanitation, bad housing, disease and destitution. Perhaps the first time poverty began to be seen not as a simple problem of the individual lacking adequate resources, but as a complex one which necessitated action on a wide front. Cholera, typhus, and other infectious diseases were no respecters of person and the comfortably off classes were shocked into action both by the danger to their own health and by the drain on their pockets through the claims on the poor rates of the ill and infirm. The fear of government interference and of bureaucratic control delayed much effective legislation for nearly half a century, and although the first Public Health Act was passed in 1848, yet it was not until the Act of 1875 that the battle for government action for promoting environmental health was really won.

The movement to ensure a more healthy working environment primarily originated with a concern to protect women and young people by regulating the hours they could work, the conditions under which they could be employed, and by a ban on the employment of young children in factories. This protective and regulatory type of legislation was not thought to conflict with individualism and laissez-faire for it did not interfere with the personal liberty or freedom to bargain of the adult male worker. In practice, however, owing to the dependence of mills and other factories on the work of women and young people, the limitation of their hours of work and the regulation of their working conditions meant indirectly that male workers too benefited from the Factory Acts. Regulation was gradually extended to include not only the textile trades but other industries, and was concerned not only with hours of work, and the like but also with the adequate fencing of machinery and the special hazards to which those working in certain dangerous trades were exposed.

The same desire to protect those unable to care for their own interests manifested itself in the long fight for the abolition of the use of 'climbing boys', for the reform of lunatic asylums and even of prisons. Side by side with this reforming legislation was a growing demand, on political, economic, social and humanitarian grounds, for a more positive and constructive government policy for better educational facilities. First by subsidies to the national religious societies for the training of teachers and later for the actual provision of schools, then by the setting up by the legislation of 1870 of school boards to fill the gaps in the provision of elementary schools by voluntary organizations, the State gradually assumed responsibility for ensuring that every child in the country had access to at least minimum educational facilities. It was not, however, until 1880 that education became compulsory up to the age of 10 (raised to 11 in 1893 and 12 in 1899), and not until 1891 that it was free. The progress of the industrial revolution demanded the development of technical education, but although subsidies were given to encourage local initiative for the establishment of technical schools, it was not until the Act of 1889 that county councils, created in the previous year, were given permissive powers to provide technical and other secondary schools, and to take part in the provision of evening and other advanced classes.

To sum up, the Victorians primarily put their faith in industrial development, through the expansion of capitalism and overseas trade in a free society, to solve ultimately the social problems caused by rapid economic change. To ease the burden on the weakest they were prepared to pour considerable sums of money into private charity and to countenance legislative reforms designed to protect some of the more vulnerable members of society as well as to look with favour on any movement which promoted thrift and self-reliance among the poor. At the same time they were forced by the pressure of political, social and economic events to accept a series of legislative reforms which began to transform environmental and working conditions. 'This adaptation of social policy in Britain to the economic changes of machine, industry and the free market', says Chambers (1961), 'was largely achieved by an alliance of forces between Benthamite interventionists under the leadership of Edwin Chadwick and the forces of traditional paternalism under the leadership of Lord Shaftesbury.' Yet by the end of the century, some thinking members of the public were becoming uneasily aware that economic growth was not curing all ills; that the thrift of the working classes could not provide adequately for their economic security and that philanthropy could mitigate the poverty of only a few of those who were the victims of industrial change. The ferment of thought and opinion in the last decades of the nineteenth and early years of the twentieth century on the proper division of responsibility between the individual, the family, the neighbourhood and the State was entangled with debate about the nature and end of man himself. This debate was given a new twist by the bitter controversy over Darwin's *The Origin of Species*, which led to a torment of doubt as to the value of any of the convictions which formed the foundations of the individual and social life of many Victorians. The influence of Marx, of the Christian socialists, and of the Fabians, was increasingly felt but resulted in no clear-cut concept of the future role of state intervention.

The Concept of the Welfare State

Kirkman Gray (1908) said,

> It is now generally recognised that in addition to such want as
> results to the ill-doer from his own ill-doing there is a vast
> amount of suffering which comes from general social causes;
> and for which the sufferer is responsible either remotely or
> not at all. For such distress society is responsible and it is
> bound to alleviate or remove it. The work which was left to
> philanthropy is coming to be accepted as an integral part of
> social politics. . . .The Movement which I describe as a
> transition from philanthropy to social politics, rests on the
> breaking down of the simple old doctrine of individualism.
> What social faith is to be substituted is yet undetermined, and
> that hesitation explains the confusion which still exists as to
> the proper spheres of philanthropy and social politics
> respectively.

Seventy years later this confusion still exists, in spite of the
development of a complex of State provision increasingly designed
not only to alleviate or remove suffering (the diswelfares) which
comes from 'general social causes', but – in theory at least – also to
ensure for every citizen *as a citizen* an optimum of health and
well-being. By the middle of the century the comprehensiveness of
this collective provision had developed to such an extent that there
was general acceptance of the title of the 'welfare state' as a fitting
term to designate this development. To many people the concept of
the welfare state is associated with the legislation of 1944–8, which
reorganized the educational system, provided family allowances,
set up a comprehensive and integrated scheme of social insurance
underpinned by national assistance, brought into being a national
health service and assumed a greater responsibility for deprived
children, the handicapped and the homeless and for providing
better housing, industrial training and more employment opportunities. Yet, if each of the measures which brought about
these developments is examined, it is not always easy to see where
the crucial changes lay or indeed what was new in them. Most
have a history going back many decades, often into the nineteenth
century.
     David Roberts (1968) sees the origins of the welfare state in the

administrative revolution of the Victorian era. The reform of central and local government, the gradual emergence of a strong, efficient and uncorruptible civil service and the advent of the inspector in factories, in mines, in public health, in education, in the administration of the Lunacy Act contained in themselves a dynamic which led inevitably to the extension of State intervention. Thus legislation of a regulatory kind developed imperceptibly into legislation providing constructive services; concern for environmental health led on to concern for personal health. Legislation to protect children from exploitation and from cruelty and ill-treatment by taking action against those responsible resulted in the necessity of making alternative provision for their victims. The hesitant experiments of pioneer philanthropists and working-class groups were used as prototypes for increasing government action. A similar model of the growth of government action, although in a different field, has been put forward by MacDonagh (1967 in Fraser, 1973), whose thesis centres on two main principles: the pressure of intolerable facts and an inherent administrative momentum.

Many factors hastened this development and there is considerable controversy over their relative importance. J. Saville (1975) suggests that,

> The Welfare State has come about as a result of the interaction of three main factors: (1) the struggle of the working class against their exploitation; (2) the requirements of industrial capitalism (a convenient abstraction) for a more efficient environment in which to operate and in particular the need for a highly productive labour force; (3) recognition by the property owners of the price that has to be paid for political security. In the last analysis as the Labour movement has always recognized, the pace and tempo of social reform have been determined by the struggle of working-class groups and organisations: but it would be historically incorrect and politically an error to underestimate the importance of either of the other factors in the situation. To do so would be to accept the illusion that the changes are of greater significance than in fact they are, as well as to misread the essential character of contemporary capitalism.

O. R. McGregor (1961) considers that,

Beneath the garish surface of political events there can be discerned the cumulative adjustment of an advanced industrial society to the inescapable imperatives, coincident in point of time, of a mass franchise, of restless technological change in an economically aggressive world, and of the menace of mechanised belligerence. The welfare state has that derivation.

The working class vote was certainly something with which successive governments after 1884 had to reckon and inevitably had its effect on policy. The development of periodic booms and slumps, of increasing economic insecurity and unemployment led to the attempt to organize the labour market through the Unemployed Workmen Act (1905) and the Labour Exchange Act (1909) and to provide a cushion against destitution by means of unemployment insurance (1911) and unemployment assistance (1934), as well as to the designation of depressed areas and to the concept of economic as well as town and country planning.

Anxiety concerning the large percentage of recruits rejected for the Boer War on physical grounds led to the setting up of an Interdepartmental Committee on Physical Deterioration. Its report in 1904 pointed the connection between the possibility of military weakness and the physical condition of the young. Partly as a result of its recommendations the school health service, school meals, care committees and the maternal and child welfare service became securely established. Two world wars hastened this development of specialized personal services. R. M. Titmuss, in *Problems of Social Policy* (1950), one of the volumes of the official history of the Second World War, shows how many services started as experimental, makeshift methods of meeting the needs of citizens exposed to conditions of total war profoundly influenced the pattern of post-war provision when subsequent legislation gave these temporary expedients a permanent place in peacetime.

Added to these factors in the genesis of the welfare state was an increasing knowledge of the facts of poverty, ill-health, overcrowding, unemployment, delinquency and other distressing aspects of contemporary life. The regular censuses, social surveys such as the pioneer inquiries of Booth and Rowntree in London and York respectively, the statistical returns of the Registrar-General, the information gained through the working of the new statutory services themselves, gradually led to the massing of more and more statistical material, which helped to delineate the size and shape of many social problems.

From one point of view, the social legislation of the late 1940s was part of an attempt at 'tidying up', at administrative simplification and integration. But perhaps the greatest difference discernible in the legislation of the period, compared with that of the previous half century, was its comprehensive universalist nature and its explicit recognition of the responsibility of the State for the provision of certain services for all members of the community and the corresponding right of individual citizens to use them. Lord Beveridge, whose famous report on social insurance and allied services in 1942 did much to shape public thinking about the scope and purpose of social provision, used an illustration appropriate to the time in the middle of the Second World War, when he wrote (1944):

> We should regard Want, Disease, Ignorance and Squalor as common enemies of all of us, not as enemies with whom each individual may seek a separate peace, escaping himself to personal prosperity, while leaving his fellows in their clutches. That is the meaning of social conscience; that one should refuse to make a separate peace with a social evil. Social conscience should drive us to take up arms in a new war against Want, Disease, Ignorance and Squalor at home.

This sentiment was in line with the philanthropic tradition of concern for others in distress which infused much of the earlier social legislation and was reinforced by wartime revelations of slums, of neglected children, of undernourished wives and mothers. But perhaps the optimistic view of the role of social policy in the immediate post-war period cannot be fully understood without reference to the contribution of that other tradition of mutual aid and fraternal solidarity which inspired the working-class movements of the nineteenth and early twentieth centuries, and which led at least one writer to describe the welfare state as one vast friendly society. This is in line with the idea that the development of mid-twentieth-century social services was one manifestation of a process which had been going on for several centuries to re-establish citizen rights. T. H. Marshall (1963) developed this theme in his essay, 'Citizenship and Social Class'. Evidence for this concept can be found in much of the legislation of the late 1940s, which sought to embody at least some degree of social rights, based not on financial need but on citizenship. Yet, as Robert Pinker (1971) has pointed out,

> The relationship between social services and citizenship is thus largely determined by subjective evaluations of the purpose of the service. For some citizenship is enhanced while for others it is debased by reliance upon social services. . . .The idea of paying through taxes or holding authentic claims by virtue of citizenship remains largely an intellectual conceit of the social scientist and the socialist . . . most applicants for social services remain paupers at heart.

The Welfare State – Myth or Reality?

During the last thirty years the euphoria of the late 1940s has given place to much disappointment and disillusion. There have been many significant advances – in access to education and health service provision, in the standard of living even of the poorest members of society, in the provision of more and better housing, in the increased life chances for many people – yet there is much evidence to suggest that many individuals and families are living in conditions of severe economic and social deprivation; that social and economic policies over the past three decades have been largely ineffective in bringing about any substantial redistribution of resources between the better-off and the worst-off in our society, and that large areas of our inner cities are in urgent need of revitalizing. The following pages attempt to discuss some of these successes and failures. The long debate concerning the role of the State, the balance between the claims of freedom of choice and genuine equality of opportunity continues.

Notes

1   For a brief account of why and how the study of social administration was established outside the disciplines of economics, politics, philosophy and history, yet relied on some parts of the knowledge derived from these disciplines, and of the way in which other universities were to develop 'social studies' departments, see *An Introduction to the Study of Social Administration*, edited by David C.

Marsh and published by Routledge & Kegan Paul in 1965. In that book we covered briefly the origins and historical development of the main fields of social administration up to the middle 1960s. It therefore serves as a useful background to this more recent study, which is concerned predominantly with the policies and practices since the 1960s. By now nearly every university in Britain and Northern Ireland has well-established courses in social policy and administration which are in most cases quite distinct and separated from the study of, say, politics, philosophy, history, and even sociology. But there is usually a close link between degree courses in social administration and post-graduate professional social work courses.

In addition to the university courses there are now a number of degree courses in social administration at other institutions of higher or further education, notably at some of the polytechnics.

2   The period 1901 to 1939 has been well documented by a wide range of authors, many of whose books are given in the references and suggestions for further reading at the end of this book.

3   For the attempts made to define the subject matter of social administration by some of the first professors of that subject, e.g. Titmuss, Lafitte, Donnison and Marsh, see *An Introduction to the Study of Social Administration*. ed. David C. Marsh, Ch. 1.

4   Some of the newer school of academics were undoubtedly influenced by the late Richard Titmuss, who, during his tenure of the chair of social administration at the London School of Economics, achieved the reputation of being the leading teacher and sponsor of research workers in the field of social administration in this country, and indeed his influence spread to many parts of the world. Professors Brian Abel-Smith, Peter Townsend, Robert Pinker and Roy Parker were in a sense protégés of Titmuss, and Professor David Donnison was a close colleague and friend for many years.

References

Beveridge, W. (1944), *Full Employment in a Free Society*, Allen & Unwin.

Booth, C. (1892), *Life and Labour of the People of London*, Macmillan.

Bourdillon, F. C. (ed.) (1945), *Voluntary Social Services*, Methuen.

Bradley, I. (1978), 'The centre of Tory thinking', *The Times*, 13 February.

Briggs, A. (1964), *The Listener*, 27 February.

Bruce, M. (1961), *The Coming of the Welfare State*, Batsford.

Chambers, D. C. (1961), *The Workshop of the World*, Oxford University Press.

Crosland, C. A. R. (1956), *The Future of Socialism*, Cape.

Crosland, C. A. R. (1974), *Socialism Now*, Cape.

Environmental Studies, Centre for, *Annual Report, 1975–6*.

Environmental Studies, Centre for (1976), *Demographic Change and Social Policy, the Uncertain Future*, June.

Fay, C. R. (1962), *Great Britain from Adam Smith to the Present Day*, 5th ed., Longmans.

George, V. and Wilding, P. (1976), *Ideology and Social Welfare*, Routledge & Kegan Paul.

Kirkman Gray, B. (1908), *Philanthropy and the State*, P. S. King & Son.

Lafitte, F. (1962), inaugural lecture delivered in the University of Birmingham.

MacDonagh, O. (1958), 'The nineteenth-century revolution in government: a reappraisal', *Historical Journal*, vol. I.

McGregor, O. R. (1961), *Sociology and Welfare*, Sociological Review Monograph, no. 4, July.

Marsh, D. C. (1965), *An Introduction to the Study of Social Administration*, Routledge & Kegan Paul.

Marshall, T. H. (1963), *Sociology at the Crossroads*, Heinemann.

Marshall, T. H. (1965), *Social Policy*, Hutchinson.

Marshall, T. H. (1972), 'Value problems of welfare capitalism', *Journal of Social Policy*, vol. I, no. 1.

More, H. (1925), *Selected Letters reprinted*, John Lane, The Bodley Head.

Pinker, R. (1971), *Social Theory and Social Policy*, Heinemann Educational.

Roberts, D. (1968), *Victorian Origins of the British Welfare State*, New Haven.

Rowntree, S. (1901), *Poverty: a Study of Town Life*, Macmillan.

Saville, J. (1958), 'The welfare state: an historical approach', in E. Butterworth and R. Holman (eds) *Social Welfare in Modern Britain*, Fontana (1975).

Social Policy, Centre for Studies in (1977), *What the Centre is and does*, September.

Social Policy, Centre for Studies in (1977), *Publications List*, August.

Tawney. R. H. (1926), *Religion and the Rise of Capitalism*, John Murray.

Tawney, R. H. (1961), *The Acquisitive Society*, Fontana.

Titmuss, R. M. (1950), *Problems of Social Policy*, HMSO and Longmans.

Titmuss, R. M. (1968), *Commitment to Welfare*, Allen & Unwin.

Titmuss, R. M. (1974), *Social Policy, an Introduction*, Allen & Unwin.

I

Social Policy and the Economic and Social Environment

2

Social Policy in Relation to Industry

Mary F. Robertson

Social policy precedes social action, which is largely interpreted through the social services. These services all depend upon financial and other resources which are permanently in short supply, so that a major part of social administration is concerned with the fair allocation of available resources.

We live in an industrial society, typical of the western hemisphere. We were the first, launched by the industrial revolution in the eighteenth century, and were known as the workshop of the world. This gave us a headstart in being financially capable of providing services for the welfare of our people. We are no longer in the lead, being neither the biggest nor the richest industrial country, but we are still entirely dependent on economic sources for our national wealth, and that means our industrial production.

If industry is allowed to decline, if it is not properly maintained with materials, money and above all, skill, there can be no surplus to provide the necessary resources for health, education, housing, social security and the rest. In a real sense, therefore, industry can be said to be the foundation of any social policy.

It was once said in a sermon by Kenneth Adams of St George's House, Windsor Castle that the Good Samaritan (surely the prototype of social workers) gave twopence to the innkeeper to care for the man found injured by the wayside. Where did the twopence come from? There is, perhaps, a modern lesson in this parable as profound as the original one expounded in the New Testament. A great many young people are eager to enter what are now often called the 'caring professions', to help others to solve their problems and to assist the disadvantaged, but few recognize that by going into industry and helping to increase our essential production of goods, they are making it possible for more people to be good Samaritans and to have twopence in their pocket for the inn-keeper.

This chapter is not intended as an introduction to industrial economics, a separate discipline from social administration. Here we are concerned with the social framework within which industry operates and with the legal and cultural constraints of the working environment.

Men have always worked and lived on the direct or indirect product of their labours but, with a few striking exceptions such as the Statute of Artificers (1563) and the craft guilds of the seventeenth century, there was no regulation or control over the conditions of work until the beginning of the nineteenth century.

The story of the so-called industrial revolution dating roughly from the middle of the eighteenth to the middle of the nineteenth centuries has been told many times and doesn't warrant repetition here. From an economic point of view, it is a story of almost fantastic success. The rapid rate of growth in technological innovation, in methods of administration and distribution and in the accumulation of wealth, created family fortunes, landed gentry, new towns, and a whole new social culture. From the workers' point of view in human terms, however, the story is not so bright and to the above examples of change we can add slums, child labour, poverty, disease and squalor. The somewhat gory details of industrial exploitation have also been described by many writers and have almost certainly been exaggerated. What is important is that the appalling conditions, the low rate of wages and the complete lack of redress for the sufferers finally succeeded in breaking the prevailing belief in Adam Smith's laissez-faire and, with the first Factory Act of 1802, State intervention began.

It is likely that the doctrine of laissez-faire, although believed in and preached by the economists of the period, was never either wholly accepted or practised. Compared with the strict regulations confining the industrialist in the 1970s, however, his counterpart in the 1870s enjoyed far greater freedom. During the greater part of the nineteenth century, there was minimum factory legislation almost entirely concerned with the mills in the textile trade and covering only the rudiments of safety and the hours of work for young children.

The sacred law of supply and demand was allowed to regulate the price of everything including labour, and a man could do what he wished with his own – which included his employees.

The Combination Acts of 1799 and 1800 forbade all association; this successfully inhibited the birth of trade unions until after the acts were repealed in 1824. Even then, their activities were severely restricted because in common law, they were interpreted as 'conspiracy', 'in restraint of trade', 'inducing a breach of contract' or as 'intimidation'. It was not until 1871, when the Trade Union Act gave statutory protection to trade union activities and virtually put them above the law, that industrial workers really began to acquire genuine bargaining power.

In the meantime, throughout the whole of the nineteenth century, factory acts were passed dealing with specific conditions in specific industries as energetic individuals succeeded in arousing sufficient interest and perhaps guilt, to pressurize Parliament into action. The first Factory Act of 1802 quaintly entitled 'The Health and Morals of Apprentices Act' seems to have been rather more concerned with morals than with health. The impression given is that long hours of labour and attendance at church twice on Sunday will hinder Satan in finding mischief for idle young hands. There seems little doubt that the acts passed during the early years of the century were not taken very seriously. Enforcement was the major problem. This was, like so much social regulation, the charge of the JPs who were, of course, also the leading employers and it is not, perhaps, surprising that they should prove reluctant to restrict their own industrial activity. In 1833, however, the first factory inspectors were appointed by central government to enforce the growing legislation. Only four in number, their task was practically impossible but the principle of inspection was accepted and the function has grown both in numbers and in effectiveness ever since. The Act of 1833 is important for another reason. It introduced what was known as the half-time system, whereby workers under the age of thirteen spent half of the working day at school and half in the factory. This was an important milestone in the progress towards compulsory education and today, with the current problems of juvenile unemployment and what became known as ROSLA children, there might be something to be said for resurrecting the idea.

This is not a history book, so it is not our intention to present a detailed account of all the factory legislation in the nineteenth century. Mention, however, should be made of the Truck Acts of 1831, 1887, 1896 and 1940 and of the Workman's Compensation Acts of 1897 and 1925. Under the first of these Acts a most popular enactment, employers were enjoined to reward their employees only in coin of the realm, thus putting an end to the pernicious habit of paying wages by means of dockets redeemable in company shops or in kind. The Workman's Compensation Acts introduced a completely new protection for workers injured, 'arising out of and during the course of their work'. Before this legislation, workers could sue their employer for damages under the common law only if they could first establish negligence. There were many flaws in the implementation of workman's compensation and the whole principle was abolished in 1946, when replaced by the Industrial Injuries Act as part of the National Health Service package, but in the 1890s it represented an enormous concession to workers' rights of protection from the hazards of their daily round.

Before we leave the nineteenth century, two other strands should be added to this brief pattern. One is a reminder of the famous reformers of the time who worked so hard to improve the lot of the helpless industrial worker and to prohibit the worst of the glaringly bad conditions. Their stories are well known. The names of Peel, Oastler, Shaftesbury and, above all, Owen, will live in the history of factory reform. They had an uphill fight and struggled against considerable opposition so that their achievements were truly remarkable.

Robert Owen deserves special mention. From the accounts of his life, he seems to have been both a brilliant manufacturer and a philosophical crank. He was also a dull and wordy orator but, as manager of his father-in-law's mill at New Lanark, he introduced a number of ideas and procedures which might be said to have pioneered the whole of what is now familiar as personnel management. He was concerned for and spent money on the welfare of his pauper child employees, seeing that they were adequately fed and housed. He opened a school for them, introduced rewards and punishments in the form of 'silent monitors' and in short, believed long before his time that it paid an employer to treat his workers as if they were almost human. In a speech (Hutchins, 1912) to a group of manufacturers in 1813, Owen said:

'If then, the care as to the state of your inanimate machines can produce such beneficial results, what may not be expected if you devote equal attention to your vital machines which are far more wonderfully constructed? When you shall acquire a right knowledge of these, of their curious mechanism, of their self-adjusting powers; when the proper mainspring shall be applied to their varied movements you will become conscious of their real value, and you will readily be induced to turn your thoughts more frequently from your inanimate to your living machines.'

The language of that quotation may be somewhat archaic but the sentiment is certainly not. It might have been written by a modern ergonomist[1] and many of today's personnel officers could describe their total function in terms of trying to turn man's thoughts more frequently from their inanimate to their living machines.

Before the end of the nineteenth century, a new concept began to gain acceptance among some industrialists. This was referred to by the clumsy name of 'humanitarianism' and is associated with the 'welfare movement' of the Quaker manufacturers of chocolate – the famous families of Cadbury, Fry and Rowntree. They were, in a sense, 'do-gooders' in that their approach was highly moralistic and somewhat patronizing, but they were also shrewd businessmen. They sponsored the habit of drinking chocolate in the pious hope that it would reduce the consumption of stronger beverages and, in doing so, they made their fortunes. It is to these Quaker firms that we owe the old term 'industrial welfare', from which grew the modern specialism of personnel management. They were pioneers in caring and catering for the welfare of workers and it is perhaps significant that they are still flourishing today.

At the turn of the century and in the first years of the 1900s, the pace quickened. The Labour movement grew rapidly so that by 1911 English workers were organized to a substantial degree and in Parliament the representation of the Labour Party grew from two seats in 1900 to twenty-nine in 1906. Before the outbreak of war in 1914, there had been several important Acts of Parliament closely concerned with industrial social policy. In 1901 Parliament passed the first Consolidated Factories Act which repealed all the piecemeal legislation of the nineteenth century and incorporated it in one act made mandatory on all manufacturing establishments.

Since then, this Act has been revised and brought up to date twice, in 1937 and in 1961. The theme of the Factories Act is health, safety and welfare, and the hours of work allowed for women and young persons.

Clearly, with the new acts concerning safety and equal opportunities of the 1970s, it is due for revision once again.

In 1909 came the Trade Board Act as well as the Labour Exchanges Act. Under the Trade Board Act, for the first time ever, minimum wages were established by especially constituted boards in certain sweated industries where the workers were not organized sufficiently to fight their own battle. These bodies still exist but now under the name of wages councils.

The Department of Employment[2]

The part played by the Department of Employment is central to the subject of this chapter both because its history reflects the changing philosophy of the times, which in turn dictated government policy, and also because it has been made accountable for so much of the relevant legislation. Its conciliation role predated its employment role.

The original department was first created in 1893, although a bureau of labour statistics had been set up seven years before. In 1896 the Conciliation Act was passed, which began the long and remarkably successful history of the government's role in both conciliation and arbitration in industrial disputes which, until the establishment of the Advisory, Conciliation and Arbitration Service in 1974 was an important service offered by the department.

As Eric Wigham points out in his interesting historical account (Wigham, 1976), there were periodic attempts to transfer the peace-keeping functions of government to the leaders of the two sides of industry.

Following some evidence to the Royal Commission on Labour, in the 1890s, the first was the appointment of the Industrial Council in 1911. Lloyd George's government made abortive attempts to set up a National Industrial Conference in 1919, and after the General Strike in 1926 there were renewed demands for a joint peace-keeping body. These resulted in meetings between the TUC and Sir Alfred Mond and others, which were known as the Mond–Turner talks, but, although a National Industrial Council was recommended, nothing materialized.

Finally, the National Economic Development Council was created in 1961. This was a joint body but it had no conciliation function.

Within industry, the government, through the Ministry of Labour, has sponsored and encouraged joint consultation ever since the Whitley Committee's recommendations of 1917. Initially seventy-four joint industrial councils were established in four years, but by the 1920s they had dwindled and were not resurrected until Ernest Bevin created joint production committees during the Second World War.

The whole subject of joint consultation in this country has a curious and fluctuating history which is, perhaps, on the margin of our present subject. There have been some famous examples of highly successful works councils and some equally feeble showpieces.

The basic concept of communication and participation has been incorporated into the latest legislation on employee protection which is dealt with below.

The idea of labour exchanges originated at the beginning of this century as an alternative to the Poor Law and the failure of the Unemployed Workmen Act of 1905, which provided temporary relief work.

The credit for such a revolutionary innovation is shared by Sidney Webb and William Beveridge, who proposed the plan, and by Winston Churchill and Herbert Llewelyn-Smith, who succeeded in implementing the scheme in 1909. Labour exchanges were set up in 1910 in a variety of makeshift buildings such as converted church halls, post offices, factories and schools. The unemployment insurance scheme was introduced in 1912 and in 1917 the new Ministry of Labour was created, which took over both this scheme and the labour (now named employment) exchanges from the Board of Trade. The business of the Ministry of Labour, to begin with, was almost exclusively concerned with the war effort, both in recruitment to the armed forces and in supplying labour for essential war work. At the end of the war came the organization of demobilization and the exchange service was expanded to meet the demands of a country returning to a peace economy.

By 1920, the temporary post-war prosperity was breaking down and there was a dramatic increase in unemployment, which soon developed into the worst recession the country has ever experienced. The long depression which followed changed the role of the ministry into one primarily concerned with unemployment rather than with employment and created the dreary image of the 'dole' (in Scotland, the 'broo'), from which it never quite recovered.

In a sense, the Ministry of Labour lived from one crisis to another and its next was, of course, the preparation for, and the demands of, the Second World War.

Its name was changed to the Ministry of Labour and National Service and, under its most famous and best respected Minister, Ernest Bevin, 1940–5, it dealt with the crucial and difficult tasks of conscription and direction of labour. It was at this time that the factory inspectorate was transferred from the Home Office to the Ministry of Labour which, therefore, took over the administration of the Factories Act.

National Service ended in 1959 and the department again became known as the Ministry of Labour. By this time, the Ministry also controlled the benefit and employment services, the wages councils and had a large role in industrial conciliation. In addition, it was attached to the International Labour Organization controlling migration and the immigration of aliens.

In 1968, the Ministry became a department of state, and for a short period its name was changed to the Department of Employment and Productivity. In 1970, with a change in government, it changed again to its present name of the Department of Employment, but this decade saw the most drastic changes, in that almost all the major functions were transferred to the new Manpower Services Commission and the old emaciated Department of Employment remains a shadow of its former self.

The Manpower Services Commission, created by the Employment and Training Act of 1973, was established in 1974. It is directly responsible to the Secretary of State for Employment and has two executive arms: the Employment Service Agency (ESA) and the Training Services Agency (TSA). It is run by a ten-man board, made up of an independent full-time chairman and nine part-time representatives of employers, workers and local government and education interests. The board is responsible for implementing broad policies laid down by the Secretary of State, and it also acts as his adviser on all manpower matters.

Both the executive arms are statutory bodies with three member boards and a chief executive. The ESA is responsible for the public employment service, professional and executive recruitment, the occupational guidance service and specialized employment services such as those for disabled people and the employment transfer scheme. The TSA is responsible for the training opportunities Scheme (TOPS) which offers free training with grants to those, whether employed or unemployed, who want to better themselves, across the whole range of jobs, from those requiring limited skills to the higher levels of management. It also co-ordinates the work of the industrial training boards and promotes training for jobs not covered by boards.

The establishment of the Manpower Services Commission and its two executive agencies has brought about both a completely new look and a fundamental refurbishing of all the old services. It was the government's intention to make a fresh start, by breaking the association of the work of the Department of Employment with the dreary exchanges, the dole queues and the payment of unemployment relief. A new body, with a new name and new premises – now called 'Job Centres' – and staffed by better qualified people has succeeded in providing a new image and, in spite of the recession which coincided with its beginning, it has already made an impressive impact on the statistics of both employment placements and training opportunities.

The Effect of Two World Wars

The First World War was an historic landmark from every point of view, not least that of industrial social policy. The urgency of wartime production, coupled with the disappearance to the armed forces of thousands of workers, created both a serious shortage of labour and a new awareness of the importance of proper selection and training. It was this situation which gave women their opportunity to show their infinite capacities. Women practically took over the munitions industry, as well as playing a full part in many others. They proved highly adaptable, acquired skills hitherto the sole prerogative of men, and opened the way to today's emancipation and equality of opportunities. And they did something else as well. By becoming injured, ill, tired and absent from work for family reasons, they highlighted the numerous human problems hitherto neglected or ignored and caused the government to set up the famous Health of Munition Workers Committee. Its report in 1915, giving official recognition to industrial fatigue and recommending the shortening of working hours, gave birth to the Industrial Health Research Board, which in turn can be said to mark the beginning in this country of industrial psychology.

In some ways, the effects on industry of the Second World War were curiously similar and in others, they were totally different. Once again, unemployment was mopped up both by recruitment to the forces and by the urgent demands for the production of armaments, so that labour, and especially skilled labour of all kinds, acquired a scarcity value on an unprecedented scale.

As had happened too, a generation before, protective legislation restricting the hours of work for women and young persons was shelved for the duration of what was euphemistically termed 'the national emergency'. Shift work for both sexes was universal in the munitions industry, and, once again, the price was paid in terms of absenteeism, sickness and accidents. The old reports of the Industrial Health Research Board and especially those on fatigue might never have been written. Again too, government intervened and hours of work were cut in 1940. This time, however, the response was quicker and much more effective. The well-meaning but unsophisticated 'welfare workers' of the First World War were succeeded by 'labour managers' in the second, who either were already qualified professionals or underwent three-month crash courses arranged by certain universities with the help of established personnel departments.

Ernest Bevin, Minister of Labour and National Service, 1940–5, possibly made his greatest contribution in the context of the human aspects of wartime industry. Under what were called 'essential work orders', for the first time in our history, workers in the engineering factories working on government contract could neither leave nor be dismissed without a certificate from the national service officer and for the first time too, such workers were given a guaranteed minimum weekly wage. These orders were among the most significant of all the wartime regulations and highlighted the supreme importance of the country's human resources.

The third report of the Select Committee on National Expenditure (1942–3) was devoted wholly to a review of personnel management, welfare and health in war factories. 'Labour management', it said, 'has in the last two years won a definite status in industry,' and it (HMSO, 1942–3) went on to explain the nature of personnel management and the work of personnel officers in these words:

> the maximum efficiency cannot be attained unless the human factor in production is recognized as being of at least as much importance as the engineering and research sides. Once this principle is accepted, the management, in order to ensure the whole-hearted co-operation from the workers, must adopt a clear policy for all personnel and welfare matters. The functions of a personnel officer can briefly be defined as those of a specialized adviser to the management, supervisors, and foremen on all questions affecting relations between the workers and the management.

This statement was a long way ahead of the tentative pronouncements of the old Health of Munition Workers Committee of 1915, but it has a recogizable echo of Robert Owen's sentiments given earlier in this chapter.

Personnel management is not our present subject, but its development was undoubtedly one of the, if not the most, significant outcomes of the war in the context of industry and society. Perhaps it can be put briefly in this way. Personnel management was born during the First World War, suffered a somewhat deprived childhood in the years between the wars and then, rather suddenly, blossomed into a brilliant adolescent during the Second World War. Adolescence, however, does not long endure and neither, mercifully, did the war. The experiences gained then had a highly maturing effect and personnel management grew into adulthood with remarkable rapidity. There is no doubt that this maturation had a profound effect both in helping to initiate subsequent legislation and in securing its acceptance by society.

Careers Advisory Service

The Labour Exchanges Act (1909) introduced local offices where both employers and job seekers could register and so obtain help in matching the work and the worker. These began under the auspices of the Board of Trade but were transferred to the new Ministry of Labour when it was established in 1917 when their name was changed to employment exchanges.

In 1910 the Education, Choice of Employment Act was passed,

which began the Youth Employment Service. This was undoubtedly a significant innovation, giving recognition to the crucial importance of helping school-leavers make a satisfactory transition from school to work.

The right match between worker and work is obviously a matter of national concern affecting the efficiency of the country's economy. It is also of vital importance to the individual. Almost all of us work for our living and spend approximately a third of our waking hours doing it. If we begin on the wrong foot and are not suited to the job, wastage accumulates in terms of time, money, effort and plain human misery. The Careers Advisory Service, the modern name for the old Youth Employment Service, therefore, attempts to facilitate the matching process from the beginning of a young person's career. The intention and objective of this service have been admirable from its beginning but its implementation rather less so. The major difficulty has always been the dual concern of both education and industry. Should the service be the responsibility of the education authorities or of the Department of Employment? It began under the original Act of 1910 with split accountability. The local education authorities were given power to establish vocational guidance schemes, and if an authority chose not to use these powers, the Board of Trade could organize such a scheme instead. This arrangement was never satisfactory. Several attempts were made to improve the situation, the most important being the committee appointed by the government during the Second World War under the chairmanship of Sir Godfrey Ince, 'to consider measures necessary to establish a comprehensive Juvenile Employment Service' (HMSO, 1945). They would have wished for a scheme accountable to and administered by one department of state, but they were forced to conclude that vocational guidance and youth employment were the responsibility of both the Ministries of Education and of Labour. Their recommendation, therefore, implemented by the Employment and Training Act of 1948, was an unusual compromise. The Ministry of Labour was given overall accountability for the service delegated to a central Youth Employment Executive, on which representatives of both ministries served. At local level, however, the old division of authority remained. Education authorities were empowered to administer the service and the majority opted to do so. Where they did not wish to undertake the task, the Ministry of Labour was obliged to do so.

With the good will of both departments, the scheme has worked pretty well, but it has suffered from other grave handicaps. As it is now called, it is and has always been, an advisory service and no one is compelled to accept advice. There is no compulsory registration of either jobs or young people, so that career advisers can help only those who seek their help and can offer only vacancies notified to them. It is not suggested that a service of this kind should be anything but voluntary but the limits which such freedom imposes on its effectiveness should be understood. In areas of the country where there is a variety of work, it is obviously easier for the service to place young people in the occupation of their choice than in areas where opportunities are limited, and although quite generous grants for transferring people and for training exist, it is understandable that few parents wish to see their children move away from home.

The Youth Employment Service was reviewed again in 1965 by a working party headed by Lady Albemarle (HMSO, 1965), which made a number of recommendations extending and strengthening the service, and in 1973, the Employment and Training Act established its present form and content.

From 1 April 1974, every local education authority had a duty to provide a vocational guidance service for those in educational institutions and an employment service for those leaving. Universities were excluded from the requirements but the services had to be available to individuals wishing to use them. The age limit, hitherto 18, was removed, so that anyone is eligible to make use of the services.

At the same time the Employment Services Agency introduced a service for young people who, being in work, may seek advice and help in furthering their careers.

In the 1970s a period of serious juvenile unemployment, the careers service, together with the Manpower Services Commission, is playing a large part in a wide variety of schemes, such as 'Job Creation', 'Work Experience' and 'Community Work'.

Disablement

This subject is dealt with more fully in Chapter 8 but the implications for employment in industry are obvious and important.

The Workman's Compensation Act (1897) was probably the first official recognition of concern for disablement in the industrial situation and in 1911 the National Insurance Act made provision for those injured at work. However, it was not until after the First World War that the concept of rehabilitation became a reality. The number of disabled ex-servicemen unable to earn a living aroused public concern and in 1917, the Ministry of Pensions set up government instructional factories to cater for them. These were taken over by the Ministry of Labour in 1919. Between the wars, several highly successful voluntary ventures were launched, such as the Queen Elizabeth's Training College for the disabled at Leatherhead and, of course, the casualties of the Second World War brought renewed interest on a major scale. By this date, there had been some important medical developments so that disabled people could no longer be 'written off' and left on the industrial scrap heap. Finally, following the recommendations of the Tomlinson Committee, which had been set up in 1941 to consider the medical rehabilitation, post-hospital rehabilitation and resettlement of the disabled, the Disabled Persons Employment Act was passed in 1944 (HMSO, 1942). Its definition of a disabled person is both simple and all-embracing. 'One who on account of injury, disease or congenital deformity is substantially handicapped in obtaining or keeping employment' and its declared purpose is 'to make further and better provision for enabling persons handicapped by disablement to secure employment or work on their own account'.

The Act established the Register of Disabled Persons, kept at the Department of Employment, also, at every employment exchange there was appointed a disablement resettlement officer, whose responsibility is to advise disabled men and women and to help them obtain suitable employment. Registration, however, is not compulsory, and the evident reluctance of the disabled to register with the department has had the effect of reducing their success in placing workers. The Act of 1944, slightly amended by another Act in 1965, also established a quota scheme. Every employer with a total of not less than twenty employees must employ 3 per cent disabled, unless he can prove that his work cannot be done by any available disabled person.

Certain special employments were 'designated' under the Act for disabled people, which meant that unless the disabled were unobtainable, no fit person could be employed on that work. Only two jobs were so designated, car park attendant and passenger electric lift attendant. In recent years this quota scheme has not proved successful, being difficult to enforce and, therefore, widely ignored. There have been several attempts to revise the whole system and the severe unemployment of the mid-1970s has emphasized the problem.

Finally, mention must be made of the provision of sheltered employment and the industrial rehabilitation units administered by the Department of Employment.

A non-profit making company, 'Remploy', was established by the government in 1945 to provide special factories for more severely disabled not able to compete with ordinary workers in open industry. Ninety factories were set up in a wide variety of trades, together with a small homeworkers' scheme. Government loans help with capital expenditure and operating costs are covered by the sale of goods in the open market. Remploy has succeeded not only in producing commercially viable products, but also in restoring a meaning to the lives of countless disabled workers.

The industrial rehabilitation units are also highly successful. They were begun in 1949 and by 1977 there were twenty-eight spread throughout the country. They are intended for men and women who need help, following accident or illness, before they can return to employment. Courses normally last twelve weeks, during which time workers are brought gradually back to normal fitness under the constant supervision of doctors, psychologists, physiotherapists and welfare workers.

The main aim of such units can be said to be to restore confidence, and their success rate is impressive. The administrative change brought about by the creation of the Manpower Services Commission in 1974, included the take-over of the Department of Employment's responsibilities for sheltered employment. The commission also assumed responsibility for policy development in relation to disabled people, and provided the secretariat for the National Advisory Council for the Employment of Disabled People.

All in all, there can be no doubt that the disabled have achieved a recognized status in the social services and this is clearly reflected in the provisions made for their useful employment.

Health and Safety

The themes of the Factories Act (1961) are health, safety and welfare which, together with the limitation of the hours allowed for women and young persons, and some miscellaneous provisions, make up its entire content. It lays down minimum conditions for both safe working and industrial hygiene and is administered by the factory inspectorate, to whom all accidents which involve absence from work of three or more days, must be reported. The sections of the Act deal inevitably with matters of safety in general terms but there are a great many detailed orders under the Act relating to special hazards in certain industries. The definition of a factory includes any premises (whether or not within a building) in which one or more persons are employed in manual labour in any process for – or incidental to – the making, altering, repairing, finishing, cleaning, washing or breaking-up of any article or the adapting for sale of any article. Such an inclusive definition appears comprehensive until one considers the thousands of workers of all grades in very many occupations who are excluded. It was for this and other reasons that the later Health and Safety at Work Act was passed (1974).

It is a curious fact that, in spite of a universal need for self-preservation, the subject of safety at work (and indeed, judging from the statistics of accidents, in the home also) lacks appeal. Sensible people acknowledge the importance of safety, but few are inspired to do much about it except in highly dangerous conditions. Accidents are likely to occur where necessary precautions are less obvious and, of course, always happen to 'other people'. Occupational psychologists have always been concerned about accident causation and prevention and interested readers should consult the literature. What is relevant here is that the Act of 1974, known by its initials as HASWA, makes a real attempt to exploit psychological knowledge and enforces by statute the involvement of each one of us in safety at work.

The Factories Act has not been repealed, nor has the Office, Shops and Railway Premises and the Mines and Quarries Acts (not dealt with in this book). The new act is superimposed over existing health and safety legislation and makes one comprehensive and integrated system of law to deal with the health and safety of virtually all people at work, and the protection of the public where they may be affected by the activities of people at work. About five million people – such as those employed in education, medicine, leisure industries and in some parts of the transport industry – who have not been covered by previous health and safety legislation, will now be protected for the first time.

The Act is administered by the Health and Safety Commission (consisting of representatives of both sides of industry and the local authorities) and by the Health and Safety Executive, a separate statutory body appointed by the commission, which enforces legal requirements and provides an advisory service to both sides of industry. The Employment Medical Advisory Service Act of 1972 is re-enacted with some minor modification. This service takes over the medical aspects of the commission and is largely involved in giving advice over the whole range of the commission's activities.

Employers, employees and the self-employed all have duties to ensure safety at work and the inspectors have strong power to enforce it. They can issue either an 'improvement notice' to remedy a fault within a specified time or a 'prohibition notice' to stop an activity if there is serious risk to safety. One of the most interesting innovations under the Act is the compulsory appointment of safety representatives of employees. At the time of writing, it is expected that they will be chosen by the unions, but exactly what their responsibilities will be, how they will carry out their duties and how the scheme will operate when there are no unions is uncertain. Indeed, the provisions of the Act are so wide ranging that its implementation has been long delayed and in mid-1977 is still not wholly in force.

Training

Industrial training has an ancient history, beginning probably with the apprenticeship system of 2100 BC in Mesopotamia and Babylon, but in Britain the story begins in 1563 with the Statute of Artificers, the only piece of legislation in this field until the Industrial Training Act of 1964.

The powerful craft guilds of the sixteenth and seventeenth centuries controlled the conditions of work relevant to their trade, which included provisions for apprentices. A seven-year apprenticeship was required which could not end before the age of twenty-four and no one could exercise a craft unless apprenticed in the prescribed manner. With changing times and lack of enforcement, the system gradually broke down and the 1563 statute was finally repealed in 1814.

The next hundred years, in spite of the growth in trade union influence, saw a decline in training. It was a period of voluntary apprenticeship, with no restriction on either the numbers of apprentices or the length of apprenticeship. The duration of the First World War and the years of depression which followed in the 1920s and 1930s saw a further decline. The war itself meant that skilled men left industry for the forces and boys were called up on reaching the age of eighteen. After the war, when the country experienced the worst unemployment in its history, there was little interest shown in training, although some large organizations were notable exceptions.

At the outbreak of the Second World War in 1939, the country was desperately short of skilled people and a number of short, improvised measures were resorted to. After the war, several further valiant attempts were made to meet the training needs of industry, but they made only a limited impact. The Education and Training Act (1948) was full of good intention but in practice, little resulted in the way of training. The Industrial Organization and Development Act (1947) was an attempt by government to intervene in training. It sought to set up development councils in certain industries, but only four were in fact created and only two survived – for the cotton and furniture industries. The industrial teams which visited America shortly after the war, under the auspices of the Anglo-American Council on Productivity, reported in 1951. Three were devoted to different aspects of education and training and all urged the necessity for increased training. They were well received but had little impact on British practice.

Changes in industrial technology were increasing throughout the twentieth century and, by the end of the war in 1945, had reached dramatic proportions. The implications for the necessary training in new skills were, however, unappreciated by industry as a whole. Both employers and unions, exclusively concerned with their own interests, resented government intervention and refused to take the long view of the country's training needs. Warnings, exhortations or threats, therefore, from whatever quarter, went unheeded.

A powerful impetus, however, came from what was known as the population 'bulge'. This referred to the exceptionally high birth rate of 1947. Children born in the last years of the war, and just after, reached employment age in the 1960s. This, of course, had been foreseen and in 1958 a report was published entitled *Training for*

Skill. It was known by the name of the chairman who led the committee of enquiry, Sir Robert Carr, and represented the views of both the CBI and the TUC. The Carr Committee was concerned with the absorption of the bulge into employment and concentrated on craft apprenticeship (HMSO, 1957). This was a period of full employment so that the problems presented by the 'bulge' were seen as those of training opportunities rather than of employment. The report was well received and training was recommended on all sides, but still insufficient action resulted until the government passed the Industrial Training Act (1964).

The Act has three main objectives: to ensure an adequate supply of properly trained men and women at all levels in industry; to secure an improvement in the quality and efficiency of industrial training; and to share the cost of training more evenly between firms.

Training was not made compulsory. Instead, a system of levies and grants was devised which, by introducing a financial element, ensured industry's close attention. Where training was concerned, firms were grouped into three categories: those doing their fair share; those doing less than their fair share; and those doing more than their fair share. All employers paid a training levy based, in most cases, on a percentage of the wage bill, but in some cases on a percentage of production; those providing training received a proportionate grant. The Act was implemented by a series of training boards set up for individual industries and representing both employers and unions with independent chairmen. As well as administering the levy–grant scheme, the boards became professional training advisers, running courses and helping individual firms, for which they received a large government grant.

The 1964 Act has been a success, in that training of all kinds and at all levels increased enormously. Firms no longer asked themselves 'Can we afford to train?' but rather 'Can we afford not to train?'

The administration of the training boards was revised, however. The levy–grant system posed financial problems which in some cases caused difficult complications. Under the Employment and Training Act (1973) establishing the Manpower Services Commission, modifications were made to the Industrial Training Act (1964). Training boards were accountable to the new commission and exemption certificates from levy could now be issued by boards to employers who satisfied certain fairly stringent training requirements. Operating expenses and grants are now provided through the Training Services Agency by the commission.

This branch of the Manpower Services Commission took over all government training services, greatly increased the amount of training offered at what are now called skill centres and at the time of writing, are concentrating on a variety of schemes to help unemployed young people.

Discrimination

In the context of this chapter 'discrimination' is confined to two categories, – race and sex. Although presenting similar problems, they have different origins and are dealt with by different legal provisions. In spite of the fact that women make up at least 50 per cent of the population, have always worked in industry and have always been discriminated against, they did not receive official attention to redress such discrimination until much later than did racial minorities. Indeed, women owe their achievement of 'equal opportunities' to the problems presented by coloured immigrants in the 1950s and 1960s and the legislation which followed to combat discrimination.

Race Relations

The peculiar aspect of industry and social policy which concerns race relations is that it is the only one not having a history beyond the 1960s. At that time it became clear that our growing immigrant population was not getting a fair deal in many areas of public life, as a result simply of the colour of their skin. Very many thinking people, the government included, saw the dangers and indeed the immorality of a possible segregated society or one with first- and second-class citizens. No doubt too, the example of the appalling racial problems in America and in South Africa acted as a spur to action. The Act of 1965 was the first Act of Parliament ever passed in this country dealing with race relations. It was, however, a very tentative affair because it dealt only with acts of discrimination in public places – that is in hotels, cafés, restaurants, dance halls, sports grounds and the like – any kind of place to which the general public normally has access.

The principle, however, was established. Discrimination was

declared unlawful on the grounds of colour, race or ethnic or national origins and defined as treating a person less favourably than another on such grounds.

The statutory body set up to administer the new law was the Race Relations Board and it soon found that the circumstances within which the Act recognized acts as discriminating were too limited. The majority of the complaints reported referred to incidents which did not occur in public places and which, therefore, could not be dealt with because they were outside the terms of the Act. Such complaints referred to alleged acts of discrimination in getting jobs, in buying houses and in obtaining all kinds of services such as insurance, mortgages and licences. In other words, the Act of 1965, although it broke new ground in English legal history, proved ineffective in providing a remedy for the unfair treatment of an increasing number of citizens in the ordinary affairs of their everyday lives.

A second and enlarged Race Relations Act was passed, therefore, in 1968. It remained in force for eight years and had a marked effect on social behaviour in many areas. Discrimination was still defined as treating a person less favourably than another on grounds of colour, race, ethnic or national origins, but now the scope of the law extended to the whole field of employment and of housing as well as in the provision of goods, facilities and services. Two bodies were set up to implement the Act. One, the original Race Relations Board, was enlarged and continued to operate through regional conciliation committees. It was charged with investigating all complaints, however trivial, relating to discrimination and, in addition, it could now initiate investigation where the available evidence seemed to warrant it. Real power, however, was lacking. Isolated cases did come to court at the instigation of the Attorney General on the advice of the board, but conciliation remained the overriding policy.

The second body set up by the Act of 1968 was the Community Relations Commission. Its main duty was not to enforce the law, but to help to establish harmonious relations by whatever means appropriate, and to support and encourage local community relations committees.

The two bodies worked well together but there was, perhaps understandably, some confusion between them in the minds of the public.

The 1968 Act, in turn, was replaced in 1976 by a third Race Relations Act. This again strengthened the law and made fundamental changes in its enforcement. A new commission with greater powers, the Commission for Racial Equality, replaces both the Race Relations Board and the Community Relations Commission and is charged with a strategic role in tackling discrimination and promoting equality of opportunity. Individual victims of discrimination now seek redress through the civil courts and industrial tribunals and in certain cases, can get help from the new commission. Local community relations councils remain and are supported and co-ordinated by the CRE.

Like its predecessor, the 1976 Act deals with racial discrimination in employment, training, education and housing, as well as the provision of goods, facilities and services and includes, for the first time, discrimination by private clubs.

The definition of 'discrimination' has been widened considerably. Victimization (because a person has asserted his rights under the legislation or been involved in its enforcement), nationality and indirect discrimination are now added to the original grounds of colour, race or ethnic or national origins.

In its form the new Act closely follows that of the Sex Discrimination Act (1975) and, like it, introduces two kinds of discrimination: direct and indirect. Direct discrimination consists of treating a person less favourably on 'racial grounds', and indirect discrimination involves practices which (whether or not intentionally) are discriminatory in their effect on a particular racial group and cannot be shown as justifiable.

This chapter is concerned with industry, so it is the law as it affects employment which is relevant. To the manager, foreman or supervisor it is as important to understand the legislation on race relations as it is the Factories Act. They are both part of the increasing legal framework within which the State obliges us to work and in many ways, the Race Relations Act like the Employment Protection Act, is more important than the Factories Act because it affects our behaviour towards other people rather than, say, the number of cubic feet allowed per person.

Discrimination must take place every time one applicant for a job is selected rather than another, every time one worker is chosen for promotion or for training, but it is illegal to do so on 'racial' or indeed, on sex grounds. It is important that all levels in an organization's hierarchy understand their legal responsibilities. Employers are held responsible for the unlawful actions of their employees and, although policies are usually made at top level, they are normally implemented lower down. As in so many other areas, therefore, communication is vital.

Sex Discrimination

Until very recently, women, with some exceptions, were paid less than men. This was accepted largely because they were regarded as inferior to men and, therefore, not worth as much. They were only seldom family breadwinners and were seen normally as dependent on fathers or husbands. When women were employed in industry, they were confined to the lower paid and less skilled jobs. The struggle for equality began with the First World War, when women took over 'men's work' on a grand and even dramatic scale, the suffragettes continued the protest and with women's repeated contribution in the Second World War the case was made out conclusively. It took many more years, however, before 'equal pay for equal work' was either recognized or accepted as a principle.

By 1918, the professions of law and accountancy were open to women and in 1920 the civil service abolished its grade of woman clerk, although women were still largely confined to the lower grades. A Royal Commission on Equal Pay sat from 1944 to 1946 and by this time, equal pay had been achieved by doctors, dentists, physiotherapists, radiographers, university teachers, journalists and architects (HMSO, 1946).

In 1951, the International Labour Organization proposed equal pay for work of equal value and in 1955, the civil service, local government and the nationalized industries agreed that women's rates of pay should be equalized with those of men over a seven-year period.

It wasn't until 1970 that the Equal Pay Act reached the statute book and, even then, employers were given five years to bring the rates for women up to those for men. By the end of December 1975, however, women were entitled to equal treatment with men when they were employed on like work, that is work of the same or a broadly similar nature to that of men, or in a job which, though different from those of men, has been given an equal value to men's jobs under a job evaluation exercise. It doesn't take very much imagination to realize how easy it was to avoid implementing this law. There are countless ways of grading or regrading jobs and of providing new names for similar roles. Many jobs too have traditionally been done solely by women and there existed no comparison with men. In some cases whole industries, such as lace finishing, were completely excluded by this legislation and so remained near the bottom of the league table and protected by a wages council. In other words, by itself, the Equal Pay Act achieved little. It was obvious that until women had equal job opportunities with men they would remain in an inferior position. The Sex Discrimination Act (1975) was intended to provide a remedy. Much had been learned from the operation of the Race Relations Acts and so this one sought to avoid some of the earlier weaknesses. From 1975, it became unlawful to treat anyone, on the grounds of sex, less favourably than a person of the opposite sex is or would be treated in the same circumstances. Although largely thought of in terms of women, it is worth noting that the law equally protects men. Sex discrimination is not allowed in employment, education, the provision of housing, goods, facilities and services, and in advertising. In employment it is also unlawful to discriminate because a person is married.

Two kinds of discrimination are distinguished: direct discrimination involves treating a woman less favourably than a man because she is a woman; indirect discrimination means that conditions are applied which favour one sex more than the other but which cannot be justified. An example of this, often quoted, is that if an employer, recruiting clerks, insists on candidates being six feet tall, a case may be made out that he is unlawfully discriminating.

Complainants who think they have been unfairly treated because of their sex can seek redress either from an industrial tribunal in the case of employment, or from the county courts.

Finally, to ensure effective enforcement of both the Sex Discrimination Act and the Equal Pay Act, the Equal Opportunities Commission was created. It has the power to hold investigations and, if satisfied that practices are unlawful, can issue non-discrimination notices requiring that they cease. It also has the power to require any person to furnish information and attend hearings to give evidence, a power which was withheld from the old conciliation committees of the Race Relations Board. The Equal Opportunities Commission can, in certain circumstances, where a matter of principle is at stake, help individuals in the preparation and conduct of complaints in both courts and tribunals. It can also promote research and, indeed, is charged to do all it sees as appropriate to promote equal opportunities between the sexes.

As is the case with much of the recent legislation, it is, at the time of writing, rather too soon to judge effectiveness, but to date (1977) the law against sex discrimination has proved disappointing. There is no doubt that the manifest situation has changed and the neutral noun 'person' is used everywhere. Some employers are keen to be seen on the right side of the law by displaying women in conspicuous posts, but it will clearly take longer than was thought before attitudes change sufficiently for women to be accepted as equal with men. Neither the country's education system nor traditional vocational opportunities can be altered by a stroke of the pen, and in addition, women themselves require time to adjust to the enormous social implications of the new opportunities now presented by law.

The Protection of Workers

In a sense, almost all the legislation of the past century can be described as being in one form or another a protection of the interests of workers. The early Factory Acts, workman's compensation and the legalizing of trade unions all contributed to restoring the balance of power between master and servant. The nineteenth century was characterized throughout by social legislation in all spheres of life but in industrial affairs, although the foundations of protection for employees and restrictions on employers were well and truly laid, the legislation was nothing compared to what was to follow in the second half of the twentieth century.

The impact of the Second World War has already been referred to and the introduction of what is called the welfare state had its effects on industrial matters. Both the Industrial Injuries Act (1946) and the Disabled Persons Employment Act (1944) can be seen as part of Beveridge's grand health package and the Employment and Training Act (1948) brought other services up to date with the immediate post-war environment.

It was the 1960s, however, which opened the floodgates and the 1970s which brought the deluge.

The Factories Act, passed in 1961, was a new edition of that of 1937. It is still in force, although somewhat surpassed by the Health and Safety at Work Act (1974), referred to above. In 1963, came the Contracts of Employment Act, which is binding on all employers and provides a measure of both security and dignity to the relationship between employer and employed. Terms and conditions of work must be given in writing to all employees within thirteen weeks of employment and, although employees only have to give one week's notice of leaving their employment, employers have to give notice of termination on a scale which lengthens according to the length of employment. This Act was amended by a second Contracts of Employment Act (1972) and yet again by the Trade Union and Labour Relation Act (1974). The most important addition to its clauses is that employers are also required to inform their employees in writing about whom to approach when they have a grievance about their employment and any subsequent steps in the grievance procedure.

The Industrial Training Act followed in 1964 (see above) and in 1965 the Redundancy Payments Act was passed. A second Redundancy Act followed in 1969 and both were strengthened by Part IV of the Employment Protection Act of 1975.

These acts represent the first legally enforced entitlement for workers to claim financial compensation when their work role becomes redundant. As with the Industrial Training Act, the fact that large sums of money were written into the provisions caused business to sit up and take notice. Both the conditions for, and the scale of, payment are generous, with the intention that as technical processes change, labour would be encouraged and enabled to seek alternative work. The scheme applies to men between the ages of 18 and 65 and to women between 18 and 60 who have been with their employer continuously for at least 2 years and who normally work for 16 hours or more per week. Employers are liable to make redundancy payments but they may claim a rebate from the Department of Employment. Employees do not pay tax on such payments but if they refuse a reasonable offer of either a renewal of their contract or suitable alternative work, they are not entitled to redundancy payment.

The Employment Protection Act (1975) gives employees job security by requiring employers to consult appropriate recognized trades unions whenever they propose to make even one employee redundant. The Act also requires employers to notify the Secretary of State if they plan to make ten or more employees redundant at one establishment within a specified period. Also, if an employee accepts an offer of a different type of job from the one made redundant, he is allowed a trial period to test its suitability. This is usually of four weeks' duration but it may be extended. Clearly, the scheme is open to abuse and the industrial tribunals are kept busy with claims and counter-claims under these acts.

> The success of Factory Legislation has been so great . . . the beneficial effects that have flowed from these Acts have been so marked and are now so universally admitted . . . and continuing evils in non regulated trades so flagrant that the time has come when . . . we may extend the principle of these Acts more largely than it has ever been extended before.

The quotation is taken from the *Parliamentary Debates* (1867) but it might have been written more than a century later when, for the first time for 100 years, industrial relations again became the subject of an Act of Parliament.

In order to appreciate both the importance and the emotional impact of first the Industrial Relations Act (1971) and its successor the Trade Union and Labour Relations Act (TULRA) (1974), it is necessary to understand the historical background in which is embedded the folk memory of the whole trade union movement.[3] There were five stages in the story of the relationship between the law and the trade unions.

(1)   From 1800 to 1824, unions were completely outlawed and any union activity was disallowed under the criminal law.

(2)   From 1824, when the Combination Laws were repealed, until 1871, unions were legal but their activities were subject to the penalties of the common law, which meant that more often than not, they were accused of 'conspiracy', 'being in restraint of trade', 'inducing breach of contract' or 'intimidation', so that their power was severely restricted.

(3)   In 1871, just a hundred years before the Act of 1971, the first Trade Union Act was passed. By this date, organized labour was seen as necessary to an industrial society but because their activities breached the common law, they had to be given statutory protection by Act of Parliament. This Act of 1871, therefore, provided immunity from acts against common law and, in a sense, put the unions above the law. For the next

hundred years – except for the Trade Disputes Act (1909) and the Trade Union Act (1913) – industry was left to settle its problems without legal intervention.

(4)   The ill-fated Industrial Relations Act (1971) was the result of increasing unrest in industry and of political dissension in labour matters. Both parties were concerned and produced documents on industrial relations. The Conservative Party's *Fair Deal at Work* was published first and recommended modernizing industrial relations through comprehensive legislation covering trade union registration, control of strike actions and improving the security of individual employees and trade union members. The Labour Government of 1965 appointed a Royal Commission on Trade Unions and Employers' Associations under the chairmanship of Lord Donovan, which reported in 1968 and recommended a complete overhaul of the system of collective bargaining, but rejected the idea that collective agreements between employers and unions should be made legally enforceable. Their paper *In Place of Strife* incorporated many of the commission's proposals but the general election occurred before such proposals became law and it was, therefore, the Conservatives who brought in the Industrial Relations Act (1971). This Act, which broke Britain's long-standing commitment to the belief in voluntary agreements, represented a return to the use of law to regulate the day-to-day transactions of employers and employed. The statutory protection introduced in 1871 was now rescinded where 'inducing breach of contract' was concerned and the Act's purpose was to enclose industrial relations within a framework of law. It introduced a number of new concepts – registration of trade unions, unfair industrial practices and a completely new set of courts to administer the law and to hear appeals.

The Act was not a success and, indeed, its claim to fame rests on the fact that it was a remarkable example of the ineffectiveness of a law which does not receive the sanction of the governed. The trade unions, almost to a man, refused to co-operate and within three years the government was forced to repeal the Act and try again.

(5)   The second attempt at legislation in industrial relations was the Trade Union and Labour Relations Act (1974), which began

a new era of legislation. This Act goes into precise detail and, together with the Employment Protection Act (1975), provides an employment package with six major objectives:

(a) A revolutionary change is made in the legal nature of the employment relationship. Status has been added to contract so that an employee now has a measure of freehold in his job, of which he can't be deprived by contract only.

(b) A whole series of new employee rights has been established. These include guaranteed payments, suspension on medical grounds, maternity rights, trade union membership and allowances for union activities, rights to time off with or without pay, unfair dismissal clauses and a legal right to an itemized pay settlement.

(c) Such rights are supported by a new legal structure. Industrial tribunals have been greatly extended and the Advisory Conciliation and Arbitration Service (ACAS) set up as an independent statutory body.

(d) There are new legal arrangements to strengthen the trade unions. The main emphasis in this total package is to give the unions both more duties and new responsibilities. They now have the right to be consulted in advance on redundancy both on its extent and on the way it is carried out. The term 'closed shop' is not used in the legislation, but unions have the right to be established by recognition and to be the body to represent workers in negotiation. A membership agreement is allowed and where one exists, an employer can fairly dismiss anyone who stays outside.

(e) Management has new obligations to disclose information relevant to proper collective bargaining.

(f) There are new anti-discrimination policies. Those on the grounds of race and sex have already been described above but in addition, part-time workers are included. Part-time work is now defined as less than sixteen hours a week, not twenty-one.

The final chapter in the story of industry and social policy is entitled 'industrial democracy'.

Although we live in a political democracy we have not yet achieved democracy at work. It is government policy, however, to do so, and a promised 'Industry Bill' is waiting in the wings, so to speak.

The enormously increased power of the unions and the greater understanding and involvement of the modern industrial employee means that a real democratic commitment is surely only a matter of time.

It is simple enough to state the principle of industrial democracy but not nearly so easy to put it into practice and it is here that controversy arises.

There are differences in the meaning attributed to industrial democracy and in recent years there has been a great deal of talk and disagreement about participation, worker directors and workers' control.

In 1975, the government appointed a committee of inquiry under Lord Bullock 'to advise on questions relating to representation at board level in the private sector'[5] (HMSO, 1977).

The Bullock report was published in January 1977 and had a hostile reception. Its majority recommended a single board divided '$2x + y$', which means an equal number of worker and shareholder representatives, plus a third group jointly agreed. Worker representatives would be appointed by a joint union committee and an Industrial Democracy Commission established to supervise the arrangements. A minority of the committee's members made alternative recommendations. They preferred to see decision-making power given to worker directors through a supervisory second-tier board concerned with general policy and not day-to-day running and only in companies that have had three years' experience of participation councils.

Some of the practical problems are obvious. For example, many workers would object to being represented by members of a trade union to which they do not belong. Shareholders may well resent having to stand down from company boards to make room for worker directors, and they in turn may have a certain conflict in loyalties in occupying two roles.

There are clearly a number of possible variations in structuring a democratic form of organization and there seems a lot to be said for flexibility to allow different companies to find the most appropriate pattern for their individual needs within a framework of the law.

At present, the whole subject is still in the melting pot and the pot is likely to be stirred several times before an acceptable solution is found.

Conclusion

There is no doubt that the theme which runs through the story outlined in this chapter is that of a steady increase in State intervention in industrial affairs. Not only have technological processes added to the complexities of industrial organization but the population also has increased so that more regulation and control appears necessary.

If you are a factory worker you are likely to interpret the effects of modern legislation as enlightened policy which has substantially improved the lot of the working man and increased the power of trade unions. If, on the other hand, you are an employer, you will see the new regulations as a strait-jacket inhibiting progress and interfering in established management prerogatives. Good employers resent the implication that employees require so much protection by law; they suggest that the recent proliferation of regulations stifles initiative, kills incentive and may even encourage unemployment because of the restrictions surrounding 'fair dismissal'.

It may be that there has been excessive legislation in too short a period for easy assimilation but it is well to remember that this country is still a long way behind almost all others in Western Europe in its range and scope of labour laws.

Notes

1   Ergonomics, a word invented by Murrell and derived from the Greek words, *ergos* (work) and *nomos* (natural law), meaning the scientific study of human work or the study of man in his working environment. It consists of the application of practical scientific knowledge gained from the basic human sciences of anatomy, physiology and psychology with the objective of improving the effectiveness and well-being of the individual through the design of equipment and the control of the environment.

2   I am indebted to Mr E. J. Pengelly, District Manager, Employment Services Agency, for providing a considerable amount of the material used in this and subsequent sections.

3   I should like to acknowledge the help of my colleague, Professor A. H. Thornton, with the content of this section.

4   ACAS describes itself as an industrial relations service to industry. It was established as an independent body under the Employment Protection Act (1975) to help improve industrial relations and assist industry to avoid and settle trade disputes. It gives impartial

and confidential advice to managements, unions, and, in certain cases, to individual employees.

The service is run by a council consisting of a chairman and nine members – three nominated by the CBI, three by the TUC and three independent. Its main functions include advice on industrial relations and personnel practices, conciliation in disputes, arbitration and mediation and help in improving collective bargaining. It also examines applications for trade union recognition under section 11 of the Employment Protection Act and has the duty to provide codes of practice in consultation with both sides of industry. These contain certain practical guidance for employers and trade unions and, to date, cover disclosure of information for collective bargaining, time off for trade union duties, disciplinary practice and procedures in employment, collective bargaining procedures and trade union recognition.

5   The full terms of reference for the Bullock Committee of Enquiry were as follows:

> Accepting the need for a radical extension of industrial democracy in the control of companies by means of representation on boards of directors, and accepting the essential role of trade union organizations in this process, to consider how such an extension can best be achieved, taking into account in particular the proposals of the Trades Union Congress report on industrial democracy as well as experience in Britain, the EEC and other countries. Having regard to the interests of the national economy, employees, investors and consumers, to analyse the implications of such representation for the efficient management of all companies and for company law.

References

HMSO (1942), *Rehabilitation and Resettlement of Disabled Persons*, Cmd 6415 (Tomlinson Committee).

HMSO (1942/3), *Health and Welfare of Women in War Factories*, House of Commons Select Committee on National Expenditure, 19, Third Report.

HMSO (1945), *Juvenile Employment Service*, Ministry of Labour and National Service (Ince Committee).

HMSO (1944–6), *Royal Commission on Equal Pay*, Cmd 6937.

HMSO (1957), *Training for Skill. Recruitment and Training for Young Workers in Industry*, report by a sub committee of the National Joint Advisory Council (Carr Committee).

HMSO (1965), *The Future Development of the Youth Employment Service*, Report of a working party of the National Youth Employment Council.

HMSO (1977), *Report of the Committee of Enquiry on Industrial Democracy*, Cmnd 6706 (Bullock Committee).

Hutchins B. L. (1912), *Robert Owen*, Fabian Society (Biographical
    series no. 2).
Parliamentary Debates (1867), vol. CLXXXV, 5 February.
Wigham E. (1976), *Department of Employment Gazette*, March.

3

Urban Planning and Social Policy

Meryl Aldridge

Planning up to 1939

The problems of urban life, and their solution, have more tangibility
and immediacy than other social policies. One may come into
contact with education and health services, social security and the
criminal law at certain stages and crises in life – or even never – but
the fabric of our urban areas is the physical expression of the social
order. Housing, employment, communications, public services,
leisure and recreation facilities – the accessibility or inaccessibility
of these are a major part of our life chances. Tacit recognition of this
has meant that since urban and rural space became accepted as an
object of public legislation and policy, planning has attracted widespread public interest and debate. The scale and complexity of
urban problems has been reflected in the heterogeneity of
approaches that have been suggested, ranging from the visionary,
Utopian – and sometimes frankly eccentric – to the gloomily pro-
saic. Indeed, the whole history of planning policy can be seen as the
outcome of a struggle of ideas between those for whom urban
problems, as a reflection of the social and political structure, should
only be approached through comprehensive analysis and change of
the whole society, and those who for principled or practical reasons
contented themselves with remedying particular issues of housing,
public health or the provision of services.

The industrial revolution in Britain shifted production from the
home or small workshop to the factory which, as products became

more complex, needed to be located not only near sources of energy, but other factories also. Thus, in a relatively short space of time, the population of Britain was transformed from being predominantly rural dwelling to urban dwelling. During the nineteenth century the population of England and Wales trebled (Ashworth, 1954, p. 7) as the death rate fell concurrently with a rising birth rate. It is hardly surprising that by the mid-century this massive social disruption had become a cause of public concern. The major crisis was of health. In the rural areas life had been impoverished, but water supply, the disposal of sewage and refuse, and space for play and recreation could be left at least in part to take care of themselves. In the towns, however, in which factories (and their effluent) and housing were crammed together with regard only for the maximum speed and profit in development, and the accessibility of worker to factory on foot, these private problems became appalling public issues.

Concentration was itself part of the problem. Anderson (1971, p. 33) writes that the population of Preston multiplied five-fold between 1801 and 1851, when it stood at 69, 542. The population had doubled between 1831 and 1851. Yet the town was still 'only about one and a half miles from east to west and one mile from north to south'. Vivid accounts of the squalor resulting from this speed and concentration of development are reproduced in Benevolo (1967, pp. 23 ff), quoting Engels's work on Manchester in 1844. Gauldie (1974, pp. 75 ff) writes of the back-to-back houses round interconnecting courts, and the cellar dwellings: 'One Irish tenant with a gift for words said that "the smell was enough to lift the roof off his skull".' Dung and refuse was collected by tradesmen – if they were paid, of course. Water too was either supplied by private tradesmen or, at a charge, by the municipality in irregular and small amounts. It was rarely filtered or treated.

Ashworth (1954, p. 48) discusses the importance of the concentration of criminality – or at least its visibility – in providing an impetus to urban legislation. The debate over private property was a continuing theme, both of nineteenth-century planning legislation, and of resistance to it by those who felt, in tune with the political philosophy of the time, that the rights of the individual to dispose of his land and wealth as he wished should not be curtailed by, for example, regulations governing building, drainage or water supply for the supposed good of the community at large. (This type of dispute continues of course, although over different issues in detail.) The spectacle of the seething urban hordes, not amenable to the informal controls of the little community nor of religion, and apparently all involved in pilfering or prostitution, was sufficient to make some controls a worthwhile compromise, he claims. Ashworth (p. 49) also reports the supposed revolutionary potential of the urban proletariat:

> the propertied classes were not likely to ignore a factor
> threatening social stability when they had seen and
> remembered rioting both in town and countryside and had
> noted with apprehension revolutionary outbreaks in half the
> capitals of Europe. The possibility of an uprising remained as
> a shadow on the British middle class mind and a persuasion
> towards some measure of reform until in 1848 Chartism
> petered out in the face of advancing prosperity.

Benevolo, too, sees 1848 as a significant date. For him it marks the point at which the Utopian tradition of men like Robert Owen, whose achievements were technical but nevertheless rooted in an ideological commitment to social change and thus to a vision of the town as a complete physical and social system, parted company from the 'specialists and officials' (p. xii). These saw their task as essentially reactive and remedial and did not seek to relate their solutions to any over-arching social philosophy. Benevolo asserts that from 1848 the working-class movement became too abstract and grandiose in its objectives to concern itself with the solution to specific urban ills. Whether or not one accepts this view, it is likely that the cholera epidemics of the 1840s in Britain propelled the reformers and their technical remedies into becoming the formative influence on planning thought and legislation which continued for a hundred years, leaving the remnants of the Utopian tradition as strident voices from off-stage.

During the period from the 1834 Poor Law Amendment Act, which Edwin Chadwick was influential in framing, to the major advance of the 1848 Public Health Act, increased collective responsibility was acknowledged over the whole area of local services. The 1848 Act was the outcome of a royal commission which made wide-ranging recommendations including the setting up of local health boards with powers to manage sewers and water supply, inspect lodging houses and slaughter houses, remove refuse and nuisances, and improve roads (Benevolo, 1967, pp. 89 ff). Even this legislation was opposed on the grounds that disease and suffering are part of the natural order, and should not, therefore, be the subject of interference. According to Ashworth (op. cit., pp. 65 ff) the period was also characterized by a conviction that profitability was the sole reasonable justification for any kind of social legislation, but the fear of infection and the decimation and disabling of the workforce in the big cities had provided the climate for a gradual extension of legislation.

The first Torrens Act (1868) and the Cross Act (1875) (Ashworth, 1954, pp. 96 ff) were concerned primarily with housing by enabling local authorities to demand the demolition of unfit houses and to prepare improvement schemes. Although weakened by conferring daunting responsibilities for compensation, and few mandatory powers, the Acts were further significant steps in the acceptance of the legitimacy of local authority intervention. Gradually this extended to other amenities such as parks, roads and bridges.

Meanwhile, the Utopian tradition was being maintained, most coherently by William Morris, who is remembered principally (but unfairly) for his concern with arts and crafts and his wish to dismantle metropolitan life by returning to a small-scale economy of agriculture and cottage trades. In *News from Nowhere* (1891) a dreamer is transported to a London of the future which has been disaggregated into villages where face-to-face contact and relationships are sufficient to maintain social control. Morris was no lover of the centralized State: the Palace of Westminster had become a fruit and vegetable market. He has been accused of being a major influence in the alleged 'anti-urban' bias of British town planning but this accusation could perhaps be more accurately levelled at contemporaries like Charles Kingsley and John Ruskin (see Petersen, 1968, for a discussion of this group).

In 1898 Ebenezer Howard published *Tomorrow: a Peaceful Path to Real Reform*, subsequently renamed *Garden Cities of Tomorrow*. This immensely influential book contained a simple – or even simplistic – scheme to try and combine the advantages of urban civilization (which Howard acknowledged) with what he undoubtedly saw as the vital and essentially superior spiritual quality of rural life. In due course, the whole population of the nation would be rehoused in a network of self-contained 'garden cities', each interdependent with an agricultural estate. Each town, Howard proposed, would have a population of about 30,000 with a further 2,000 living on the agricultural estate. The total area would be about 6,000 acres, of which 5,000 acres would be agricultural.

Little attention is paid in the book to aesthetic or economic issues, but much more to finance. Howard's intention was that the land, initially bought by private subscription, would be held by the municipality and all property leased. Surpluses after the 'rate-rents' had been used to provide services and payments towards the debt on the land, would be used to extend municipal facilities. It was central to Howard's concerns that migration to the garden cities would be voluntary and that housing, and industrial and commercial foundations would be privately owned. Although he had the aim of abolishing the private landlord, he had no more extensive designs upon the social order and seems very much to have been of the view that ill-health and bad housing were the only inequalities that should be the object of intervention. Otherwise the moral order was acceptable. Howard was not a Utopian in the sense that Benevolo defines – and indeed he never claimed to be. The major influences on him seem to have been writers like H. G. Wells and he acknowledged his debt to another technocratic visionary, Bellamy, who had published *Looking Backward* in 1887. In this, another book with a 'dream' motif, the sleeper awakes in the Boston (USA) of AD 2000.

Ebenezer Howard was very much the 'plain man', remaining a parliamentary shorthand writer and ferocious self-educator all his life. But his book (1965 edn) uniquely combined vision, apparent accessibility of its objectives and wide-ranging political appeal. As a result of it the Garden City Association was founded in 1899. This subsequently became the Garden City and Town Planning Association and, through a very fortunate combination of politically influential and tenacious, almost monomaniac, members and employees like C. B. Purdom and F. J. Osborn, succeeded in keeping garden cities on the political agenda until the Second World War. (The GCTPA became the Town and Country Planning Association in 1941, under which name it flourishes and publishes the influential monthly journal *Town and Country Planning* still.)

In 1902 the GCA, through the associated Garden City Pioneer Company started to raise money for Letchworth Garden City, which was begun in 1903. This was not an outright success, but nevertheless Welwyn was founded in 1920. The influence of these projects, aided by the GCTPA, was far in excess of their scale or success. Through the well-known architects associated with them, notably Raymond Unwin and Barry Parker, they became synonymous with the low-density, low-rise, cottage-style development which characterized public and private house building both before 1914 and in the inter-war period. Ironically, 'garden-cities' and 'garden-suburbs' became confused in the public mind and the latter were more enthusiastically adopted by municipal and private builders alike, despite their being the antithesis of what Howard had had in mind. They were almost exclusively dormitory housing areas at the periphery of cities from which residents commuted increasing distances to work. Far from being Howard's 'town-country', they were neither town nor country! It is this style of planning against which Glass (1959) and Jacobs (1964) inveigh but which the propagandists of garden cities claimed to reject. (More detail on this period of the garden cities movement can be found in Aldridge, 1979; Ashworth, 1954; Purdom, 1949.)

Many of those who espoused the garden cities movement were also influential in framing the first real town planning legislation: the Housing, Town Planning etc. Act of 1909. Ashworth (1954, pp. 168 ff) describes this as having more symbolic than actual importance, because it merely enabled local authorities to prepare planning schemes for undeveloped land if they so wished. It was 'a mild, uncertain affair' (p. 188) hampered by the permissions needed from central government and the safeguards to land owners. The 1919 Housing, Town Planning etc. Act (pp. 199 ff) made the preparation of town planning schemes mandatory on local authorities of more than 20,000 population, although this was never fully enforced, and removed the necessity for ministry permission for the preparation of schemes. In 1932 a further Act enabled local authorities to introduce development control but the planning powers of local authorities remained, in effect, essentially optional until the Second World War. Ashworth remarks (p. 224) that the most effective interventions were under the Housing Acts, but that the tenor of legislation showed how far planning had become an accepted part of public policy.

The period between the two world wars saw the biggest expansion of house building that has ever occurred in this country. Railways and then trams and buses had transformed the physical form of urban areas. Hall *et al.* (1973, pp. 76 ff) graphically illustrate the spreading of London and other major cities along railway routes in the last quarter of the nineteenth century, providing for the growing population and reducing densities at the centres. Between the wars a similar process occurred along major roads, partly by the process of 'ribbon development' where builders, untrammelled until 1935 by effective legislation, bought land along radial routes and built housing one deep, thus reducing the extent and cost of the infrastructure that they had to provide. Public authorities were providing large-scale public-housing schemes for the first time. One of the most famous is the London County Council scheme at Becontree and Dagenham, where houses for 120,000 people were built between 1921 and 1934. Given the extremely limited powers of the LCC, which was building outside its boundaries, there was no co-ordination of employment, transport, health, education, welfare, retail or leisure facilities. All these were allowed to arrive spontaneously as the local authorities and private enterprise thought appropriate. Ruth Glass (Durant, 1939) recorded the early days of Watling, a smaller LCC estate on the Edgware road, in pessimistic terms calling it a 'vast hotel without a roof' she lamented the lack of civic and political activity of residents and the financial and physical drain of commuting.

The private sector of house-building was expanding just as rapidly, if in a more piecemeal fashion. Why this conjunction of events should have occurred is still being debated, but a government policy of cheap money was a major factor. Building costs were sufficiently low for the cost of buying a house in the Dagenham area to be very close, for a period, to the rents being paid by LCC tenants nearby. Young (1934) records that people were leaving the estate to buy their own homes and then having to return because they could not manage the cost of maintenance, so small were the margins on their income after paying for household expenses and travel.

Towards the end of the 1930s this explosion of the area of cities had made commuting and anomie on peripheral estates into new social problems, alongside the continuing concern about epidemic diseases like TB, rickets and diphtheria in the central city. All this was taking place in the context of the depression, a major feature of which was the gross disparity in its effects as between the 'traditional' areas of primary and heavy manufacturing industry in Scotland, Wales and the north, and the relatively prosperous Midlands and south-east. Not only the state of the cities but the whole distribution of the population and industry became subjects of scrutiny. In 1937 the 'Barlow' Royal Commission on the Distribution of the Industrial Population (1940) was set up.

The Barlow Commission and Post-war Legislation

The Barlow Commission's primary focus was the 'tide of forces' which concentrated people and wealth in the cities, in particular in London and the south-east of England, and the social, economic and strategic problems that these processes caused. Evidence was received from many influential individuals and organizations, including the GCTPA and the Council for the Preservation of Rural England (CPRE). These two groups were locked in combat over the impact of planning policies on agricultural land, yet a prominent member of the commission, Patrick Abercrombie, was both a member of the former and one of the founders of the latter!

The Commission undertook a comprehensive review of economic changes in Britain, charting the environmental and social consequences of the growth of primary and heavy industry and then its relative eclipse by the light manufacturing upon which the wealth of the west Midlands and south-east was then built. It reviewed population trends and changes in transport policy and took specialist evidence on the effect of urban life on physical health. Despite this wealth of information, Hall has called the conclusions of the Barlow Commission 'muted' (1973, vol. II, p. 47). On the one hand the commission did not accept the GCTPA's arguments that policy should be directed towards the virtual abolition of metropolitan areas, but on the other hand they rejected the CPRE's view that population should be concentrated so as to protect agricultural land and productivity. The commission was naturally preoccupied with air attack and this must have influenced their general recommendations, which inclined towards limiting any further growth in the area or population of existing urban centres and the decentralization of both population and industry to ease congestion. These new developments would be satellite towns, garden suburbs and cities, the expansion of existing towns and trading estates (Barlow, 1940, p. 136). The most significant of Barlow's specific recommendations was that central government should take powers to control the location of industry in an attempt to redistribute employment, through a national industrial board. In a dissenting report, Abercrombie and others argued for a central ministry with more comprehensive planning powers.

Both the Barlow Commission's diagnosis and its proposed cure for urban decay and congestion and regional inequalities have been fundamental influences upon the philosophy of post-war British planning. Whilst many of the problems that expressed themselves in tangible environmental terms were acknowledged by the commissioners to be the outcome of economic and social processes, nevertheless they were to be solved by control of the built environment. The economic decline of the depressed areas could be arrested by redirecting industry to them, transport problems by cutting the journey to work, health problems by a house and garden on a properly planned estate segregated from industrial areas.

During the war Lord Reith, as Minister of Planning, appointed two other influential committees. The Committee on Land Utilization in Rural Areas (1942) (Scott Report) produced anodyne recommendations that towns and villages be strictly controlled and not allowed to encroach upon the countryside. It did, however, reinforce the trend toward accepting more wide-ranging planning legislation, and developed the important principle that the 'onus of proof' should fall on those who wanted to take prime agricultural land for development, rather than those who wanted to preserve it (p. 233).

At the same time a far more radical and overtly influential committee was meeting under Lord Justice Uthwatt. The Expert Committee on Compensation and Betterment (1942) was a small group of lawyers and surveyors. It produced a review of the history and status of the concepts of compensation and betterment which is still a standard reference.

These remain contentious issues in policy on land use. Compensation is the sum that might be paid to a property owner if he loses the right to develop his land or if permission to do so is refused, or if the property is bought from him compulsorily. Betterment is the unearned increase in the value of property brought about by the granting of permission to develop, or by the activities of other public or private bodies. (The classic example of betterment would be where a village, hitherto a sleepy inaccessible place, finds itself near a new motorway to London and is transformed into an ideal base for commuters. Anyone who owns land and is granted permission to develop is likely to make a large profit on the price paid for the land before the motorway was known about.) If the State is to make any effective impact on planning the environment, controls must be enforced that will involve deciding principles of compensation. Collecting betterment for the community at large has had a far more haphazard history, partly because of the practical difficulties of assessing the cause and extent of any supposed rise in value, and partly because of profound political differences over the legitimacy of the profits of land ownership. (The whole melancholy story to date, including the detailed findings of the Uthwatt Committee, the provisions of successive planning Acts, the 1967–70 Land Commission and the 1975 Community Land Act can be found in Cullingworth, 1976, Ch. 7; Ratcliffe, 1976.)

Uthwatt and his colleagues considered a range of solutions to the problems of compensation and betterment, including land nationalization, and concluded that what was needed was the nationalization of the right to develop.

Like the Barlow and Scott reports before it, the Uthwatt Committee was significant not only for its findings, but their general tone. Lawyers and surveyors are not noted iconoclasts, yet they prefaced their report with a brisk affirmation of the necessity to subordinate the 'personal wishes and interests of landowners' to the public good (p. 11). In accordance with the general climate, far-reaching legislation was being framed before the war ended and culminated in the 1945 Distribution of Industry Act, the 1946 New Towns Act and the 1947 Town and Country Planning Act. Significantly, the 1945 Act, which gave central government control over the location of industrial plants above a certain size (currently 15,000 square feet) through a system of industrial development certificates, vested the operation in the Board of Trade, now the Department of Industry. Thus a crucial separation of urban planning and economic policy was created and is still perpetuated.

The 1947 Town and Country Planning Act

Under the new planning legislation both undeveloped and developed land became subject to planning control and the right to develop was nationalized. (£300 million was set aside to compensate, once and for all, those who had acquired land expecting to be able to develop and were thus denied the right.) The intention of the Act had both a positive and a negative dimension. Positively the responsible local authorities (the then counties and county boroughs) were to prepare maps of their entire area, showing present and future land use. After public inquiry, possible modification and the approval of the minister, this would then provide guidance for orderly development, both by the local authority itself and by other public and private agencies. The more negative aspects of planning were the carrying out of 'development control', giving or withholding permission to build or modify buildings in the light of the development plan, amenity, aesthetic and other considerations. The 1947 Act also contained powers to control advertising and caravan sites and to protect the countryside.

Issues of compensation and betterment were approached boldly: compulsory purchase was to be at existing use value and betterment to be levied at 100 per cent. There would be no compensation for the withholding of planning permissions. Only the last of these provisions has survived. The betterment levy was abolished in 1954 and the compensation for compulsory purchase returned to full market value (i.e. with any planning consents) in 1959.

The 1946 New Towns Act

In 1945 the new Labour Minister of Town and Country Planning appointed a New Towns Committee under Lord Reith. Between January and July 1946 the committee produced three reports on the economic, social and cultural prescriptions for new towns and the agency that should develop them. The New Towns Act completed its passage through parliament a week after the *Final Report* (New Towns Committee, 1946) appeared, which suggests that there was powerful government commitment to the idea. Stevenage was started in March 1946 and designated under the Act in November 1946.

The new legislation allowed the minister to designate an area, subject to public inquiry, and to appoint a chairman and board to supervise the new town. The board would then appoint full-time staff to design and execute the town and to manage it once it was under way. The development corporation, using funds borrowed from central government, could build housing and the necessary infrastructure such as drainage and water supply, local facilities like play space, community centres and shops, and some commercial and industrial premises. Within the designated area, the local authority's powers would be unaffected and it would fall to them and to other State, voluntary and commercial bodies to provide the employment, shopping, leisure, welfare, educational, health and other facilities that were their normal responsibility. The development corporation could only liaise, bully and cajole – even over the matter of jobs, which were seen as a crucial element of the new towns as 'self-contained and balanced communities' (New Towns Committee, 1946 – terms of reference). From the earliest days it was decided that eligibility for housing in a new town should be linked with holding a job in the town, a policy which was to have profound and largely unintended consequences for the age and class profile of the towns.

New town corporations did have some major advantages over conventional local authorities. First, they had powers of compulsory purchase at a price below full development value making comprehensive development both possible and potentially profitable. Second (for good or ill), they had no direct political accountability (nor the conventional structure of departments linked 'vertically' to committees but not 'horizontally' to each other) and third, they were able to go and sell themselves to industrialists and others.

Between 1946 and 1950, fifteen towns were designated, principally to serve the housing needs of London and Glasgow (see Table 1) but progress was slow. There were shortages of manpower, cash, building materials and building licences. What had been debated in Parliament as a vision embodying all the high hopes of the new peacetime seemed to be producing very little.

The 1950s

For a number of years planning legislation was allowed to rest, except for the passage of the 1952 Town Development Act, which allowed major expansion of towns by local authorities themselves. This was a more congenial concept to the new Conservative administration, which designated only one new town (Cumbernauld) in the 1950s (for a fuller account of this legislation and its application see Harloe, 1975, Levin 1976). Two key assumptions were widespread: that the population was static or only rising very slowly and that the upward trend of the economy would render interventionist policies, which were anyway distasteful to the administration, redundant.

Around 1960, however, the climate changed dramatically. Even before the census of 1961, the Ministry of Housing was responding to findings that the south-east of England was rapidly growing in population by natural increase, rather than by migration. The physical impact of this was being exacerbated by a tendency to household fission (with more single people and couples setting up home alone, for example) and by the expansion of high technology manufacturing and the service sector of the economy (commerce, retailing, distribution, etc.). The government was suddenly converted to the notion of planning in general and set up a number of regional projects of which *The South-East Study* (MHLG, 1964) and *The North-East* (MHLG, 1963) attracted most attention. These generated another round of new town designations, some based on existing towns such as Peterborough and Northampton (see Table 1). Town and country planning was ripe for re-evaluation in terms of a more regional scale of operation and including social and economic processes as part of its scope. The Labour government of 1964–70 had anyway come in determined to institute national planning.

The PAG Report and the 1968 Act

In 1965 the Planning Advisory Group of the Ministry of Housing and Local Government published a critique of the operation of the 1947 Act and proposals for new legislation. While development control had worked reasonably well, it concluded, the tendency had been towards plans that had become rigid and acquired an unrealistic and unresponsive 'appearance of certainty and stability' (PAG, 1965, p. 5). No sooner had the counties struggled to complete their plans than they were out of date, superseded by events. This type of 'blueprint planning', the group said, could not respond to, for example, revised population estimates or the impact of the widespread redevelopment of town centres by private developers which was taking place together with – or sometimes in spite of – local planning authorities.

Many local authorities, short of trained and experienced staff, were slow to submit their plans to the ministry for approval. The ministry was even slower to grant approval and the backlog built up into a wait of several years. In some cases the statutory five-yearly review fell due before the initial plan had been approved. All this produced, as McLoughlin (1973) has observed, a curious and unsatisfactory mixture of flexibility and rigidity. The plans, once approved, were out of date and excessively detailed so that the objectives they embodied were restricted and unresponsive to change. At the same time this encouraged local authorities to keep plans at a tentative stage and to prepare non-statutory 'bottom-drawer' plans to meet particular contingencies. These, although flexible, were of ambiguous status and not amenable to proper public scrutiny.

The recommendations of the advisory group were accepted without major modification by the government and transformed, via a 1968 White Paper, into the 1968 Town and Country Planning Act (for England and Wales, with a parallel Act for Scotland in 1969 and subsequently consolidated by Acts in 1971 and 1972). Under the new system, planning was to become more comprehensive in scope, less detailed, more responsive, by being linked to general rather than specific objectives, and more decentralized. The main agents for planning would be the counties, which would prepare structure plans. These would be primarily written statements of the environmental policy for the area. The strategy would be generated in the light of all the relevant information – including social and economic material – available to the planning authority both from its own and from national, regional and other sources. Diagrams and drawings might be used to illustrate the strategy, but should not be detailed, would have no status in law nor should be interpreted as firm statement of intent – the GLC had its knuckles rapped for trying to use a structure plan as a map at the inquiry on the Greater London Development Plan (McLoughlin, 1973, p. 158).

This strategic plan would then be subject to examination in public and approval by the Secretary of State, but the hope was that because of the emphasis on high level and generalized policy objectives, which would be subject to continuous updating by research, it would not become obsolete in the way the 1947-type plans had. Once approved, the structure plan would provide the basis for local plans. These could be either district plans of an entire area (which might be a part of a large town or the whole of a smaller one) or action area plans, where the local authority intended comprehensive redevelopment or subject plans, dealing with specific policies on housing or conservation. Local plans would be shorter-term and more specific than structure plans and would rely more heavily on detailed maps. They would not have to be submitted for central

Table 1 Facts and figures on British new towns

	Date of designation **	Source of designation **	City housing need	Housing needs of industry	Regional regeneration	Putting in infrastructure	Land reclamation	Arresting rural depopulation	Original population **	Target population at designation	Subsequent targets	Target population at 31.12.77 †**	Present population **
Aycliffe	19.4.47			✓					60	10,000	1957 20,000 / 1966 45,000	Undecided / 45,000	27,500
Basildon	4.1.49	Advisory Committee for London Regional Planning 1946	✓ London			✓ ?	✓		25,000		1951 80,000 by 1975 / 1960 86,000 / 1967 103,000 by 1976	103,600 / 130,000	91,420
Bracknell	17.6.49		London						5,000	25,000	1961 54,000	55–60,000 / 55–60,000	47,500
Central Lancs New Town	26.3.70		Manchester		✓				234,500	430,000 by 1991	1973 420,000 *in 2001*	285,000 in mid 80s / Not estimated	248,200
Corby	1.4.50	Local initiative	✓ London	✓ Steel		✓ ?	✓		15,700	40,000	1963 55,000	Not estimated / 70,000	53,500
Crawley	9.1.47		✓ London						9,100	60,000 by 1965		CNT††	75,500
Cwmbran	4.11.49			✓		✓ ?			12,000	55,000		55,000	45,000
Harlow	25.3.47	Greater London Plan 1944	✓ London						4,500	?	1961 71,000 by 1966	Undecided / Undecided	79,500
Hemel Hempstead	4.2.47	Greater London Plan 1944 (as Redbourn)	✓ London						21,000	60,000	1961 63,500 by 1963	65,000 / 85,000 now CNT	78,500
Milton Keynes	23.1.67	The South-East Study 1964	✓ London						40,000	250,000 by 1990s		150,000 / 200,000	80,000
Mid Wales (New Town)	18.12.67	1965 A New Town for mid-Wales	London			✓		✓	5,000	11,500	13,000	11,500 / 13,000	7,900

Town	Date	Origin / Plan	Near								
Northampton	14.2.68	*The South-East Study* 1964	✓ London				133,000	?	1969 230,000 by 1981	173,000 180,000	147,000
Peterborough	1.8.67	*The South-East Study*	✓ London		✓	✓	81,000	176,000 by 1985	1970 187,900 by 1985	150,000 160,000	112,000
Peterlee	10.3.48	Local initiative	✓ Mining	✓?			200	25,000		28,000 30,000	27,500
Redditch	10.4.64		✓ Birmingham	✓			32,000	70,000 by 1979		70,000 90,000	56,000
Runcorn	10.4.64		✓ L'pool				28,500	70–75,000 by 1979		71,000 by 1980 90–95,000	57,900
Skelmersdale	9.10.61	Lancashire Development Plan 1956	✓ L'pool				10,000	70,000 by early 1980s		52,000 60,000	40,000
Stevenage	11.11.46	Greater London Plan 1944	✓ London	✓	✓	✓	7,000	?	1967 80,000 by 1965	Both under review	74,500
Telford	12.12.68	Started as Dawley – expanded after 1965 W. Midlands Economic Planning Council report	✓				70,000	70,000	90,000 by 1978 220,000 by late 80s	130,000 150,000	98,500
Warrington	28.4.68		✓ Birmingham	✓	✓	✓	122,300	?		160,000 170,000	135,400
Washington	26.7.64	*The North-East* Cmnd 2204	✓ Manchester		✓	✓	20,000	65,000 by 1983		65,000 80,000	48,000
Welwyn Garden City and Hatfield	20.5.48	Advisory Committee for London Region Housing 1946	✓ London (Welwyn)	✓			18,500	36,500	42,000	42,000 50,000 (CNT)	41,000
			de Havillands (Hatfield)				8,500	25,000		25,000 29,000 (CNT)	26,000

	Date of designation **	Source of designation	City housing need	Housing needs of Industry	Regional regeneration	Putting in infrastructure	Land reclamation	Arresting rural depopulation	Original population **	Target population at designation	Subsequent targets	Target population at 31.12.77 †**	Present population **
Cumbernauld	9.12.55	Clyde Valley Plan 1949	✓ Glasgow						3,000	70,000	100,000	70,000 70,000	45,600
East Kilbride	6.5.47	Clyde Valley Plan 1949	✓ Glasgow		✓ ?				2,400	82,500	90,000	82,000 90,000	73,000
Glenrothes	30.6.48	Clyde Valley Plan 1949	✓ Glasgow	✓ (mining)					1,100	55,000	70,000	55,000 70,000	35,000
Irvine	9.11.66	Central Scotland: a Programme for Development 1964	✓		✓ ?				34,600	116,000	120,000	116,000 120,000	57,300
Livingston	16.4.62		Glasgow ✓ Glasgow		✓		✓		2,000	70,000	100,000	70,000 100,000	33,340

† Two figures are given: the first is the population size when planned migration is to stop, the second the projected ultimate population, allowing for natural increase.
†† Handed over to commission for New Towns.
* Expenditure Committee 1974, p. 545, and *Town and Country Planning*, February 1976.
** *Town and Country Planning*, February 1978.

approval, although the Secretary of State has extensive powers of veto.

Cullingworth (1976) points out, in his evaluation of the legislation, that at the time of the Act counties were expected to be unitary authorities. When local government was finally re-organized in 1974, it was into a two-tier system of counties and districts, which has introduced considerable ambiguity.

There has, up to now, been little opportunity to examine even the process of producing structure and local plans, let alone to evaluate the effectiveness of the legislation. Producing the new-style documents has not been helped by the alleged failure of planners to comprehend the rationale of the intended relationship between structure plans and other policies on the one hand, and between structure plans, local plans and development control on the other (McLoughlin, 1973, Chs 5 and 6). Neither has their task been simplified by the confusion that the two-tier system of government has introduced. Are local plans a district council responsibility? If so, how can they be legitimated (and exempted from central control) by their relationship to the structure plan when the county authority has no legal control over the district? Cullingworth (1976, pp. 89 ff) observes wryly that the Department of the Environment 'clarifications' have so far proved to be the opposite! In the long term however, the problematic aspects of the 1968 Act are likely to be the logical, yet potentially explosive, issues of public participation built into the legislation, and its dependence on social and economic data. These propel into the open the inherently political character of planning, so effectively disguised by the technical presentation of 1947 blueprint planning.

Planning and Pluralism

Land use planning has, since its inception, been part of the conventional structure of national and local democracy. Planners are subject to the committees of the local authority. Plans are approved by the minister, who is answerable to Parliament and the electorate. Additionally, complex mechanisms of public inquiry and examination in public have been developed to scrutinize structure plans, new town sites, major road proposals and one-off issues such as the proposed third London airport. Despite these paraphernalia of accountability, however, there has, since the late 1960s, been a growing tumult over the right of planners to plan. L. J. Sharpe (1975) has called this the 'breakdown of the operating ideology' and seen it as a loss of public trust in policy-making and its institutions. He says there has been a 'reassertion of the primacy of the electorate' but in fact many protagonists see direct action as the only solution, by-passing the elected decision-makers altogether.

Some responsibility for the dissatisfaction must rest with the planning profession itself. As we have seen, the 1947 Act presented land use planning as an essentially technical procedure, merely executing the political decisions made elsewhere. Indeed, in the case of new towns, there was a general assumption that this was not a political issue at all, because there was no *party* political disagreement over the policy. Foley (1960) suggested that there has always been an ambiguity about the ideology of planners themselves. The transformation of social and economic concepts into such technical devices as housing densities and greenbelts was a convenient – but not calculated – way to give planners room to manoeuvre over sensitive issues. It was perpetuated because of the composition of the profession itself: 'planning in the county boroughs, even in some of the biggest cities, was an outgrowth of the borough or city engineer's department and often remained subordinate to it' (Hall, 1973, vol. II, p. 94). The key staff were engineers, surveyors and sometimes architects. Glass (1959) has acerbically observed that the former two are 'used to a mechanistic mode of thought – a fairly straightforward sequence of cause and effect, in terms of a limited number of material factors'.

Much of the training of those executing planning post-1947 was carried out while in employment, producing a loyalty to the bureaucratic ideal of disinterested public service in the British tradition, rather than the more radical orientation that can – but does not always – arise from identification with an autonomous professional group. Latterly planning education has been moved out into universities and polytechnics, but recruits to post-graduate courses are still predominantly from disciplines with a preoccupation with the physical and material – architecture and geography, for instance – and much of the training is still at the drawing board. McLoughlin (1973, pp. 150 ff) discovered that many local authority planning departments were divided into 'design' and 'plan' sections. The first were dominated by architects, the second by geographers or those with first degrees in planning. Despite the emphasis upon continuous research flows in the 1968 planning legislation, sociologists, economists and others concerned with non-physical data and techniques remain under-represented in both planning schools and departments. Besides, the general approach of a planning department is not determined by newly recruited graduates but by chief officers and their immediate subordinates, who probably developed their skills in the 1940s and 1950s.

It would be unfair to imply that the planning profession is unaware of these issues. The Royal Town Planning Institute has been seething with debate about whether planning is one profession or several, and what kind of people should be embraced in membership, since the mid-1960s. Ironically the identity crisis reached a peak shortly after the former TPI received its royal charter. A discussion paper on membership policy (RTPI, 1971) was published which proposed a range of alternative models of professional organization, some of which implied the demise of the RTPI in its existing form. No solution to these issues has yet been found.

When the 1968 planning legislation was being framed, 'consumerism' was sufficiently well advanced for some element of direct public participation to be provided for in the Act. Sharpe (1975, p. 337) has attributed this trend to the expansion of the professional middle class and of the public services that they consume, and to a rising level of general education. Certainly in the 1960s, unlike in the inter-war period, when the changes in the built environment were even more rapid, planning became a noisy public issue. One can speculate as to the reasons: perhaps it was the sheer scale and cost of motorways and airports and the large numbers of people potentially affected; perhaps it was because many changes involved the destruction of existing town centres and residential areas, rather than mere suburban growth. It may have been a major shift towards the recognition of conflict as endemic in society or merely that more people had formed a negative view of planning because their contact with it had been limited to direct or hearsay experience of apparently pettifogging development control. In the minds of many of the public, 'planners' are clerks who tell you that you can do what you like with the back of your house but dictate the minutest detail of any alterations to the front.

Only the barest outline of public participation procedures are included in the 1968 Act. The planning authority must give 'adequate' publicity to their report of survey and plan, and 'adequate opportunity' for the public to make representations. These representations must then be taken account of in the drawing up of the structure plan and the plan placed on deposit for public inspection (Cullingworth, 1976, p. 258). It was no doubt expected that the Skeffington Committee's report, *People and Planning* (MHLG, 1969), would fill in the fine detail. The committee's principal recommendations were that there should be 'four pauses' in both the structure and local planning process to enable the reaction of the public to be sought. This would be carried out by the maximum use of publicity media such as local radio and newspapers, exhibitions, etc. and by the local authority's employing a community development officer to act as a 'catalyst for local opinion' (MHLG, 1969, para. 82). It was also suggested that a 'community forum' (paras 60 ff) should be set up as a sort of standing committee of such local interest groups as chambers of commerce, the civic societies and other voluntary associations – but not political parties.

The unkind commentator would say that the Skeffington report contrived to recommend the worst of all possible worlds. On the one hand it encouraged the direct contact of planners and public, producing both avoidance and concealment of the realities of local democracy and of the working of pressure groups and lobbies. It suggested 'pauses' in a process that is neither linear, nor mechanical. It spoke of the need to canvass the views of the unaffiliated and powerless, but made no effective suggestions as to how this could be achieved. Finally it implied a slowing down of the already slow planning process, thus exacerbating the fundamental problem of 'planning blight'. This occurs when major redevelopment schemes for an area are announced, resulting in an immediate drop in property values and the gradual abandonment of maintenance, let alone improvement, by private landlords, owner-occupiers and statutory agencies alike. The outcome is a downward spiral of decay which is almost impossible to halt.

Conversely the Skeffington Committee avoided the central issue of power. In terms of Arnstein's pungent, and now classic, taxonomy of supposed 'participation' (1969) the recommendations went no further than that the public should be informed of planning proposals and that their views should be sought, on the topics and at the time that the planners felt appropriate. Indeed, the introduction to *People and Planning* declares its acceptance of what Davidoff (1965) has called a 'unitary' model of planning. 'Responsibility for preparing a plan is and must remain that of the local authority . . . the completion of plans . . . is a task demanding the highest standards of professional skill and must be undertaken by the professional staff of the local planning authority' (MHLG, 1969, para. 56). In other words there is to be no opportunity for other interested parties to put up rival proposals for serious consideration, whether it be the tenants' association on a piece of squared paper or a group of the more affluent by employing consultants. Davidoff (1965) has suggested that genuine participation is unlikely until this kind of 'plural planning' is possible. Acceptance of this notion would, however, imply abandoning the idea of a single, common, public interest which can be identified given resources, time and goodwill. This has, of course, much wider implications for political institutions far beyond mere planning schemes.

Social Planning and Positive Discrimination

Elsewhere in the Skeffington report, the committee cosily asserted there was no need for public debate of social goals in Britain (MHLG, 1969, para. 136). Even if the goals were not to be questioned, however, the thinking that had led to social and economic objectives being seen as part of land use planning had also produced the concept of 'positive discrimination', which first appeared in the 'Newsom' report (CACE, 1963) on education, and in the US poverty programme (Marris and Rein, 1974). The central assertion was that the mere availability of public services and welfare benefits was not enough. In some areas the combination of economic problems, population movement, housing decay and low public investment justified identifying them for special help, particularly in housing, education and social services.

In 1967 the Home Office launched its Community Development Project. Twelve areas all over Britain were identified. An action team set to work in the area and a research team based in a nearby university or polytechnic was to monitor their activity and effectiveness over the duration of the project, which was usually five years. Relations with the local authority varied from cordial to disastrous, as the action team's work inevitably led to implied or outright criticism of the local authority's policies and practices. Gradually a more profound political issue emerged, as many of those working in the CDP concluded that the problems they were dealing with arose out of large-scale social and economic processes and could not be resolved by piecemeal support directed to particular localities. They claimed, for example, that the low income of many inner-city residents was neither because of their personal inadequacies, nor of lack of knowledge about other employment opportunities, but because the structure of the economy as a whole demands some low paid and insecure employment. Unsurprisingly, since the radicalization of CDP and the workers' increasingly trenchant publications coincided with the end of the first five-year period of many projects, neither central nor local government was keen to prolong the experiment and it has been allowed to lapse. A summary of the history and development of CDP and some of their research can be found in the *Interproject Report* (National CDP, 1974) and in *Gilding the Ghetto* (CDP, 1977b).

Inner City Decay

If the 1960s were characterized by simultaneous calls for more comprehensive and yet more accountable planning, the 1970s could be said to be notable for less planning with more conflict over it. National economic difficulties have led to massive expenditure cuts and the deferral of controversial schemes for new airports, motorways and the Channel tunnel. Regional policies, never very effective because of the longstanding lack of mobile profitable industry, have become even more passive. Sharpe (1975) has argued that the new mechanisms of structure planning may be over-ambitious, seeking to intervene in processes where they can have no influence and relying on flows of information which departments are ill-equipped to obtain. If this is so, then the revelation that the emperor has no clothes may have been delayed by present circumstances, in which there is very little public or private investment to direct and while the population remains static.

The problem of the 1970s is not containment and reconstruction but the regeneration of the inner city. While the economy expanded, both population and employment had been leaving the central areas of our major cities. This process has been brought about by the need of successful industry for more space, the 'death' of the less successful, and by the desire for better housing standards in both the public and private sector. In many cities the redevelopment of the city centre with offices and branches of the big retail chains, all part of the growth of the service sector of the economy, has reduced both the land available for housing and eliminated much of the low-paid but accessible employment of the residents.

Paradoxically, now that economic decline and a static population have brought into sharp focus a process which has been going on since the end of the Second World War, planning policies are being blamed, attributing to them an effectiveness which they never possessed. Much of the change in city centres has been undertaken by private capital. In some cases this has been in co-operation with the local authority, seeing in it an opportunity to modernize the town in a way that it could not by itself afford. In other cases, notably in London (Ambrose and Colenutt, 1975; Marriott, 1967) the city has been redeveloped in spite of planning controls. Migration of population and industry has been largely voluntary and uncontrolled. The expanding types of employment have been in the service sector, which falls outside industrial development certificate control, and has been subject to vacillating government policies, and in high technology manufacturing, often in plants below the IDC threshold.

The contribution of the new and expanded towns to this process has been relatively puny. Nevertheless they have been the subject of much criticism. Giving evidence to the Expenditure Committee (1974, p. 571) the London Boroughs Association complained vigorously that the new towns had attracted both their young, fit and employed population and the industry that contributed significantly to the revenues of the boroughs. Inner London local authorities were being left, they claimed, with a very expensive residual population in which the elderly, the handicapped and others dependent on public services were over-represented, while the income to provide these declined. In London the problems manifested themselves in dramatic ways as people left the inner area in search of better or cheaper housing or were driven out by the 'gentrification' of multi-occupied houses back into family homes for the middle class. Faced with ever-increasing transport costs, many then could not afford to travel back into the central city to work. Public authorities have been finding increasing difficulties in attracting teachers, firemen, policemen and bus drivers.

In provincial cities the process has been the same, although the outcome has been a shortfall of well-paid employment for those who remain. Many of the jobs available are part-time, or for women or both, and most are poorly paid. While in London the problems of the local authorities are manifesting themselves in pot-holed and unswept streets, in Liverpool there are vast tracts of derelict land and demolished houses (see Donnison and Eversley (eds) (1975) on London and CDP (1977a) on general employment issues).

In recognition of the inner city 'crisis' the government announced a new policy in September 1976, since detailed in a White Paper (DOE, 1977a) and an act. The White Paper draws on the three inner area studies (DOE, 1977b,c,d) of Stockwell in London, Small Heath in Birmingham and Liverpool 8, commissioned by the Department of the Environment and carried out by planning and economic consultants. It is not a dramatic document and does not announce fundamental policy departures, rather it formalizes a number of *ad hoc* trends in urban policy and announces some modest innovations. There are two main groups of recommendations. The first is to modify earlier policies of containment. IDC control is to be (officially) slackened so that industry can relocate in the inner city, and local authorities are to be encouraged to relax their segregation of housing and industrial development. They are further to be allowed to offer loans and grants to assist industry to remain in or return to the inner city. The Location of Offices Bureau which had been set up to channel office employment out of London has been reviewed and 'part of its new role will be to give particular attention to the promotion of office employment in inner urban areas, including London' (DOE, 1977a, para. 56). A review indeed.

New town population targets have been reduced and it is formally stated that no new designations are planned. (This change was widely regarded as inevitable in the light of the precipitous drop in population projections since the last round of new town designations.)

The second group of recommendations is a package of positive discrimination, through modifications of the rate support grant and urban programme grants, and the elaboration of the experimental comprehensive community programmes into partnership schemes between the government and selected local authorities. These appear to be intended to offer management support for an evaluation of local circumstances by the local authority itself, together with a significant portion of the £125 million per year over ten years (at 1977/8 prices) made available to the urban programme (DOE, 1977a, para. 64). Liverpool, Manchester/Salford, Birmingham and

Lambeth and the Docklands in London are named as the first authorities to be offered partnerships (para. 76). Despite the indeterminacy of the partnership notion, and the relatively modest sum of money involved, when compared with the scale of the problems, many other local authorities were quick to question the rationale of the decisions on partnership. Two more partnerships were subsequently announced, with Newcastle/Gateshead and Hackney/Islington in London. Fifteen further 'programme authorities' are to receive special help from urban programme funds. Whether either is a prize worth having remains to be seen. Many commentators believe that real change will only be possible through significant 'bending' of expenditure towards inner city areas both by the local authorities themselves and by government departments other than DOE.

In 1969 Ray Pahl presented a conference paper (Pahl, 1976, Ch. 10) which suggested that cities should be understood as sociospatial systems in which 'gatekeepers' like planners, housing managers, building society managers, social workers and others play a crucial role in determining access to urban resources. These scarce urban resources include not only housing but access to cheap shops, good quality schooling and recreation facilities and to employment, and they are, Pahl claimed, part of real income. Conflict over them is inevitable. The paper seemed to have a catalytic effect upon researchers in sociology, social administration, politics and economics by crystallizing their conviction that they, too, could contribute to understanding the urban environment, despite not knowing a gross housing density from a net housing density. Research reports on groups of these gatekeepers in the urban system have followed (for example: Ford, 1975; Lambert, Blackaby and Paris, 1975). It could be argued that the White Paper on the inner cities demonstrates an acceptance of this type of approach as its recommendations include fiscal and management strategies – albeit vague – together with approaches more traditionally defined as within the province of urban planning.

Pahl has also been vigorously criticized, directly and by implication, in the growing volume of Marxist urban research, both in Britain and abroad, notably in France (see Pickvance, 1976 for a selection of essays in this tradition). In a later essay (1975, Ch. 13) he has defended his 'Weberian' position that opportunities and conflicts in the urban system cannot be explained solely in terms of the relations of production, i.e. a person's employment – or unemployment – status. A Marxist analysis of the city clearly raises both practical and principled difficulties for students, researchers and those who make and execute urban policy, but it cannot be denied that the debate about urban problems and their solutions has been rescued from technologism and revitalized. It is no longer possible to maintain that urban planning is merely about buildings, roads, infrastructure and their location. The problems have once more come to be debated within a larger perspective that Robert Owen and William Morris might have approved.

References

Aldridge, M. (1979), *The British New Towns Programme,* Routledge & Kegan Paul.

Ambrose, P. and Colenutt, B. (1975), *The Property Machine*, Penguin.

Arnstein, S. (1969), 'A ladder of citizen participation in planning', *Journal of the American Institute of Planners*, July.

Anderson, M. (1971), *Family Structure in Nineteenth-Century Lancashire*, Cambridge University Press.

Ashworth, G. (1954), *The Genesis of Modern British Town Planning*, Routledge & Kegan Paul.

Barlow Commission (1940) *see* Royal Commission on the Distribution of the Industrial Population.

Bellamy, E. (1951), *Looking Backward: 2000–1887,* Random House (first published 1887).

Benevolo, L. (1967), *The Origins of Modern Town Planning*, Routledge & Kegan Paul.

Central Advisory Council on Education (1963), *Half our Future*, London, HMSO.

Committee on Land Utilization in Rural Areas (1942), *Report*, London, HMSO, Cmnd 6378 (Scott report).

Community Development Project (1977a), *The Costs of Industrial Change*, CDP.

Community Development Project (1977b), *Gilding the Ghetto*, CDP.

Cullingworth, J. B. (1976), *Town and Country Planning in Britain*, (6th edition), Allen & Unwin.

Davidoff, P. (1965), 'Advocacy and pluralism in planning', *Journal of the American Institute of Planners*, November (also in Faludi, A. (ed.), 1973).

Department of the Environment (1977a), *A Policy for the Inner Cities*, London, HMSO, Cmnd 6845.

Department of the Environment (1977b), *Unequal City* (inner area study of Small Heath, Birmingham by Llewellyn-Davies, Weeks, Forestier-Walker and Bor), London, HMSO.

Department of the Environment (1977c), *Inner London: Policies for*

Dispersal and Balance (inner area study of Lambeth by Shankland, Cox *et al*.), London, HMSO.

Department of the Environment (1977d), *Change and Decay* (inner area study of Liverpool by Wilson, Warnersley *et al*.), London, HMSO.

Donnison, D. V. and Eversley, D. (eds) (1975), *London: Patterns, Problems, Policies*, Heinemann.

Durant, R. (1939), *Watling*, P. S. King & Sons.

Expenditure Committee (1975), *Thirteenth Report*, New Towns: I, IV and V, HC 616 I, IV and V.

Expert Committee on Compensation and Betterment (1942), *Report*, London, HMSO, Cmnd 6386 (Uthwatt report).

Faludi, A. (1973), *A Reader in Planning Theory*, Pergamon.

Foley, D. (1960), 'British town planning, one ideology or three?', *British Journal of Sociology* vol. 11, no. 3.

Ford, J. (1975), 'The role of the building society manager in the urban stratification system', *Urban Studies* vol. XII, pp. 295–302.

Gauldie, E. (1974), *Cruel Habitations : a History of Working Class Housing, 1780–1918*, Allen & Unwin.

Glass, R. (1959), 'The evaluation of planning', *International Social Science Journal* vol. II, no. 3 (reprinted in Faludi (ed.), 1973).

Hall, P. *et al*. (1973), *The Containment of Urban England, vols I and II*, Allen & Unwin.

Harloe, M. (1975), *Swindon, a Town in Transition*, London: Heinemann.

Hayward, J. and Watson, M. (eds) (1975), *Planning, Politics and Public Policy: the British, French and Italian Experience*, Cambridge University Press.

Howard, E. (1965), *Garden Cities of Tomorrow*, Faber (first published in 1898 as *Tomorrow: a Peaceful Path to Real Reform*).

Jacobs, J. (1964), *The Death and Life of the Great American Cities*, Penguin.

Lambert, J., Blackaby, R., Paris, C. (1975), *Neighbourhood Politics and Housing Opportunities, Proceedings of urban change and conflict conference*, Centre for Environmental Studies.

Levin, P. (1976), *Government and the Planning Process*, Allen & Unwin.

McLoughlin, B. (1973), *Control and Urban Planning*, Faber.

Marriott, O. (1967), *The Property Boom*, Hamish Hamilton.

Marris, P. and Rein, M. (1974), *Dilemmas of Social Reform*, Penguin.

Ministry of Housing and Local Government (1963), *The North East*, London, HMSO, Cmnd 2206.

Ministry of Housing and Local Government (1964), *The South East Study*, London, HMSO.

Ministry of Housing and Local Government (1969), *People and Planning*, London, HMSO (Skeffington report).

Morris, W. (1891), *News from Nowhere, or an Epoch of Rest*, London.

National Community Development Project (1974), *Interproject Report*, National CDP.

New Towns Committee (1946), *Final Report*, London, HMSO (Reith report).

Pahl, R. (1975), *Whose City?* (2nd edn) Penguin.

Peterson, W. (1968). 'The ideological origins of Britain's new towns', *Journal of the American Institute of Planners*, May.

Pickvance, C. (ed.) (1976), *Urban Sociology*, Tavistock.

Planning Advisory Group (1965), The Future of Development Plans, London, HMSO.

Purdom, C. B. (1949), *The Building of Satellite Towns*, Dent.

Ratcliffe, J. (1976), *Land Policy*, Hutchinson.

Royal Commission on the Distribution of the Industrial Population (1940), *Report*, London, HMSO, Cmnd 6153 (Barlow Commission).

Royal Town Planning Institute (1971), *Town Planners and their Future: a Discussion Paper*, RTPI.

Sharpe, L. J. (1975), 'Innovation and change in British land-use planning' in J. Hayward and M. Watson, (eds), *Planning Politics and Public Policy: The British, French and Italian Experience*, Cambridge University Press.

Young, T. (1934), *Becontree and Dagenham*, The Pilgrim Trust.

4

Social Policy and Housing Need

John S. Ferris

Structurally sound and healthy housing is a fundamental human need and is an important component in the quality of life experienced by people everywhere. It is therefore hardly surprising that housing not infrequently becomes the subject of intense political controversy and a central feature in national social policies.

There are rather special problems which arise out of the peculiar nature of housing as a commodity. In industrialized societies houses are fixed in their location, are very expensive to produce, and have a very long useful life. The occupants of a particular house will generally be as concerned with external aspects of the situation – for example access to work, schools, shops and other communal and environmental amenities – as they will be with the intrinsic aspects such as space, design and facilities. In any area of social policy a major problem is the definition and interpretation of need. This is particularly difficult in the sphere of housing because of the very wide range of objective and subjective factors that must be taken into account by those responsible for the formulation and implementation of policy.

It is useful initially to make a distinction between housing need and effective demand. Both of these concepts have emerged and acquired their present meaning with the development of housing policy in Britain. They are defined here with reference to current administrative and professional conventions. Housing need for government officials and planners is essentially the extent to which existing housing accommodation fails to meet in terms of quality and quantity the requirements of each household for accommodation of a specific minimum standard. This is regardless of ability to pay or any idiosyncratic preferences.

Effective demand is basically a concept, most commonly used, by such market professionals as building society managers, estate agents, surveyors and solicitors. They are mainly concerned with the quantity and quality of housing that a household can afford to pay out of present and anticipated future income. It is an economic concept and does not have any normative implications.

Both of these definitions are useful to the officials and professionals who use them because they make it possible to measure and quantify existing housing provision and the performance of the housing system. To this extent they are objective and are valid, regardless of subjective housing preferences. The difficulties arise when attempts are made to assess the preferences and aspirations of households because these are likely to include elements of 'need' and 'effective demand'. There are problems with the validity of professional and official judgments regarding what constitutes a 'sound investment' or 'satisfactory minimum standards'. Both market professionals and government officials are involved in imposing standards, although in different ways. It is often incorrectly assumed that only government officials impose standards – there is a demonology of bureaucracy which forgets that market institutions are also involved in the imposition of standards which seem arbitrary.

The idea of housing need can be extended in ways that attempt to take into account the requirements of households seeking to realize their aspirations in the housing system. From the point of view of an individual household seeking to meet what it perceives as its housing needs there are more or less tangible objective elements and less tangible, but nevertheless important, subjective considerations. The three most important objective elements will be, the physical standard of the dwelling, its location, and the security of tenure attached to a dwelling. These objective elements can to a large extent be legislated and planned for. The subjective factors are of course potentially limitless but one writer has identified three important factors which are quite likely universal – identity, security and opportunity (Turner, 1972). According to Turner, identity has to do with the fact that housing is often a reflection of personal status; by security he means the role that housing can play in crystallizing past achievement; opportunity refers to the role housing circumstances play in facilitating access to social and economic advancement.

The point in including these subjective elements in the calculus of housing need is to stress that any housing policy aimed simply at realizing the quantifiable objective factors however energetically pursued may still fail to meet the aspirations of many households. The priorities accorded by households to both the objective and subjective factors will vary with income. Even if we include only the six elements mentioned here it will be a very complex calculation. A further extension in the conception of housing need is necessary in order to incorporate the legitimate requirements of the community. There is a social concern with housing provision which must somehow be reconciled with the aspirations of households. Historically this social interest in housing has figured prominently in social policy.

Throughout the nineteenth century and up to the First World War the 'housing problem' was overwhelmingly a preoccupation with what used to be called the 'health of towns'. Government involvement in the housing conditons of the poor and the 'working classes' was not primarily benevolent. It was a by-product of the attempt to impose sanitary control on the anarchic unplanned nineteenth-century city. The great sanitary reformers like Chadwick and Simon were concerned with the necessity for adequate drainage, fresh water supplies, clean air. These were essential to combat the recurrent epidemics of cholera and typhoid which struck at rich and poor alike.

Public health reforms later involved reducing urban congestion by means of slum clearance, the imposition of building regulations, the imposition of density standards, and the control of building plots and street layout. These measures were not always popular with the Victorian public but the reformers managed to 'sell' their programme by establishing a link between disease and moral laxity in the slum areas. They argued that opening up the slums meant not only exposing the poor and the unwashed to fresh air and sunshine but also to the clergy and the police.

This sanitary policy was negative and probably restricted the production of necessary housing for the poor. Despite the confused attempts at reform by such philanthropists as Octavia Hill and housing trusts as Peabody, Guiness and Sutton Dwellings there was little awareness during the nineteenth century that the 'solution of the housing problem' involved providing new housing within the means of ordinary working-class families (Gauldie, 1974).

The influence of nineteenth-century sanitary policies persists in modern housing policy – and quite properly so, in the sense that public health is a collective need and one in which the community must assert its interest. It is reflected in three separate bodies of legislation that impinge directly on the provision of housing: the town planning acts; the public health acts; and the building regulations. This legislation is concerned with the establishment of minimum standards in one way or another. Added to this framework are those government policies which aim to prevent overcrowding, homelessness and unfit dwellings by more positive means.

First by direct provision – council housing – where tenants are selected on specific criteria of need. Second the State is involved in private housing markets where it attempts in various ways to increase the level of effective demand, notably by means of a range of direct and indirect subsidies: for example improvement grants to owners; rent control; rent allowances; tax relief on mortgage interest payments. However complex and difficult in practice it is to apply consistently, the concept of housing need is inescapable and important. The economic concept of effective demand, which has its uses, is altogether too narrow and restrictive to provide a satisfactory basis for housing policy. Such policy must also concern itself with aspirations as well as legitimate collective needs like those represented in the public health legislation.

The British Tenure System

Perhaps one of the most significant features of housing in Britain is that, in contrast to other areas of social policy, such as health and education, the State has not considered it necessary to develop a comprehensive plan for meeting need. Even more surprising perhaps, given the prevalence of 'welfare state' ideology in the post-war years, is that there has been no attempt to give an explicit definition of acceptable minimum standards, or establish unambiguous rights to housing. There have been attempts to raise standards and to assist in the provision of housing. State housing policies have always been fragmentary and pragmatic in character – a series of *ad hoc* responses to particular problems within tenure sectors.

During the late 1960s and early 1970s the first tentative moves were made towards a more comprehensive approach to housing policy on the part of government. One of the more explicit statements of this approach was provided in a government White Paper (HMSO, 1973): 'The ultimate aim of housing policy is that everyone should have a decent home with a reasonable choice of renting or owning the sort of house they want.'

The assumption behind this statement was that housing policy would necessarily involve a diverse range of housing agencies and programmes, both public and private, producing a variety of housing for the diversity of needs that exists. As a general aim it was rather bland and uncontroversial. It became the core of what for a period amounted to a bipartisan housing policy. Initiated by a Labour government it was taken over by a Conservative government in 1970.

To the extent that this comprehensive approach was actually, rather than rhetorically, followed by government and the local authorities it appears to have failed dismally (Harloe, Issacharoff, Minns, 1974). There are clear indications, with the publication of the Housing Green Paper (HMSO, 1977a), that this strategy has already been abandoned. Why is it that what were really quite modest and uncontroversial changes in housing policy lacked credibility and were dropped so rapidly?

The answer to this question must be sought in the nature of the British system of housing tenure, and in its institutional organization. Between 1951 and 1971 there has been something of a revolution in tenure patterns.

Public housing and owner occupation are now firmly established as the two major forms of tenure in a housing stock which has grown by over 40 per cent in two decades. There are two main reasons why the distinction between tenures is important in the British system. Firstly, even though an owner-occupier and a council tenant may be living in physically identical houses their respective legal rights and obligations will diverge quite markedly. In practical everyday terms this will involve differences in security of tenure, freedom to alter and use the property, the right to sublet all or part of the property. Citizens in the modern 'welfare state' may be equal before the law, but as far as housing is concerned they are not subject to the same laws. The legal framework reflects very different degrees of effective control over housing circumstances. Second, the distinction

Table 2   Types of Tenure – Great Britain

	1951	1971	
Owner occupation	29%	52%	
Public authorities	18%	31%	
Privately rented	51%	17%*	(figures for private renting include housing associations, tied accommodation, etc.)

Source: *Social Trends*, 1972.
*Before the First World War about 90 per cent of all dwellings were privately rented.

between tenures is important because State housing policies have always operated along tenure lines. Housing law is tenure specific and no atttempt has been made to reconcile the differences that have emerged historically. The financial framework developed by successive governments has been a major factor serving to sharpen and crystallize the purely legal distinctions between tenures. The cost of housing to a particular household depends on what tenure they are in as much as income or family circumstances.

These differences between tenures, which derive from the legal framework and State interventions in the different sectors of the housing system, will be considered in terms of three main factors – finance, standards, access.

Private Renting

The Financial Framework

During the nineteenth century a system for the provision and management of housing that we now call private renting became the dominant form of tenure. Basically the system was simple enough, the transactions between landlord and tenant were not really very different from any other commodity transaction. The price and availability of housing was determined by impersonal laws of supply and demand. From the aspiring landlord's viewpoint to have access to capital presented no problem, for most of the century, because of the availability of trustee funds and small savings. These were often directed into housing investments by local solicitors. From the point of view of tenants, it was necessary to have sufficient income to be able to pay economic rents for a given standard of accommodation. Private renting during the nineteenth century was very much a form of petty capitalism – although large-scale employers often built housing to rent to their workers.

As personal incomes were low for the bulk of the population for most of the century housing standards were also primitive compared to modern standards. Such a system could only remain viable if investors and landlords were able to achieve a satisfactory return on capital invested: at the very least housing had to be able to show returns comparable with those from alternative forms of investment offering similar security.

Although quite complicated systems of leasehold developed in some urban centres – particularly London, where major landowners such as the Duke of Westminster were unwilling to relinquish ultimate control over land use – it was a system easily understood by tenants. They had minimal legal protection and got what they could pay for in a world where subsidies were virtually unknown. This system provided a wide range of house types and conditions of tenure but by the end of the century there was growing awareness that it was far from perfect. For most of the twentieth century private renting generally has not been competitive with alternative forms of investment except in rather exceptional circumstances (Nevitt, 1966). Although rent control has been blamed for this there is evidence that a full explanation is more complicated. There are at least five factors operating together which help explain the decline:

1 Constraints imposed by the State

Ever since the first Public Health Act of 1848 there has been a gradual but nevertheless relentless pressure on landlords to raise their standards. Housebuilding becomes more expensive and therefore less accessible to those with the lowest incomes. Someone has to pay for higher standards and if State subsidies in one form or another are not forthcoming then investors are going to put their money elsewhere.

2 The lack of suitable financing institutions

One of the major elements in the rapid expansion of private renting during the nineteenth century was the existence of an informal but nevertheless effective system for steering savings into housing investment. When alternative avenues of investment opened up, this locally based system collapsed and no comparable source of finance for landlords has since evolved. Banks do not normally lend for long enough periods, building society terms are not generally acceptable to landlords. Because of this, small landlords are obliged to resort to informal networks at higher interest rates or withdraw from the field.

3 Competition from owner-occupation

With the expansion of building societies since the 1920s, owner-occupation has offered competition to landlords. In particular the favourable tax position of owners who receive tax relief on mortgage interest payments means that they can pay more for a property than a prospective landlord obliged to make a profit. Moreover, there is now a well-developed system of finance supporting owner-occupation. Savings now find their way into building societies that might in the past have been invested in rented housing.

4 Tax position of landlords — rent control

Compared to other businessmen the private landlord is in a peculiarly disadvantaged position. The inland revenue assume that a house will last for ever and no allowances are made for depreciation and obsolescence. Most businessmen can deduct the cost of new building and equipment from their tax payments. With rent regulation and control it is very difficult for a landlord to recover his costs on improvement let alone make a profit.

5 Competition from local authorities

In renting houses to people in housing need, local authorities are not required to make a profit; council housing is normally subsidized. This means that local authorities can provide high standard housing at low cost to people who would otherwise turn to private landlords. In their slum clearance programmes they have been obliged to replace privately rented housing with public housing.

Standards

The overwhelming statistical fact about the privately rented sector has to do with the age of such property and its rate of obsolescence. According to the 1973 general household survey most of the property was built before 1914. Nearly half of all private tenants occupy terraced housing, about 20 per cent were in non-purpose-built flats and rooms. These proportions are much higher than for any other form of tenure. The 1971 house condition survey (DOE) found that 23 per cent of all privately rented housing built before 1919 was statutorily unfit, compared with an average of 7 per cent for all other tenures. Private tenancies in general are lacking in basic amenities like use of bath or shower, hot water, internal W/Cs and so forth.

Improvement grants were intended primarily to be taken up by private landlords in order to assist them in rectifying these conditions. The economic position of landlords, however, has made most of them unwilling to invest in improvement. The general standard in the private rented sector is greatly reduced by the fact that there has been virtually no new building for renting for many years – apart from a minimal amount of luxury accommodation.

During the course of the 1960s, following the Milner Holland report on housing in London, there has been general concern about the existence of 'housing stress' areas in the larger cities where there are particularly high concentrations of renting and poor housing conditions. Successive governments have introduced new policies and legislation to alleviate these problems, so far without making any great impact (CDP, 1977).

Access

Although the private sector has declined dramatically since 1951, and standards are generally much lower than elsewhere, it is still important for certain categories of household who have not been able to meet their housing needs elsewhere. Such households are faced with the fact that a very high proportion of privately rented dwellings are occupied by households aged over 65 and that when these tenancies become vacant they are more likely than not to disappear, either through clearance or into owner-occupation.

In some areas of the country there is virtually no privately rented accommodation available; in others, London for instance, 25 per cent of all dwellings are still privately rented. It is now clearly recognized that certain types of household are more likely than others to seek this form of tenure, if only because they have no alternative. Two main categories of household can be identified.

1 Single persons under retirement age

Single persons generally, particularly those below retiring age, have been considered low priority by local authorities and if their incomes are low will not qualify for a mortgage – in any case building societies prefer lending on orthodox 'family size' property.

2 New households and migrants in a local authority area with low incomes

New households and recent migrants generally receive low priority from local authorities and their low income can preclude them from ownership. In urban areas such households constitute a very heterogeneous group; and include young professionals, clerical workers, students, single-parent families, low-income families, ethnic minorities. They are not equally well placed to compete for a dwindling stock of private tenancies. Although, in contrast to other forms of tenure, there are no formal criteria governing access other than ability to pay, the fact of scarcity allows landlords and their agents considerable discretion as to whom they will accept as tenants. There is evidence that non-economic criteria, such as ethnic identity or social status – whether a household has children or not – can all influence the degree of access to a dwindling stock of privately rented property (Harloe et al, 1974; Smith, 1977).

Owner-occupation

More than 50 per cent of the housing stock in Britain is now in owner-occupation. Although owner-occupation is effectively controlled by market institutions it has nevertheless been strongly supported by State housing policies. The State has been as closely involved with home ownership as it has with the other major tenures in different ways, something that is often forgotten in discussions of the relative merits of the different tenures and the role of government.

The Financial Framework

The average new house built in Britain costs about three and a half times the average income. Very few households dependent upon earned income could afford to buy their home without some form of State assistance. Above all it is government fiscal policies which have enabled so many households to become home-owners. This help increases effective demand for home ownership and at the same time provides the necessary incentive for investors to invest in housing. There are three principal ways in which the State encourages home ownership and provides an incentive for those with capital to invest.

1 Tax relief on mortgage interest payment

By far the most important form of State help is the tax relief given on mortgage interest. Home-owners are allowed to deduct each year's mortgage interest payments from their taxable income. In 1977 each new owner-occupier paid on average over £1,000 mortgage interest. With tax at 35 per cent this meant in effect £350 was paid by the government to those with money to lend on behalf of those with mortgages. In 1977 this assistance cost the Treasury £957 million. This does not appear as public expenditure in official statistics but the volume of this *de facto* subsidy could be held to support those who argue that, left to itself, the market would not be able to respond to those requiring housing.

2 The tax position of building societies

The major source of finance for home ownership are the building societies – currently more than 80 per cent of all new mortgages are provided by them. The building societies spend a considerable amount of money in promoting the image of being rather modest self-help institutions for the thrifty small saver and young couples with limited financial resources seeking their first home. This is to misrepresent the reality: although there are of course many small savers and many first-time buyers are given mortgages, building society finance today is big business and without it the residential property market would collapse.

The building societies dominate housing credit because they have a dual competitive advantage over such alternative lending institutions as banks. First they are able to borrow money from investors at lower interest rates. Second they lend money to mortgagors more cheaply than their competitors. They are able to do this because of preferential tax arrangements conferred on them by the inland revenue. Building societies are allowed to deduct tax on behalf of inland revenue at what is called the composite rate. This is simply an average rate for all investors. In effect large investors pay the same tax as the small investors who would otherwise have paid no tax at all. In 1977 the composite rate of taxation was about 27 per cent – about 8 per cent below the standard rate. The effect is dramatic as a high proportion of building society funds come from large investors.

Large investors are very sensitive to even minor fluctuations in interest rates. Even a half per cent change can overnight, as it were, attract or repel millions of pounds. Building societies have become repositories for 'hot money' and this has important implications for national housing policy, which will be dealt with below. The composite tax arrangement gives the building societies their competitive edge and also means that the 'little old lady' in Bognor or the young couple in Ruislip in effect subsidize the large investor. This is then another subsidy conferred on money lenders by the State which encourages investment in housing.

3 Stabilization policies

One of the consequences of the bulk of building society funds coming from the big investors is that the system has become less predictable. If there is an outflow of funds from the societies as a result of higher interest rates elsewhere, this will mean a drastic restriction of new mortgage lending and higher interest charges to borrowers. Both reduce effective demand and can drastically curtail new housing construction. Conversely, when the societies are attracting money the resulting increase in the rate of lending can have inflationary effects on house prices, as in 1971–3. Inflation means the exclusion of potential buyers from the market and many others paying a higher proportion of income for housing.

The political pressures arising from both of these consequences means that governments have a direct interest in promoting stability in the flow of investment funds to housing. Since 1973 there has been a joint government-building society advisory committee charged with the task of devising ways of regulating mortgage funds. In 1974, when mortgage interest rates were rising to politically unacceptable levels, the government loaned the societies £500 million to assist them in keeping down the interest rate. The building societies are now expected to regulate their lending so as to end the stop–go cycle in house building programmes. To date these arrangements have been informal and voluntary but stronger powers could be invoked by government if for any reason they prove inadequate. The fact is that no government can sit back and ignore the destabilizing effects of unregulated markets. At the same time they will be careful to avoid draconian measures that will act as a disincentive to investors.

Standards

The stock of housing within the owner-occupied sector is immensely varied and this precludes any general statements about standards. At one extreme it includes nineteenth-century terraced housing in the inner cities and urban conurbations. Much of this has been bought by migrant workers obliged to borrow at high interest rates from fringe banks and finance companies. For these home-owners, owner occupation is not so much the outcome of choice as a strategy of necessity with a declining privately rented sector. Not surprisingly, given its age, much of this housing is unfit or lacks basic amenities. High mortgage repayments preclude investment in improvement. This is an aspect of owner-occupation that is often overlooked in a political climate where there is strong support for home ownership.

At the other extreme there is of course a substantial amount of expensive residential property of a very high standard: detached suburban houses with large gardens, the fashionably restored town houses of inner London, much of the latter highly subsidized by improvement grants and indirectly by town planning policy. In between, there is the suburban and new housing that encircles virtually every town and city in Britain. As most of this housing has been built since the 1930s it is generally in good condition and of a reasonable standard.

Leaving aside the older pre-1919 owner-occupied housing – where there are rather special problems – it is probably true to say that two main factors have operated to raise standards in the owner-occupied sector. First, post-war inflation in wages and house prices has meant that many owners have found the proportion of income spent on mortgage repayments has been falling steadily and this has enabled them to finance their own improvement with credit from the building societies and banks. Such improvement has been generally tax deductible (credit and fiscal assistance that has not been available to landlords). Second, although government improvement policies were originally devised with the problems of low standards in the privately rented sector in mind, they have in practice been more beneficial to owners able to match the grants with their own savings. Thus the raising of standards in the owner-occupied sector has been quite heavily subsidized.

Access

There can be little doubt that home-ownership is popular. Politicians are often inclined to attribute this to a somewhat mystical, almost atavistic 'deep-seated aspiration' among the people. The truth is more mundane. Given the prevailing structure of housing finance and tenure law, the preference for home-ownership is hardly surprising. There are advantages in home-ownership, although not all home-owners enjoy these. State housing policies have done much to create this situation. This has important policy implications. With the emergence of bipartisan support for extending home-ownership there is a strong possibility of a dual-sector housing system: a privileged owner-occupied sector and a public sector seen as a kind of ambulance service – highly stigmatized and starved of resources. Thus the issue of access to the 'privileged' sector is important. There are two main issues involved in this question of access to home-ownership – individual opportunity and spatial justice. To what extent do the practices of the market institutions influence individual opportunity in the housing system? Is the spatial allocation and distribution of scarce housing resources in accordance with the wider communal interest? Both of these issues have received a great deal of attention in the literature on housing and town planning in recent years (Pahl, 1976).

The most important market professionals who exercise control over access to home-ownership are building society managers, estate agents, solicitors and surveyors. They have been described as 'urban gatekeepers', because their function is to regulate access to housing. These professionals do not operate autonomously, but are parts of a widespread system and are mutually interdependent. Estate agents often act as agents for building societies, and find it easier to sell houses if they can offer mortgage facilities to the right applicants. In return they attract savings into the societies. A similar relationship exists between solicitors and building society managers. Solicitors invest trust funds in the societies and expect them in return to extend mortgage facilities to their clients. A solicitor with good building society and estate agency contacts is able to maintain a high level of house conveyancing work – the bread and butter of his profession. Similarly, chartered surveyors, often estate agents in their own right, advise building societies on the value of property they lend on. It is the surveyor's job to keep himself informed about local planning policies and all the various factors which affect property values. When a property is sold, anything up to 10 per cent of the sale price will be paid in fees to the various professionals and institutions involved. As they make their living out of the residential property market it is in their interest to collaborate closely and maintain market stability by reducing uncertainty and risks.

The individual wishing to buy a house simply wants to know whether a mortgage can be raised on the property that fits his or her circumstances and pocket. Whether this is possible or not depends on the judgments of the professionals. The building society is interested in two things when they receive a mortgage application: Is the property worth what they are being asked to advance? Is the borrower in a position to meet the monthly mortgage repayments out of present and anticipated income?

In reality these two sets of factors are extremely complex because individuals, like houses, vary enormously. The market institutions through long experience have developed procedures and 'rules of thumb' which make these judgments virtually automatic. Building societies are cautious and have shown themselves unwilling to lend on older property and houses of unconventional design. Likewise, they tend to favour borrowers with good career prospects or at least regular incomes, as they are better credit risks.

This caution means that certain kinds of individuals have found themselves less favoured by the building societies: manual workers, single women, and coloured applicants are examples. For these and other categories this means a lack of the chance to exercise choice in a housing system that is becoming more monolithic and can have important consequences for individual liberty and opportunity. Market institutions are concerned with 'ability to pay', but the outcome of their decisions may be that many individuals end up paying more for less suitable housing elsewhere in the system.

On the second question of spatial justice, the investment

priorities of the market institutions and 'urban gatekeepers' go beyond individual opportunity and react back upon it. It has to do with a social interest akin to that of public health. If there are differences between the urban investment priorities of local authorities and the market institutions this can give rise to serious social problems. The issue of building society 'red-line' districts illustrates this possibility (*Roof*, 1976). Red-line districts are those where building societies draw a red (or blue) line on the map around certain neighbourhoods – usually inner-city districts – and then refuse to grant mortgages within these areas, the justification being that the houses within such districts are a poor risk for investors' saving. This issue extends further than formally designated 'red-line' districts: the societies refuse to lend on certain kinds of property – back-to-backs, houses with doors opening on the street, three-storey housing, etc. As house types tend to 'cluster', the cumulative effect can amount to a virtual red-line policy. Not all building societies adopt identical policies for identical localities but the general effect, if these policies are pursued by the larger societies consistently, can be to starve a district of new housing investment.

If the local authorities are able to step in and lend in these districts the consequences can be minimized. However with public expenditure restrictions this has not been possible. The government now has an explicit policy of promoting inner-city revitalization (HMSO, 1977b). This, among other measures, means concentrating house improvement resources. If the red-lining practices are as extensive as suggested by Shelter and some academic research (the building societies deny that they red-line at all), then the local authorities will be cast in the role of King Canute in trying to reverse the tide of urban decay. A possibility associated with this issue that has received less comment and discussion but may be just as important is that the market institutions will for obvious reasons continue to promote and finance suburban development. This means that the local authorities will have to follow market priorities (ability to pay) and invest a greater proportion of resources in the already affluent suburbs because of the new needs for roads, schools, clinics, parks, public transport and so forth. The big question hovering over these possibilities is whether public planning is merely reactive or whether it can shape market decisions, so as to make them compatible with public priorities.

Public Sector Housing

The first local authority in Britain to build homes for rent was Liverpool Corporation in 1869. Other local authorities made similar experiments before 1914, notably the old London County Council. This early council housing was intended to replace houses lost through slum clearance. By 1914 less than 2 per cent of all dwellings were owned by local authorities. Two underlying economic factors explain this slow start.

Slum housing was concentrated in the cities where land values were highest; households in need of rehousing from the slums were precisely those least able to pay the higher rents for accommodation of higher standards.

The necessary subsidy for clearance and replacement housing could come only from local rate income and most local authorities were committed to low rates. Slum clearance was only viable where the local authority permitted new land uses for industry and commerce. The question posed by nineteenth-century experience was how to pay for higher standards, given the low income of potential tenants. The solution was found with the 1919 Housing and Town Planning Act when the State undertook to subsidize local authority housing for rent.

Since 1919 an elaborate system of subsidy arrrangements has been developed in order to bridge the gap between an economic rent and minimum acceptable standards decreed by the State. The essentials, if not the details, can be described here. Contrary to popular opinion council housing is not primarily paid for by taxing the wealthy. Rather it is the wealthy – those with money to invest – who are paid by the community for lending money to the local authorities in order to finance their housing programmes. The system has to be understood at two levels, first that of local authority finance generally, second at the level of the housing revenue account (HRA). The two levels of course are interrelated.

1 Local authority finance
The money for local authority housing programmes comes from each authority's consolidated loans fund. This is a general fund which finances all local authority capital projects such as schools, old people's homes, libraries and so forth. The money for this fund is raised by the local authority issuing bonds for varying periods

which are repaid at the rate of interest prevailing at the time of issue.
For example, 5-year bonds issued in 1974 would be repaid in 1979
with interest at about 15 per cent. Bonds issued in early 1978 would
earn about 10 per cent. The total local authority debt will depend on
when it borrowed money and this in turn reflects the range of past
investment programmes. The consolidated fund lends money for
each project at pooled historic interest rates – the average rate of
interest payable on its total debt. This debt is repaid from income,
which includes rate income and subsidies given for general and
specific purposes by government.

Since 1945, despite short-run fluctuations, the long-run tendency
has been for interest rates to rise, thus increasing the cost of all
social programmes to local authorities, including housing.

2 *The housing revenue account*

The money for new housing and improvement is loaned to the local
authorities housing revenue account. The basic form of this means
of financial control over council housing can be simply conveyed for
the purposes of exposition as in Table 3.

Table 3   Housing Revenue Account of Local Authorities

Income	Expenditure
Loan (from consolidated fund)	Loan repayments (principle + interest)
Rents	Management (includes wages, salaries, administration and communal facilities)
Rate subsidy	
Central government housing subsidies	

The major item of expenditure on the HRA is almost invariably the
interest element of loan repayments. Currently these average about
70 per cent of all rent and subsidy income, and as such have become
the dominant factor in council house finance. Because of inflation
the repayment of principal is in real terms constantly declining.
Interest rates conversely tend to rise. Normally loans for housing are
repaid over sixty years, land eighty years.

Rents

The aspect of finance which most immediately concerns council tenants is how much rent they have to pay. Since 1936 local authorities have been able to pool their historic costs in the HRA. With inflation, new houses cost more than old houses of identical standard. Most local authorities aim to equalize the housing costs of tenants by setting rents at lower than cost on new homes and by allowing the rents of older houses to rise above costs. It is this capacity to socialize capital gains from inflation which confers a considerable advantage on council housing. In the private sector such gains accrue to the individual household and over time reduce their housing costs. Rent pooling enables local authorities to respond to new needs – for example sheltered housing for the aged. The sale of council houses can undermine this system – unless they are sold at a price which covers the cost of replacement, which is unusual. If rents are allowed to rise in line with incomes, council tenants are to some degree protected from the vagaries of the capital market.

Finally, with respect to public sector finance, there is no reason why a government should not decide to pay for housing out of general taxation, just as it pays for defence and roads. Another option for governments is to hold interest rates below market level, obliging those with capital to accept lower returns. This policy was adopted by the post-war Labour government, when local authorities were enabled to borrow from the Public Works Loan Board at low interest rates. Such policies would, of course, be more strongly redistributive than current policies but would no doubt arouse fierce opposition from those who believe in free market principles and the containment of public expenditure.

Standards

There are now over 6 million dwellings in the public sector in Britain; of these just over 1 million were built before 1940, the remainder since 1945, and this means that housing standards are high. The public sector has the lowest proportion of unfit dwellings and dwellings lacking basic amenities. Since 1918 a number of government committees have been concerned with defining and establishing acceptable public sector standards: Tudor-Walter

(1918), Dudley (1944), and Parker Morris (1961) (HMSO, 1961). They have generally been responsible for laying down the standards which local authorities have adopted. Currently local authorities are obliged to meet Parker Morris standards in their new housing developments.

Within this picture of generally adequate standards there are problems not revealed by the conventional statistical measures of standards. First, although much of the high rise and deck access housing in recent decades meets Parker Morris standards, it has given rise to dissatisfaction among many tenants. It is now felt that such housing is not really suitable for families. Similarly, many pre-war council estates which have not been adequately maintained or modernized are seen as less desirable, a problem compounded by selective allocation policies concentrating low income and 'difficult' families on such estates. Second, differential standards have emerged within the public sector because of economic constraints imposed on local authorities at different periods. These pressures have obliged local authorities to build to lower standards and cut back on maintenance and improvement programmes. A constant problem in the public sector is striking the right balance between meeting current needs and anticipating the expectations of future generations. Too much emphasis on the present can mean premature obsolescence.

Access

With the decline of private renting for many low income households, the only effective chance of adequate housing at a price they can afford is that offered by council housing. This makes the issue of access particularly acute in the public sector. Local authorities have a wide area of autonomy and discretion in this sphere of allocation. The 1957 Housing Act laid a general duty upon them to give reasonable preference in selecting tenants to those who occupy insanitary or overcrowded houses, have large families, or live in generally unsatisfactory conditions. Beyond this it is very much up to each local authority how they set about allocating their houses. Each local authority's system is, therefore, to a certain extent unique, reflecting local priorities and political values. They also, of course, have many common features. In recent years attempts have been made by government to standardize allocation procedures along the lines proposed by the Cullingworth report (CHAC, 1969). Local authorities, nevertheless, continue to create their own rules and retain wide powers of discretion.

At the root of the allocation problem in the public sector is the fact of scarcity. As public sector allocation is governed by non-market criteria, formally that of need, scarcity means that local authorities are obliged to operate some form of rationing system. Ideally, applicants would choose the house that meets their requirements; in practice it is more accurate to say that local authorities choose tenants for houses that fall vacant. Every local authority attempts to rank needs in order of priority by means of a waiting list, usually on a points system reflecting factors such as current housing circumstances, size of household, length of residence in the area, and so on. Extra points are given for medical or other socially stressful circumstances. Against the priorities of the waiting list must be set the demands for rehousing clearance area households, requests for transfer from existing tenants and urgent 'cases' put forward by social services departments.

This generally is the kind of rationing system operative in most local authority areas. It is at best only a very crude indication of what actually governs allocation in the areas of greatest housing need – the larger cities and towns. However sophisticated the system for defining need and priorities, in practice many authorities have a greater number of households with equal qualifications for housing than houses to allocate. The problem is managed by recourse to administrative discretion. Such discretion can be justified in terms of the flexibility it gives housing officials to respond sensitively to individual problems and needs. On the other hand, there has been considerable research into allocation policies which lends weight to the view that sensitivity is something that many authorities – especially the larger urban authorities – are not in a position to display. Rather the operation of discretion is frequently quite arbitrary, and sometimes is governed by political interests (Niner, 1975; Lambert et al., 1975). This poses legitimacy problems for a system formally governed by criteria of need. One common way out of the dilemma is to invoke what can be called the ideology of the queue.

This ideology involves the idea that those at the top of the waiting list are rewarded for their fortitude by being able to move into a decent home. It is an idea that has been promoted by local politicians and officials and is widely accepted by the public. This is by no means what actually happens in many of the authorities with the most pressing needs. For example one recent study into the extent of racial discrimination found that some local authorities give priority to indigenous residents at the expense of immigrant applications (Smith, 1977). Clearance families often receive priority. Relatively few, it seems, get housed from the top of the list. In these circumstances many applicants find it more effective to press their claim with all the support they can muster from doctors, social workers, local councillors and local advice centres. In the areas of acute housing need, it is persistence rather than merit and need that is rewarded. The ideology of the queue serves to displace resentment at the failure of central government and the local authorities to provide sufficient housing on to those who are considered to be indulging in that most un-British activity, 'queue jumping' – homeless families and social service families, for instance.

The only conceivable solution to these problems of access and the realization of a situation where applicants choose homes rather than officials choosing tenants is a sustained commitment to building more public sector housing for those who lack the means or desire to become owners.

Conclusions

In 1967 Professor David Donnison (1967) in an authoritative comparative survey of government housing policies throughout Europe wrote:

> The distinctions between the 'public' and 'private' sectors of housing – distinctions which are central to the thinking of those accustomed to a 'social' pattern of housing policies – have lost most of their significance. Private enterprise usually has a large part to play, often a larger one. But it operates within the context of a plan determined by government.

We would question whether private enterprise operates within 'a plan determined by government'. Perhaps it would be more accurate to say that government operates within a plan determined by private enterprise. Either way the point that the distinction between private and public has been blurred has not been invalidated by any subsequent developments in British housing policy. One of the major problems for students of housing policy is discerning with any clarity what the logic and purposes of government intervention are. As Professor Donnison pointed out, the distribution of the housing available does not accord with any politically defensible views about social justice and human rights. We would add that the present system of housing finance – apart from the overriding concern to provide incentives to those with capital to invest – lacks any clear economic rationale.

Easier to discern are the political pressures on government that emerge out of the tangle of vested interests in the housing system that has been developed during this century. Any attempt to reform the complex subsidy arrangements and fiscal policies that govern the distribution of housing resources appears likely to cause a major political controversy. What seems to be emerging as a response to those ever-present political pressures is a dual sector, or two-tier system of housing.

First, there is an extensively state subsidized owner-occupied sector, powerfully politically supported, for those who have the adequate incomes and job security to meet the market institutions' requirements of ability to pay. Second, there is a public sector where there is no longer any intention to provide much more than a residual 'ambulance service' to those defined as being in special need – low-income families, the homeless, single-parent families, battered wives, the elderly, and ethnic minorities (HMSO, 1977a). The housing strategy indicated by the Green Paper implicitly rejects the option of creating a real and meaningful choice between owning and renting. Although it was a discussion document offered by a Labour government, it does not even consider the more radical option that has inspired previous Labour governments and has done so much to make the British public housing sector one of the best in the world. Ministers of Health such as Wheatley in 1924 and Bevan in 1945, with responsibility for housing, believed in high-quality housing for everyone, and many had cause to be grateful.

Is it really possible to solve the problems of the poor, the ethnic minorities and the homeless without a firm commitment to an expanding and vigorous public housing sector? There is a vast amount of historical and comparative evidence which lends support to the argument that wherever public housing has been treated as 'welfare housing' it has tended to stigmatize and isolate the groups it was claiming to integrate and assist.

References

CHAC (1969), *Council Housing, Purpose, Priorities and Procedures*, MHLG.

Community Development Project (1977), *Gilding the Ghetto – the State and the Poverty Experiments*.

Donnison, D. V. (1967), *The Government of Housing*, Penguin.

Gauldie, E. (1974), *Cruel Habitations*, Allen & Unwin.

Harloe, M., Issacharoff, R. and Minns, R. (1974), *The Organisation of Housing*, Heinemann/CES.

HMSO (1961), *Homes for Today and Tomorrow*, Report of the Sub-Committee of the Central Housing Advisory Committee, MHLG.

HMSO (1973), *Widening the Choice – the Next Steps in Housing*, Cmnd 5280.

HMSO (1977a), *Housing Policy – a Consultative Document*, Cmnd 6851.

HMSO (1977b), *Policy for the Inner Cities*, Cmnd 6854.

Lambert J., Blackaby, R. and Paris, C. (1975), *Neighbourhood Politics and Housing Opportunities*, Centre of Environmental Studies Conference paper.

Nevitt, A. A. (1966), *Housing Taxation and Subsidies*, Nelson.

Niner P. (1975), *Local Authority Housing Policy and Practice – A Case Study Approach*, Occasional Paper no. 31, Centre for Urban and Regional Studies, University of Birmingham.

Pahl, R. E. (1975), *Whose City?* Penguin.

Roof (Shelter's housing magazine), (1976), article by Stuart Weir in, vol. 1. no 4, July.

Smith, D. (1977), *The Facts of Racial Disadvantage*, Penguin.

Turner, J. F. C. and Fichter, R. (1972), Ch. 7 in *Freedom to Build*, Macmillan.

II

Policies and Services Designed to Meet Basic Individual Needs

5

Education

Roger E. Cox

Great Britain, like all advanced industrial societies, has a complex arrangement of educational services run by the State or by institutions closely associated with it. In recent years the cost of education has amounted to 10 per cent or more of all public expenditure, and is by far the major item of expenditure for the county and metropolitan district councils which administer it at the local level. Indeed, it represents one of the major growth areas in post-war Britain and draws into employment around one million people, including a significant proportion of those (particularly women) who have high educational qualifications.

Yet the function of such a large and complex system is far from obvious. At the most superficial level, the humanitarian arguments that might justify a bare minimum of provision in the fields of health, housing or income maintenance will not justify even the most rudimentary service of mass education: the formal knowledge schools provide is not a prerequisite for survival. As Musgrave points out, our view of the function of educational institutions is the result of an ever-changing process of negotiation and bargaining which *defines* it. These 'definitions' can be seen to be the result of contrasting views of what the function of education ought to be (Musgrave, 1968, p. 2).

Two pairs of competing aims can be identified throughout the history of education as a State enterprise. The first of these pairs clusters around, on the one hand a concern with social order in society, and on the other with a concern to liberate the uneducated from their ignorance. Education as a civilized means of social control has been the dominant ideology informing much educational policy. It encompasses the character-building ethos of the public schools; it has been apparent in the long and powerful association of the Churches with education (a pedagogic version of 'education is next to Godliness', where ignorance is sinful); it has been explicitly stated in the attempts of some dominant groups to impose their will upon others, and used as a specific instrument, as in the USA, for the fostering of a national consciousness. But perhaps most significantly for this country it has been used as a response to demands for the extension of democratic rights, in the belief that a State system of education should inculcate not only the correct moral values, but also the appropriate political attitudes.

By comparison, the belief in education as a process of liberation has always been the assertive ideology of minority groups or movements, or the creed of individual writers from Rousseau to A. S. Neill, who have had little contact with systems of mass education. Nevertheless it has had influence within the educational world (far more than outside it), and is evident in some aspects of the 'progressive' movement in primary education and more generally in the claims of universities for 'academic freedom'. In the political sphere, sections of the Labour movement have espoused the cause of education as a means of emancipating the working class, but even here it has competed with calls for more vocational education.

The second pair of competing aims places emphasis either upon the utilitarian function of education and its relation to economic growth, or upon the importance of formal education in passing on from one generation to another those aspects of a society's culture that are most highly prized. The former sees education as an economic investment (both for the individual and for society as a whole) and therefore part of the competitive arsenal of industrialized nations in their continual search for better technologies and higher productivity. By contrast, the latter sees education as the guardian and careful distributor of precious knowledge, conserved and nurtured through generations. It is the utilitarian view which has tended to dominate successive definitions of the function of State education, but elites have often attempted to reserve for themselves access to the realms of 'high culture', whilst regarding a more mundane, skill-orientated education as being sufficient for the majority of society.

Rarely, in the day-to-day negotiations that go towards the making and implementation of educational policy (nor, indeed, in the more ruminative discussions of government-sponsored committees and councils), are such aims seen to be so distinct. They do however underlie many of the attitudes which shape policy, and occasionally surface with a startling clarity, especially in periods when superficial consensus begins to crack. The publication in 1969 of the first Black Paper on education (Cox and Dyson, 1969), for example, exposed the fragility of a political consensus nurtured at central government level by ministers such as Boyle and Crosland (Kogan, 1975).

More often debates are conducted in terms of less generalized objectives, and again, for simplicity, it is useful to distinguish two pairs of competing objectives concerned with the process of teaching and learning and hence with the organization of educational provision. First, there are opposing views, one of which holds knowledge, and the divisions of knowledge, as the basis of educational activity, and the other which takes the individual learner and his particular stage of development as its starting point. On the one hand there are institutions such as universities which (having admittedly selected a very homogeneous group of learners) take little further notice of their individual differences, and rather concentrate attention almost exclusively upon the knowledge to be learned. On the other hand there is the image of the modern primary school where (at least in the imagination) each child learns in a way appropriate to his individual development.

Second, there is a tension between the belief that education should be a process which differentiates according to the learner's abilities and inclinations (and provides a differentiated curriculum), and the belief that the educational experience should, to a large extent, be common to all children. It is this conflict, in particular, that has produced so many decisive debates about the organization of the State system, and since the war has been the focus for the conflicts surrounding the reorganization of secondary education.

Even before the Second World War, however, the discussions which surrounded what is now called 'secondary' education and which culminated in the 1944 Education Act, raised in many ways the tensions and conflicts described above. Indeed it was the problem of differentiation, and its attendant problem of selection that dominated pre-war thinking about the organization of post-elementary education.

It is important to realize that there had developed in this country a dual system of education, confirmed as part of the State system by the Education Act of 1902. First, there was elementary education designed for the majority of the population and described by the novelist H. G. Wells as being intended to, 'educate the lower classes for employment on lower class lines, with specially trained inferior teachers', but which constantly sought and often achieved a standard and level of education far beyond the government's intention. Second, there was a system of secondary education developed through the nineteenth-century revival of the public schools and endowed grammar schools which charged fees and aimed specifically at attracting the middle class and the 'gentry', often abusing the original intention of their endowments in the search for a high-class clientele (Simon, 1965). The 1902 Act then allowed local authorities (which succeeded the potentially more radical School Boards) to develop their own secondary schools – the State grammar schools of the twentieth century.

Before the 1944 Act, this arrangement of parallel systems of education was still to a large extent intact, although in some areas there had developed a range and quality of provision in the non-secondary sector good enough to be seen by some as a threat to the more prestigious secondary schools. In addition there had developed the idea that there should be a 'ladder' from elementary to secondary education for a limited number of bright children. This was climbed with the help of a system of 'scholarships' for children from elementary schools, enabling them to receive free, or partially subsidized, secondary education. It is interesting to note that the practice of streaming children from an early age was one of the consequences of the need to select the potentially bright child and foster his development as a possible scholarship pupil (Simon, 1974).

It had been accepted as early as 1926[1] that there would have to be some rationalization of educational provision for adolescents, but there was far less agreement about the form that such a rationalization should take. It was not even accepted that they should all receive a 'secondary' education. For example, one Tory MP, in 1932, expressed the fear that free secondary education for all would mean 'secondary education for none', and that it would 'turn the whole country into a vast educational soup kitchen' (Simon, 1974, p. 186). Even the Labour movement, whilst advocating free and universal secondary education, was critically uncertain about the value and viability of a 'common' secondary school. In fact there had long been a commitment amongst certain sections to the expansion of a segregated system. As early as 1908 Sydney Webb, a leading Fabian, had claimed that what was needed was 'a progressive differentiation of the publicly provided schools each more accurately fitting the needs of a particular section of children' (Rubinstein and Simon, 1969, p. 6).

But perhaps the most crucial factor in the pre-war debate was the general confusion of 'ability' with 'interests and aptitudes'. It was a confusion that allowed far too much reliance to be placed upon the capacity of psychometrics (then still in its infancy) to differentiate between and to categorize types of children as being suitable for particular kinds of education. Uncertainty and ignorance often lead to dogmatism and this is all too evident in the now notorious Norwood report of 1943 (MacLure, 1965). This report, concerned with the curriculum and examinations in secondary schools, postulated three types of child: first, children who were 'interested in learning for its own sake'; second, those 'whose interests [lay] markedly in the field of applied science or applied art', and last, children who dealt 'more easily with concrete things than with ideas'. The report, according to Musgrave, purported to find 'psychological justification for a system of secondary organization that was fundamentally based on historical developments and on social attitudes that had been stronger in the pre-1914 period than in the 1930s' (1968, p. 103). Indeed Simon sees something rather more sinister than ignorance in much of the pre-war debate, claiming the rationalization presaged by this emphasis upon pseudo-psychology was aimed at 'turning the school system into a vast self-regulating selective machine' (1974, p. 227).

The 1944 Act itself made no direct statement on the actual organization of secondary schooling, and apart from making the important declaration that secondary education was to be universal, free and 'end-on' to primary education, it achieved little more than a tidying up of the old elementary system and a better harmonization of denominational schools with the State system. It was passed under the aegis of a wartime coalition government maintaining a necessary but insubstantial consensus on matters of social policy, and implemented by a Labour government ambiguous and divided about its own educational policy (Lawton, 1977).

The Political Organization and Control of Education

One of the problems with the study of educational policy is that the wording of legislation reveals very little about the values inherent in the accompanying debate, or about the political, social and economic interests that lie behind those values. To locate the sources of power that manipulate and shape policy one has to seek beyond the public statements of governments and their committees. This leads into the details of negotiations that take place behind public utterances, or out to the broader themes that attempt to relate policy to more slow-moving changes in the social structure. The danger of the latter is that it can lead to abstractions far removed from the everyday reality of policy-making; the danger with the former is that the mass of detail obscures the very patterns being sought. Nevertheless both are necessary if one is to avoid accepting superficially rational explanations of policy-making, or concluding that the whole process is so muddled as to be purposeless.

Most social policy aims at making interventions in the affairs of men in a more or less systematic manner, but the level at which the intervention is attempted reflects not merely the constraints under which it is implemented, but also the broader aspects of the power context within which it has been formulated. As will be discussed later, positive discrimination programmes have been crippled not simply by inadequate resources but also by having to operate within so restricted a frame of reference that their potential for success was severely limited from the outset. The problem is compounded with respect to education by the fact that no solutions of a more impersonal structural nature (such as might be envisaged in relationship to poverty or bad housing) are likely to be adequate, simply because, in the end, all policy has to be mediated through the mind of the individual pupil or student. The end product of educational policy needs to be seen, at the same time as personalized to the individual, and yet related in its aims and in its effects to the wider social structure.

In a discussion, then, of the politics of the policy-making process, it is important to remember that such an analysis can only provide a partial explanation of the particular form that the education system takes at any one time. The more limited objective of accurately describing the process is no easier to achieve: as Kogan remarks in his study of post-war educational policy making, 'The sources of policy generation are so difficult to locate, let alone place in any logical pattern, that detecting the change in values, or the pressures by which change is effected is more a matter of art than of analysis' (1975, p. 23).

Later in the same book Kogan describes the education system as, 'pluralistic, incremental, unsystematic, reactive' and remarks, 'how untidy the whole system is' (1975, p. 238). Such a conclusion provides a useful starting point for a discussion of the political organization and control of education. Each of these four adjectives, together with their implied opposites, provides a simple but useful tool for an analysis of a few selected aspects of the political process.

'Pluralistic', the first of Kogan's adjectives, implies that there are many groups, none of which has absolute dominance or authority, which negotiate in a political market place, reaching decisions through a process of negotiation. Its implied opposite in this context would perhaps be that of a bureaucratic system with clear lines of decision-making springing from the apex and achieving rational, planned decisions. If such a bureaucratic structure did exist, control would presumably lie with the Secretary of State, and decisions would be passed down to the local authorities and thence to the schools and into the classrooms. Clearly such a description bears little relationship to the reality of the situation, and the imagery more often used is of a 'partnership' between central and local government and of the head being 'first amongst equals' in his school. Whilst such images may be nearer the truth, they over-estimate consensus and under-estimate the conflicts inherent in the system. The duties and responsibilities of the Secretary of State and of the local authorities (and the rights of parents) are expressed only in generalities in the 1944 Act, and their implementation is ringed with ambiguity. In fact central government rarely attempts to exercise control directly, preferring to exercise its strong financial control than to risk the legal entanglements sometimes consequent upon using the Act. The recent Tameside dispute amply demonstrates the point, when the Secretary of State tried unsuccessfully to prevent a local authority from reversing an earlier decision to establish comprehensive schools, following a change of political control in the council. The final ruling of the House of Lords implied that the authority was correct to heed what it believed to be the will of the local electorate, rather than submit to the stated policy of the current government.

This however should not lead one to believe that local electorates (or more specifically parents) can exercise control in any direct way. Buxton (1970), in his discussion of the Enfield case, where a small group of parents sought to prevent the reorganization of the local grammar school into a comprehensive school, shows quite clearly that, though both central and local government must operate within the strict letter of the law, they cannot be prevented from pursuing their own policies. Even if the legality of the policy may be in question, as Batley (1970) points out, 'a legal struggle between citizens and a Minister is never equal, because it is always open to the Minister to change the law.' Indeed, not long after the final ruling on the Tameside dispute, the 1976 Education Act was passed which gave the Secretary of State more power to prevent local authorities from operating selective systems of secondary education.

Another aspect of the pluralism of which Kogan talks is the origin of innovation in education. Very little, in fact, seems to be initiated from the centre, whereas a great deal of change in the organization of schools has come from the local level, and within schools from the institutions themselves. Kogan and van der Eyken, for example, quote the remark of a chief education officer that it is these officers who carry the 'thrust of innovation' (1973, p. 14), and in certain areas the same might well be said of the head or even of the classroom teacher.

Clearly, when using the term 'pluralistic', Kogan was also thinking of the activities of various interest groups – the teachers' associations, the local authority associations, Parliament itself, and of various pressure groups such as the Confederation for the Advancement of State Education or the Black Paper movement. He also refers to the more general influence of the 'intelligentsia' and of the media. The teachers' associations, for example, effectively prevented the working of a ministry-controlled curriculum study group set up in 1961 to act, in David Eccles's words, as a 'commando-like unit' which would lead central government into the 'secret garden of the curriculum' (Kogan, 1975, p. 142). Its replacement, the Schools Council, is relatively autonomous of government and dominated by the representatives of the teachers' associations, even though they are not necessarily representative of the aggregate of teacher opinion on curriculum matters and, indeed, are not especially interested in curriculum development as such. In more recent years the Schools Council has come in for considerable criticism, and between central government and the teachers' associations there exists what can best be described as a 'cold war' atmosphere.

Turning to the second of Kogan's adjectives, he describes the system as 'incremental', perhaps implying something which is unplanned and certainly not planned from any 'first principles'. Elsewhere in a discussion of the role of the Central Advisory Council (Kogan, 1973),[2] he gives some illustration of what he means. 'The C.A.Cs.', he says, 'were evidently devised to provide a continuing ruminative and contemplative service to the D.E.S. [Department of Education and Science] . . . and no dramatic results were ever expected' (1973, p. 164). They had, he argues, an evangelical role in describing the 'best' educational practice, a legitimating role (particularly in giving respectability to the 'radical' sociology of the 1960s), and a sponsoring role in advocating changes of policy 'that have already been mooted within education and the wider social service world' (1973, p. 166). They were, he concludes, 'the tug boats of gradualist radicalism'.

In a more detailed discussion of the Plowden Report (1967), Kogan describes the lingering (and incidentally illegal) death of the CACs. The result of the Plowden Report, he claims, was a great deal of acclaim but very little action – there was no systematic follow-up or attempt to convert general recommendations into policy, so that 'as an immediate planning and social engineering exercise' it 'scored no great successes' (1973, p. 185). Nevertheless, he claims for the report a success in its evangelical role, producing a 'ripple' effect which passed on to teachers and the public at large some of the commonplaces of educational sociology and development theory.

Certainly there have been attempts by central government to plan part of the education system – mostly in the fields of further and higher education, and especially in the area of teacher-training – but they have had more to do with questions of manpower planning than with education as such, and have not been notably successful. The idea of planning perhaps has more relevance for the short- to medium-term operations of the local authorities, but very little again at the school level, where change is often dictated by the movement of staff, with their individual problems and idiosyncrasies.

The third of Kogan's adjectives is 'unsystematic', by which he may simply intend to emphasize the pluralistic and incremental nature of the political process. Yet he does refer to the power of individuals within the system to act decisively, and to exercise personal authority and leadership. King (1970), in a discussion of the role of the head, considers the basis for his authority. Clearly, King argues, the role and function of the head have a strong rational legitimation.[3] The education system as a whole has certain expectations of the head: that, for example, some kind of mathematics and English will be taught, or (in secondary schools) that children will be prepared for external examinations. It would require particular circumstances for such expectations to be flouted and for the head to retain the confidence of the wider educational world.

Nevertheless, the head is widely regarded as having a large degree of autonomy, and though schools, as organizations, often appear bureaucratic on paper, the 'style' of their operations is too untidy, too dependent upon personalities, too bound up with the everyday interaction of staff and pupils ever to be considered remotely like the classical model of a bureaucracy. It is in the ritualistic and charismatic aspects of the head's authority that the wide variations in ethos and style of schools become apparent. Heads enforce their authority through carefully designed ceremonies which may range from annual speech days or carol services, to ceremonial checks upon the length of hair or the shortness of hemlines. Even caning, as King points out, is a ritual carefully carried out and executed upon a ceremonial part of the offender's anatomy.

Similarly, the charisma which the head cultivates is an important part of the school ethos. A head who hides himself away in his study and issues memoranda to his staff (however efficient an administrator he may be) is not likely to keep their approval. He needs to be seen, and be seen to have a coherent set of attitudes and a decisive style that are clearly his own, because in the eyes of the world – parents, staff and pupils – it is *his* school and must bear the imprint of his personality. Many of the objections to large schools, one suspects, have less to do with the quality of the knowledge they impart than with the inability of such institutions to project the personality of their head.

It is however too easy to over-estimate the ability of the head to indulge in personal whims, and King makes an important distinction between autonomy and autocracy: '"Autonomy" refers to the ability to control one's own actions and this head teachers clearly have. "Autocracy" refers to rule, controlling the behaviour of others, which does not relate to a higher or external authority. This head teachers do not have' (1970, p. 94).

The last of Kogan's adjectives is 'reactive', and it may be useful to consider this briefly in relation to decision-making on the curriculum. Several writers, notably Eggleston (1973), have pointed to a conflict between those who hold to a traditional curriculum which reacts only slowly to external pressures, and the more creative approach of those who see curriculum development as initiating change and innovation. Eggleston in fact argues that during the course of the last hundred years or so there has been a movement away from curricula which are a reflection of dominant values and interests, to a position where assertive groups – teachers, parents, employers – more frequently challenge the orthodoxy. Teachers in particular have increasingly claimed autonomous control over the curriculum, rejecting text books and devising their own exams (e.g. Mode 3 of the Certificate of Secondary Education). Elsewhere however Eggleston makes it clear that it is an increasing challenge to 'dominant or received ideologies rather than the overthrow of such ideologies' (1977, p. 49), which is taking place. 'Reactive', then, is perhaps too weak a word to describe the process by which curricular innovation takes place. More creative forces are at work that have, in recent years, jostled and nudged received opinion into a position of uncertainty, and generated considerable discussion.

As a final example of the political process in education, it is worth turning to one of the major (and politically most contentious) developments of the post-war period. Whilst the expansion of higher and further education has been more dramatic and possibly of far greater overall significance, it is the reorganization of secondary education that has attracted most of the critical attention of educational commentators. The very 'newness' of the tertiary sector and the relatively firm grip of central control makes it a less attractive subject for historians and political scientists. Equally, the role of the private sector in education deserves debate, but in spite of its undoubtedly strong influence upon the structure of British society and two commissions having deliberated upon its future since the war, it remains a curiously peripheral subject of discussion. The attempt to phase out the direct grant schools has probably strengthened rather than weakened the private sector, whose very independence shields it from the glare of public debate. The reorganization of secondary education, on the other hand has never been far from the forefront of research and debate. The evolution and development of the comprehensive school has been well summarized elsewhere (Rubinstein and Simon, 1969; Bellaby, 1977), but a few comments here will serve to illustrate the insights to be gained from the study of the political process and also give some indication of their limitations.

The idea of the common school lay deep within the ideology of the Labour movement and has long been central to the policy of the TUC, but Labour Party education policy has too often been ambiguous or simply non-existent, leading to the characteristic 'yes, but not now' approach. Indeed, finding the Party pregnant and about to give birth to comprehensive schools was a shock which some senior members of the Party never overcame. Gaitskell had never shown much enthusiasm and as late as 1970 Wilson was still asserting that the comprehensive school would be a 'grammar school for all' (Kogan, 1975, p. 220). Without the expert midwifery of some staunchly conservative local authorities, it is perhaps unlikely that the child would ever have been born alive.

Within the Labour Party, the National Association of Labour Teachers campaigned long and hard at constituency level for the implementation of comprehensive schools and, building upon the frustration which was increasingly being felt by the staff and parents of children at secondary modern schools, gained the support of some Labour-controlled councils. But outside the Labour movement, in some of the rural counties, local problems and needs militated against the effective expansion of segregated schools and forms of comprehensive reorganization were introduced in the 1950s. One of the most interesting developments was the decision of Leicestershire in 1957 to introduce a two-tier system of secondary education, allowing the more effective use of existing resources to produce junior and senior high schools. It is true that under Labour control in London, some comprehensive schools (which were to gain considerable reputations) were set up, but London also had a large number of established grammar schools which the Ministry refused to allow the authority to close. And this – the closure of grammar schools – rather than the setting-up of comprehensive schools was, and still is, the principal point of contention.

When a Labour government came to office in 1964, there was sufficient force in its own grass roots and enough credibility given to the comprehensive school by existing experiments, for reorganization to be made an official and explicit policy, though it was 1976 before the force of law was added to that of persuasion. It was a policy which could by the 1960s be legitimated (partly through the CAC reports) by reference to the growing body of sociological and psychological writing which was often sharply critical of the effects of selection at the age of 11, and by implication in favour of non-selective secondary schools. Further legitimation was sought by reference to the need to produce more highly skilled and adaptable workers and by talking of the 'wastage of ability' that segregated schools were supposed to produce. It must be said however that it was never very clear how the reorganization of formal schooling was supposed to relate in any direct way to the demands of technological innovation.

The Conservative Party, to a large extent, acquiesced in reorganization – though here it was the leadership (particularly Boyle) who were in favour and the grass roots of the party who were far less enthusiastic. Even so Mrs Thatcher, on becoming Secretary of State for Education in 1970, attempted to slow the movement down and to move the focus away from secondary education. At the present time, whilst careful to show their acceptance of comprehensive schools for the majority of children, the leadership is strong in its defence of the remaining grammar schools.

The pattern of schools that has emerged from the process of reorganization is more varied than that which preceded it. The country is now dotted with schools catering for every conceivable age range, and one of the most dramatic results of reorganization (coupled with the trend to stay longer at school) is to throw into complete uncertainty the organization of educational provision for the 16 to 19 age group.

As an example of the political process in education, the process of comprehensive reorganization illustrates well Kogan's claims about pluralism and incrementalism. All major political parties have given it their support, though scarcely with any wholehearted commitment and the main teachers' associations have been ambivalent, reflecting perhaps a continuing uncertainty amongst the members of the profession. Local authorities have demonstrated once more that they have an inventiveness of their own, and some of them can claim to have led an unwilling central authority into more or less decisive action.

Yet none of this provides a really convincing explanation as to why secondary education should have undergone the transformation that it did at that particular time. Kogan talks of how 'issues arise from the conjunction of changes in popular attitudes, perhaps spurred by the consumer boom, and social values' (1975, p. 224), but this is a weak explanation of social change and provides no explanation (apart from the consumer boom) of why attitudes and values have changed.

Elsewhere, on the general question of the policy process, Kogan admits, 'We have no adequate explanatory framework of how local pressures and decision making add to the national aggregate' (1975, p. 223), and in his general conclusion he uses the metaphor of a kaleidoscope saying that, 'In looking at the education service and its politics we have to reckon with unpredictable sequences and patterns of change in ideology, in received concepts of human development, and in the economy' (1975, p. 237). To consider whether such changes are really so unpredictable and consequently inexplicable, it is necessary to step outside the education system as such and to consider the social implications of education in a more general way.

The Social Implications of Education

In each of us, it may be said, there exist two beings which, while inseparable except by abstraction, remain distinct. One is made up of all the mental states which apply only to ourselves and to the events of our personal lives. This is what might be called the individual being. The other is a system of ideas, sentiments, and practices which express in us, not our personality, but the group or different groups of which we are a part: these are religious beliefs and practices, national or occupational traditions, collective opinions of every kind. Their totality forms the social being. To constitute this being in each of us is the end of education.

Here, Durkheim (1956, p. 124), writing at the beginning of this century, is stressing that education is not simply of value to the individual, nor merely of value in increasing the individual's contribution to the whole. It is, he claims, concerned to constitute the 'social being', which shapes not only people, but also the interconnections between them; the relationships between people that make up the totality of what is called society. In this Durkheim makes two basic and essential points – one explicitly and one by implication. First he points quite clearly to the social implications of education. It has never been doubted that there is a strong connection between education, in a general sense, and the kind of society we live in, nor that formal systems of education reflect that society in some way. The directions in which the causal lines of force run have often been debated, but that the connections exist is beyond dispute. It follows therefore that the effects of education should be sought in the wider context of society and that in society should be sought the forces which shape the form and organization of education. Second, Durkheim refers, in his distinction between the individual and the social identity of man, to what is perhaps the most crucial dilemma that so much educational research has faced – the relationship of the individual to the social structure within which he lives. Or, as Tyler (1977, p. 100) puts it, the 'connection between structure and biography'.

In a discussion of the problem of inequality, Tyler (1977, p. 33) elaborates upon this point, saying,

> theorists tend to see inequality as a set of relationships
> between large groups of people based on occupation, income,
> or, at a deeper level, on their power and wealth. Education is
> then considered either justly or unjustly, as the instrument
> for reproducing and maintaining these relationships. On the
> other hand social policy makers are more concerned with
> individual biographies, with the distribution of people across
> these groupings and with the characteristics of ability,
> background and training that determine individual life
> chances.

It is the search for solutions to this problem which had led educational research of the last twenty years or so in a variety of directions which must briefly be traced here.

Karabel and Halsey (1977), in their review of recent educational research, refer to the 'political arithmetic' studies prevalent in the early post-war period. These studies were concerned with 'calculating the chances of reaching various stages in the educational process for children of different class origins'; concerned with 'matching ability with opportunity' and preoccupied with 'wastage' (1977, p. 11). Linked to economic arguments for the expansion of education, these studies found powerful support in CAC reports of the 1950s and early 1960s, as well as in the very influential Robbins Report on higher education, and constituted one of the significant factors in the massive expansion of further and higher education. They pointed, also, to the relative failure of the working-class child to benefit from the expansion of education and began to question the validity of rigid segregation of children from the age of 11. Further, some commentators such as Little and Westergaard (1964), questioned the effect of expanded educational opportunities upon social mobility, arguing that as the educational channel widened and the possibility of acquiring educational credentials increased, so 'career mobility' declined. Tyler uses the image of an 'escalator of life chances which moves everybody up but preserves the differentials,' and he adds, 'We may be able to perceive too why educational expansion may be popular and at the same time relatively powerless to change the orginal inequalities between its "passengers" ' (1977, p. 43).

In exploring the relative failure of the working-class child at school, several studies went beyond the abstract notion of class to try to identify those factors in the environment which correlate with success and failure. Research carried out for the Plowden Report (1967), attempted not only to identify the factors involved, but also to rank them in importance. The research concluded (see Morrison and McIntyre, 1971, for a useful summary) by placing great emphasis upon the importance of parental attitudes – in particular, the educational aspirations of the home, the 'literacy' of the home and parental interest in the child's school work. It also pointed to a number of factors grouped under the heading 'home circumstances' as being of considerable importance in explaining the difference in achievement between schools, some of the most important being the father's occupation and the parents' education as well as the physical amenities of the home. Certain aspects of the school itself, in particular the experience and competence of the teachers, were also found to be significant. The report itself supplied the metaphor:

'The apples on a tree in a good situation will do better than those on a tree in a poor situation' (1967, para. 91).

These attempts to break down the monolithic concept of class, provide interesting and valuable 'snap-shots' of the child in his home environment, but they reveal little about the process (either at home or at school) which produces the picture. They lead inevitably back to the dilemma that was referred to earlier, and to the need to explore 'biography' whilst not losing sight of the structure. Swift (1968) explains the difficulty in more detail describing two basic approaches to educational research. One takes a 'societal' view, analysing the relationship of the education system to the stratification system, showing the support one gives to the other, whilst the second 'psycho-dynamic' approach asks how the experience of the individual affects his adaptation to the education system. The 'societal' view employs concepts which remain at a high level of abstraction, whilst the 'psycho-dynamic' approach, attempting to isolate separate, more concrete, factors is faced with the problem that 'the number of potential single variables is limitless' (1968, p. 287). To illustrate the point, Swift refers to a study which found 'an association between climatic temperature changes during foetal development and subsequent ability'. Whilst such information may not be abstract, it contains little of value to the policy-maker.

Swift however makes a further point about the implications of the 'psycho-dynamic' approach: 'Taking the education system and its adaptation to society as given involves concentrating upon the problems of adaptation it raises for the individual. But these very problems may be aspects of its own adaptation to the wider social structure, and as such may be better solved at that level' (1968, p. 287). In other words it can lead too easily to the view that the child who fails at school is deficient, without in any way questioning the validity of the school experience for that child, and without consideration being given to the relationship of education to the wider social structure.

Faced with the seeming intransigence of this problem, more recent educational research has tended to fragment and to pursue several different lines of enquiry. Some has been mesmerized by its own methodology into a conclusion that education has no more effect upon life chances than personality, competence at work or simply good and bad luck.[4] Others, equally pessimistic in their conclusions, have argued that the education system is so deeply embedded in the existing class structure of capitalist societies that it can only ratify and reinforce existing inequalities. They see so tight a 'fit' between the existing social order and the education system, that the only possibility of change lies in the eruption of the conflicts they find to be inherent in the societies they describe.[5]

More optimistically, a few have attempted to trace the effects of the input of hard cash and resources upon educational achievement. Byrne, Williamson and Fletcher, for example, conducted a sophisticated study of several local authorities in Great Britain and concluded that 'the kind of policy a local authority pursues influences the extent and character of what it provides. This provision, in turn, is related to measures of educational attainment. Where provision is high there is a tendency for attainment to be high' (Byrne *et al.*, 1975, p. 165). Such research, however, whilst suggesting that educational provision can mediate the impact of class background, leaves open the question of the extent to which resources really affect outcomes for the individual child and precisely the process by which they do so.

One of the most fascinating areas of contemporary research has been within the school itself. Researchers such as Hargreaves (1967), Lacey (1970) and Nash (1973) have gone inside the school and deep into the classroom itself to study the effects of teacher–pupil interaction and pupil–pupil interaction. They have provided some of the most brilliant insights into the importance of teachers' perceptions of the children they teach and of the pupils' perceptions of each other, exposing the naivety of the belief that 'ability' could be abstracted from the interaction of personalities. Nevertheless their value to the practising teacher is perhaps somewhat limited, since any teacher who took their insights too much to heart would end up in a state of paralysis, unable to move for fear of producing the wrong response.

Equally problematic for the practising teacher, but possibly also the most exciting current writer in the field of educational research, is Bernstein.[6] He has accepted the challenge of the structure/biography dichotomy and attempted to trace the relationship of one to the other by focusing upon linguistic development in the child and the process of cultural transmission in the school. He attempts 'to set the analysis of the school against a broader canvas of changes in forms of social control' without losing sight of the 'grim consequences of class relationships' (Bernstein, 1975, p. 1). His importance in the field of the sociology of education is undoubted, but his significance to the student of policy is less obvious. Unlike much of the 'political arithmetic' or 'psycho-dynamic' research, his work does not easily suggest policy reforms (though his early socio-linguistic work has been much used and abused), yet he does have the virtue of insisting that every change in policy or practice, however trivial it may appear, be examined as the consequence of causal agents operating at a higher level of generality. Karabel and Halsey remark: 'No matter how intimate the phenomenon being examined, Bernstein believes that it should be possible to show how its form and development are influenced by the larger patterns of power and control' (1977, p. 62).

Perhaps the honesty of Kogan, in admitting to the inability of political analysis to find the patterns behind apparently 'unpredictable sequences', needs to be matched by a determination to explore the 'order' that controls the changes of the kaleidoscope. At the present time however it must be said that social research provides few answers to the problems posed by Kogan. The concentration upon the distribution of education has led to the neglect of the social changes which give rise to new forms of education and to new curricula. In this country a few historians (for example Musgrave, 1968; Simon, 1965, 1974) have set out to relate educational change to broader patterns of social change, but there is less work of this nature upon more contemporary educational policy. On the actual emergence of the comprehensive school, which so puzzled Kogan, for example, there is very little, though recently Bellaby (1977), using an explicitly Marxist perspective, has made a valuable attempt to relate its appearance to changes in the capitalist mode of production. Again one can only emphasize the importance of the approach of Bernstein when he stresses the need to examine the 'range, variation and change' in the content and organizational forms of education 'at both societal and school levels' (1975, p. 170).

As an example of the way some of the problems thrown up by research have plagued educational policy, a few comments will be made here upon the history of the educational priority areas. The bare facts of the story are told by Robinson (1976), and a considered verdict upon the action-research programmes attached to a few of them is given by Halsey (1972). Only some of the more general issues raised by them can be touched upon here. Initiated by the Plowden Committee and implemented by a government growing cynical about the ability of the education system to solve social problems, positive discrimination was intended as a way of concentrating extra resources upon geographical areas of particular deprivation which would be designated as educational priority areas. The belief was that by improving the quality of the schools in such areas and by concentrating upon the relationship between home and school, some children would be rescued from their origins and be given a better start in the competitive race that lay ahead.

The difficulties associated with the implementation of such a policy lie in two main areas: the theoretical framework upon which the policy was based, and confusion about the appropriate level of intervention to be employed. As far as the theory is concerned two aspects have to be considered. The first of these has to do with the interpretation of theories of poverty in connection with the policy. Halsey (1972) suggests three such interpretations:

(i) 'cultural deprivation' as the cause of poverty, where the focus is upon the inadequacy of parents in socializing their children,

(ii) 'educational deprivation', where the focus is upon the failure of the school to provide the appropriate 'educational' socialization, and

(iii) poverty as the result of the restricted 'opportunity structure of society' (1972, pp. 17–19).

The emphasis upon the 'psycho-dynamic' approach to research – evident in Plowden and reflected in the 1960s – leads to a concentration upon the first two interpretations, but whilst they offer concrete opportunities for reform, they remain only partial explanations of poverty and thus immediately restrict the opportunities for positive change. As Halsey, himself, comments, 'no amount of success with work on either the culture of poverty of the home or the educational poverty of the school will result in anything but frustration if socialisation cannot be translated into opportunity at the end' (1972, p. 19).

The second theoretical problem concerns the model of the child implicit in Plowden and dominant in the developmental psychology taught to prospective teachers. It was, claim Bernstein and Davies (1969, p. 57), an 'essentially biological' view of the child, with natural stages of development – rather like a turnip or a carrot. It concentrated upon the individual child and ignored the social factors associated with age, sex and subcultural differences that would affect socialization. Such a theory is again only a partial explanation of the forces at work and opportunities for change are thereby restricted.

On the question of the level of intervention, there are two main problems. One of these relates to the usefulness of using geographical areas, rather than social categories, as the unit for implementation. It has often been pointed out that, however the line is drawn round an area, there will be more deprived children outside it than inside. Similarly, the general social indicators that define an area as being deprived cannot be taken to describe the circumstances of each individual child within it. When these two factors are taken into account, the use of geographical areas begins to lose some of its attractiveness.

The more serious problem of implementation, however, relates back to the difficulties associated with the interpretation of theories of poverty, and has to do with effectiveness of isolating education from the other social services, and indeed from economic policies. Halsey points to the danger of confusing 'astronomical ends' and 'minuscule means' (1972, p. 5), and Coates and Silburn, whilst accepting the value of an attempt to use schools as 'centres of regeneration: growth points of a new social consciousness among the poor', conclude, 'Education, in itself will not solve the problem of poverty. The social structure that generates poverty generates its own shabby education system to serve it' (1970, p. 73).

Conclusions

Education, it might well be said, is in the doldrums. Kogan (1975) subtitles one of his chapters, 'From Expansionism to Pessimism, 1960–1974', and he traces growing uncertainties in the aims of educationalists, doubts about education's value amongst consumers and a growing challenge to the established government of education at all levels. Several hopeful innovations have been deemed failures, or have never been properly launched. Nursery schooling, for example, remains a poor relation competing ineffectually for limited resources,[7] and adult education has, if anything, been even less successful. Central to the education system, comprehensive schooling has too often been regarded as a panacea, prompting hypercritical reactions from those who can all too easily point to its difficulties and failings. Even at the core of so much post-war educational policy there has been failure. As Halsey remarks, it was assumed that the expansion of educational facilities would produce 'a marked change in the social composition of student bodies and in the flow of people from the less favoured classes into the secondary schools and higher educational institutions'. And he concludes that 'the essential fact of twentieth century educational history is that egalitarian policies have failed' (1972, p. 7).

To the extent that these failures have demonstrated the limitations of education in achieving broader social and economic objectives, and the folly of treating education as 'the waste paper basket of social policy – a repository for dealing with social problems where solutions are uncertain or where there is a disinclination to wrestle with them seriously' (Halsey, 1972, p. 8), they have served a useful purpose. They have served another purpose too in revealing some of the cracks in the veneer of consensus, exposing some of the more fundamental conflicts that lie beneath. In particular they have led in recent years to a change in emphasis away from the learner and his social environment towards a consideration of the content of education – the knowledge that is to be learned – and of the social implications of the way it is organized and distributed in schools, colleges and universities. It is the content of education that surely should be the focus for the generation of both educational theory and policy in preference to the increasingly sterile debate on the nature/nurture controversy, or even in preference to continued arguments about the form of organization for secondary education where, as Bernstein suggests, *'plus ça change, plus c'est la même chose'* (1975, p. 170).

In a recent study of social justice in education, Lawton has argued, 'that the weakness of the argument for social justice in education, or equality in education in the past, is that it has been stated in terms of equality of the right to x years of education or the right to enter a certain kind of educational institution, but what has not been done is to specify the kind of educational benefits to be made available in terms of curriculum content' (1977, p. 9). There are dangers in the current emphasis upon knowledge, however, which can lead to assumptions being made about what knowledge is appropriate for different kinds of children, producing formulations as banal as those of the Norwood Report. Equally, the obvious fact that knowledge is as subject to differentiation on social grounds as schools are, has led some to make the rather dangerous claim that all knowledge is relative and that no one fact, concept or attitude is more valuable than any other. As Karabel and Halsey remark, 'the ideological impetus behind ultra-relativism is a powerful one, for if sociologists cannot eradicate glaring inequalities in the real world, they can perhaps do away with them on the conceptual level by denying that they are, appearances to the contrary notwithstanding, inequalities at all' (1977, p. 56). Such a view, if taken seriously, would inevitably lead to the conclusion that there is no need for, and no purpose to be served by a State system of formal education. Such positions cannot be easily dismissed and some of those who adopt these views have often had important comments to make upon the operation of the education system,[8] but perhaps their main weakness is that they present no substantive challenge to those who would prefer private resources to be the main determinant of educational opportunity, or see the current emphasis upon a 'core curriculum' as a means of restricting the content of the education provided by State schools. In Musgrave's (1968) terms, the content of the curriculum and its distribution is likely to be the focus for the process of negotiation and bargaining that will define the educational situation for the next few years, perhaps decades. It also contains elements of the competing ideological objectives referred to at the beginning of this chapter, often stated with renewed clarity. It is after all through knowledge that people seek to liberate or control; the institutions and the credentials they offer are only the means by which knowledge is organized – even if the brightness of their masquerade is sometimes dazzling.

Notes

1   The Report of the Consultative Committee chaired by Hadow, called *The Education of the Adolescent*, recommended a radical reorganization of what it termed 'post-primary education', as well as suggesting that the age of transfer from elementary to secondary schools should be fixed at 11.

2   The Central Advisory Council was set up by the 1944 Education Act and has produced some of the major reports on education in the post-war period. It was the successor to the Consultative Committee set up as far back as 1899, and has had several chairmen who have given their names to the reports their committees produced – for example, Crowther (15–18), Newsom (*Half Our Future*), Plowden (*Children and their Primary Schools*). The principal exception to the list of major education reports since the war is the Robbins Report on Higher

Education, which was produced by a committee personally appointed by the Prime Minister.

3   King is using a framework of analysis taken from Weber – see Gerth, H. H. and Wright Mills, C. (1948), *From Max Weber: Essays in Sociology*, Routledge & Kegan Paul.

4   This is the general conclusion of a book by Jencks (1972), published in America, but widely reported and exerting a great deal of influence amongst academics and educationalists in this country. Jenck's disillusionment with the American liberal social reforms of the 1960s, and his consequently pessimistic interpretation of his data, found a sympathetic response in some educational circles in Britain.

5   See Karabel and Halsey (1977) for an evaluation of the contribution of conflict theorists (Weberian and Marxist) to the study of education, and in particular to the question of social change and education.

6   Bernstein has suffered too much from attempts to provide brief summaries of his work. Karabel and Halsey (1977) provide a useful introduction, but the best source is undoubtedly Bernstein's own collections of his articles and essays (1971 and 1975).

7   The failure of nursery education to attract attention on a long-term basis is an old story. Blackstone (1971) recounts the history of pre-school provision, and attempts to explain why successive governments have been so ambivalent towards it.

8   Examples are to be found in Young (1971) and Keddie (1973). The view is perhaps also implicit in the writings of Illich and others who seek to make a distinction between 'schooling' and 'education' – a distinction of dubious relevance when discussing formal systems of State education.

References

Batley, R. *et al.* (1970), *Going Comprehensive*, London, Routledge & Kegan Paul.

Bellaby, P. (1977), *The Sociology of Comprehensive Schooling*, London, Methuen.

Bernstein, B. (1971, 1975), *Class, Codes and Control*, vols 1 and 3, London, Routledge & Kegan Paul.

Bernstein, B. and Davies, B. (1969), 'Some sociological comments on Plowden', in Peters, R. S. (ed.), *Perspectives on Plowden*, London, Routledge & Kegan Paul.

Blackstone, T. (1971), *A Fair Start*, London, Allen Lane.

Buxton, R. (1970), *Local Government*, Harmondsworth, Penguin. (An extract is reprinted in Fowler (1973).)

Byrne, D. *et al.* (1975), *The Poverty of Education*, London, Martin Robertson.

Coates, K. and Silburn, R. (1970), 'Education in Poverty' in Rubinstein, D.

and Stoneman, C., *Education for Democracy*, Harmondsworth, Penguin.

Cox, C. B. and Dyson, A. E. (eds) (1969), *Black Paper One*, London, Critical Quarterly Society.

Durkheim, E. (1956), *Education and Sociology*, Chicago, Free Press.

Eggleston, J. (1973), 'Decision Making on the School Curriculum: A conflict Model' in *Sociology* (Sept., vol. 7, pp. 377–94).

Eggleston, J. (1977), *The Sociology of the School Curriculum*, London, Routledge & Kegan Paul.

Fowler, G. *et al.* (eds) (1973), *Decision Making in British Education*, London, Heinemann.

Halsey, A. H. (1972), *Educational Priority*, vol. 1., Dept. of Education and Science, London, HMSO.

Hargreaves, D. H. (1967), *Social Relations in a Secondary School*, London, Routledge & Kegan Paul.

Jencks, C. *et al.* (1972), *Inequality: A Reassessment of the Effect of Family and Schooling in America*, New York, Basic Books.

Karabel, J. and Halsey, A. H. (1977), *Power and Ideology in Education*, New York, Oxford University Press.

Keddie, N. (ed.) (1973), *Tinker, Tailor . . . the Myth of Cultural Deprivation*, Harmondsworth, Penguin.

King, R. (1970), 'The Head Teacher and his Authority' in Allen, B. (ed.), *Headship in the 1970s*, Oxford, Blackwell. (Reprinted in Fowler (1973).)

Kogan, M. (1973), 'The Function of the Central Advisory Council in Educational Change', in Fowler (1973).

Kogan, M. (1975), *Educational Policy Making: A Study of Interest Groups and Parliament*, London. Allen & Unwin.

Kogan, M. and van der Eyken, W. (1973), *County Hall*, Harmondsworth, Penguin.

Lacey, C. (1970), *Hightown Grammar*, Manchester University Press.

Lawton, D. (1977), *Education and Social Justice*, London, Sage Publications.

Little, A. and Westergaard, J. (1964), 'The Trend of Class Differentials in Educational Opportunity in England and Wales' in *British Journal of Sociology* (Dec., vol. 15, pp. 301–16).

MacLure, J. S. (1965), *Educational Documents, England and Wales*, London, Methuen.

Morrison, A. and McIntyre, D. (1971), *Schools and Socialisation*, Harmondsworth, Penguin.

Musgrave, P. W. (1968), *Society and Education in England since 1800*, London, Methuen.

Nash, R. (1973), *Classrooms Observed*, London, Routledge & Kegan Paul.

Plowden Report (1967), *Children and Their Primary Schools*, Central Advisory Council for Education (England), London, HMSO.

Robinson, P. (1976), *Education and Poverty*, London, Methuen.

Rubinstein, D. and Simon, B. (1969), *The Evolution of the Comprehensive School*, London, Routledge & Kegan Paul.

Simon, B. (1965), *Education and the Labour Movement, 1870 – 1920*, London, Lawrence & Wishart.

Simon, B. (1974), *The Politics of Educational Reform, 1920 – 1940*, London, Lawrence & Wishart.

Swift, D. F. (1968), 'Social Class and Educational Adaptation' in Butcher, H. J. and Pont, H. B., *Educational Research in Britain*, University of London Press.

Tyler, W. (1977), *The Sociology of Educational Inequality*, London, Methuen.

Young, M. F. D. (1971), *Knowledge and Control*, London, Collier-MacMillan.

6

Health

Gillian Pascall

Health in Social Policy

The scope of State involvement in health services

The National Health Service is an extreme case in social policy. Much social service provision is piecemeal; in many areas direct public provision competes with publicly supported private provision; much social policy legislation discriminates actively between different sections of the community. The National Health Service does not stand completely apart from other social policy areas – as will become clear – but it does go further than the others in its concern with equal, universal, and comprehensive provision. If anywhere in the 'welfare state' we are to find a system of provision which is not dominated by market principles and class divisions, it is to the National Health Service that we might reasonably look. Such a view, at least, appears widely accepted in social policy literature (see especially Titmuss, 1970). The NHS, then, may be seen as a key subject in studying the nature of the welfare state; it is the prime example of a service which is provided almost wholly by government agencies, financed by taxation rather than individual payment, available to everyone in need without other qualification, and provided with a generosity which makes alternative private provision generally unattractive.

The 1946 NHS Act and the objectives of health policy

The legislation on which the present National Health Service is based was passed in 1946, and the Act came into force in 1948. There has, subsequently, been some legislative change, but for such a major work it has been small. The legal framework for the existing health service, then, was firmly established in the post-war period. The political setting of that time and the principles that emerged from the debate about a new health service are thus of continuing importance today.

The 1946 Act was produced by a Labour government, and has, indeed, been described as their 'only piece of pure socialism' (Eckstein, 1959). On the other hand during the war there had been wide support for some kind of new health service. Wartime emergency services had revealed the poverty of existing services (Titmuss, 1950), and a return to pre-war conditions was rejected on all sides. In planning post-war social security provision, Beveridge – a Liberal working for a coalition government – made the important and radical assumption that there would be 'comprehensive health and rehabilitation services' (Beveridge, 1942). The coalition government, and thus the main political parties, accepted this assumption, and both they and the medical profession began planning a state service. There is a question, then, about how far the NHS was truly a product of the subsequent Labour government, and how much it was based on socialist principles.

Perhaps the best way of answering this is to look at the Act itself, but it is worth making some comments about the political setting first. There was, it is true, fairly broad agreement about the general issue of a more comprehensive health service; but this consensus covered quite varied conceptions of the extent of State involvement and the method of financing, organizing and distributing services. Negotiations and debate over the 1946 legislation turned into a bitter political wrangle, which concerned more than mere detail. Furthermore, the positions adopted in the early planning stages under the coalition government are not necessarily direct pointers to what might have happened afterwards under a different government. Proposals for a National Health Service met with great hostility (Willcocks, 1967), and required determination and ingenuity for their fruition. The commitment, then, was made by Bevan and a Labour government, and the legislation owes much to its political origins.

Key features of the legislation were its universal coverage, its almost total reliance on taxation for finance, and its nationalization of the major physical facilities for medical care, the hospitals. In these respects it made striking innovations, and in these respects it is still different from health services in many other industrialized countries.

Providing universal coverage – one service for everyone – meant on the one hand including the richest by discouraging private practice, and on the other including the poorest by eliminating charges and contributions. Private practice was not banned, but its users were not to be exempt from the taxes which paid for the NHS; there would therefore be little competition from a large and wealthy private sector. There were to be no charges at the time of use, and no insurance requirement; therefore the poorest would not be excluded by inability to pay or by inadequate contribution records. Finally, one service for all meant that there would be no means tests to establish eligibility; need was to be the only criterion for using services. This was strikingly new. The government had long been involved in providing health services, but not in this way. General practitioner services, for example, had been organized since 1911 under National Health Insurance, but coverage was limited to insured workers, thus excluding most women and children, and anyone without an adequate insurance record. Universalism, then, was new, and – as has already been remarked – it was more thorough-going than in the other social service legislation of the period.

Universalism was backed – and necessarily backed – by funding from general taxation through central government. This eliminated charges and the need for records of contributions. It was also a first condition for eliminating regional variations in the standard of service. As Bevan argued in the House of Commons:

> 'Furthermore – and this is an argument of the utmost importance – if it be our contract with the British people, if it be our intention that we should universalize the best, that we shall promise every citizen in this country the same standard of service, how can that be articulated through a rate-borne institution which means that the poor authority will not be able to carry out the same thing at all?'

Funding through general taxation meant, in theory at least, that people would pay according to their ability. The combination of services according to need and payment according to ability would not be universally recognized as a total recipe for 'pure socialism', but it fits well the philosophy of the Fabian socialists whose ideas of social reform permeated the British Labour movement. The question of how far in fact services are provided according to need will be one of the themes of the second part of this chapter. It may be remarked here, though, that Britain's taxation system has not in practice levied only according to ability to pay (Field *et al*., 1977).

The third key and novel feature was the nationalization of the hospitals. This meant the taking over, administering and financing of the main physical assets of the previous system, and transforming them into a national service whose resources could be centrally planned. This was a big step, in view of the previous chaotic system and the prestige of its independent hospitals; it was also a step not contemplated in coalition plans. It, too, was a condition of a truly universal service, as it provided a basis for bringing the standards of the poorer areas up to those of richer ones.

The principles of universal provision, funding through taxation and national ownership of the main physical assets were bold, clear and new. They remain important and little changed as the basis of today's service. The machinery for implementing these principles, however, was quite another matter. The administrative structure owed a lot to the past and was extremely complicated. It was much criticized, and eventually modified in 1974. There were other, more enduring debts to history in the character of the services offered and of the personnel employed, for the NHS did not challenge these. It took over the hospitals, general practices and clinics, and the specialists, general practitioners and medical officers of health; with them it took over, virtually unaltered for the time being, the whole structure of medical care facilities.

The legislation and the principles, however, are by no means the end of the argument. Legislation provides only a framework. Its operation in practice may be very different from the way it appears on paper. Its practice will certainly be moulded and changed by social, economic and political pressures. Development and change may require little legislative action – and there has been very little relating to the health service – but may nevertheless affect crucially the way even the most basic principles operate in practice. Thus part two of this chapter attempts to survey developments in the way the NHS actually works and tries, in particular, to show how far the service has met the objective of universality – the provision of services according to need.

A further question, though, concerns the effect of the health services provided under the NHS upon health. Health services are not just a means to an end, but health is clearly one of their ends. If one of the basic objectives of the NHS is to detach the supply of health services from market forces, then it must be assumed that its second basic objective is to make the same break between health itself and economic conditions. The third section of this chapter therefore looks at the view of health that seems to be reflected in the NHS, at the continuing link between economic status and state of health, and at the relevance of the NHS strategy for breaking that link.

The Health Care System

Introduction

In this section it is hoped to give a descriptive account of the health services as they exist today and to highlight some of the important trends since 1948. In the light of the objectives analysed above, particular attention will be given to the way in which the NHS distributes its resources. One of the most striking features to emerge from any consideration of health statistics in the period since 1948 is the massive increase in the real resources available to the NHS. No legislation has deemed that we shall have more doctors, more nurses, more technicians of many kinds, more patients treated, but more of all these we have, and in dramatic numbers (Cochrane, 1972). There has, then, despite continued claims of shortage, been enormous potential for developing services, equalizing standards, and changing the pattern of services available to people. A main theme of this section will concern how that potential has been used and not used. The next part is mainly descriptive, but the trends described in it are of key importance in understanding the tenacity of the problems of distribution recounted in the following two parts. Finally, the political structure, through which flow the decisions about developments and resources, is described.

Hospitals, general practitioner and preventive services

As has already been noted, the NHS adopted the technical characteristics of services that previously existed under different auspices. There were, to simplify slightly, specialist services based on hospitals, general medical and related services based on independent practices, and preventive services based on clinics. In the hierarchy of prestige and of spending these almost certainly fell in descending order before the NHS and they continued to do so under it. The two latter have become more integrated: GPs have formed group practices and preventive services have become attached to these, and furthermore, health centres housing both facilities have spread in recent years. The process has not been without its difficulties (HMSO, 1976/7), but it does now make reasonable sense to consider them together as domiciliary services.

The majority of people who become sick do not in fact spend much time in hospital. They receive care from the domiciliary services – from general practitioners, home nurses and health visitors; they are looked after mainly by relatives, but also by the social services; they may visit hospital as out-patients. An acute phase of an illness may require a short spell in hospital, as an in-patient, but even for seriously ill people this will probably be only a small – though intensive – part of the care they receive. They will most likely leave hospital still requiring care, and go back to the domiciliary services. The length of time people spend as in-patients has in fact been gradually declining: in 1976 it was, on average, 21·6 days, compared with 49·3 days in 1949. These figures include very long stay patients, and most people's stay will be shorter than these average figures (HMSO, 1977a, Table 4.9).

This does not, incidentally, mean that hospitals do less work. Instead they treat more patients more intensively. But more important for the moment is the fact that the task of the domiciliary services is a major part of the health care task. It is a task of maintenance of many sick, disabled – especially elderly – people who do not require constant in-patient care; it is a task of before- and after-care for those going into hospital; a task of sifting and diagnosing to find those whose symptoms need more sophisticated attention; and a task of prevention – preventing illness from arising at all, and preventing symptoms from becoming more disabling than they need be. The size of this task is indicated by General Household Survey findings about the number of chronic sick in the community. Only people living at home were interviewed, and they were asked whether they had any illness which limited their activities compared with people of their own age: 134 per thousand men and 150 per thousand women reported limiting illness of long standing (HMSO, 1977b, Table 5.8).

On the other hand the hospitals – at first glance – appear to be the centre of the health care system. It is in hospitals that medical students are mainly taught – very important this for the future direction of medical interest – and it is from hospitals that we hear of exciting new developments in curing patients. Here, it appears, are the situations of life and death, glamorous enough to be turned into television programmes. Perhaps rather mundanely, in view of all this, it is here that the money is spent.

At the beginning of the NHS, domiciliary services had lower status and resources than hospitals, but they nevertheless commanded a fairly large share of the budget and of the people needed to run a health service. There were more general practitioners than hospital doctors, though they worked often in poor and isolated circumstances; the army of 'medical auxiliaries' now mainly based on hospitals had not yet emerged; the midwifery service was home-rather than hospital-based. Without there having been any explicit major rethinking on the part of governments, the picture is now markedly different. It is not that the absolute standard of domiciliary services has declined, rather that these services have not been allocated the growth in resources that others have enjoyed. The emphasis has thus been shifted subtly, but inexorably away from them. The proportion of doctors in each service is a good indicator, as other workers tend to depend on them. In 1976 there were 23,377 general practitioners in England and Wales – just a few more than in 1948 – but there were the equivalent of 29,264 whole-time medical staff in hospitals, compared with 11,735 in 1949 (HMSO, 1969, Table 3.1; HMSO, 1977a, Table 3.1). Financial statistics, naturally enough, show the same picture, with the share taken by all domiciliary services showing a steady decline: by 1975/6 general medical services were taking only 6·2 per cent of the resources devoted to all health services (HMSO, 1977a, recalculated from Table 2.4).

At the heart of this change has been the ever-increasing sophistication of the hospital medical enterprise: elaborate machinery has become central to hospital activity; the drug industry supplies more and more elaborate preparations; hospitals compete with one another to do more complicated operations, requiring special equipment and extra personnel. The teaching hospital, and especially the new teaching hospital, epitomizes these developments. The scale of an enterprise such as the new medical school in Nottingham dwarfs all other health facilities in the district and its vast and elaborate new buildings are a monument to medical care as viewed in the 1970s.

Some preliminary conclusions may be drawn together concerning these trends. First, the medical machine has an insatiable appetite for resources. It has grown many fold and yet there are always 'shortages'. The situation is not a once and for all crisis, but a continuing one – more resources do not in fact solve the problem.

Second, the call for more resources in the hospital sector is a very effective one: it is claimed that lives are at imminent risk and may be saved, and the claim is sometimes justified. The power of the claim is demonstrated by the historical trend, by the success with which hospitals have virtually monopolized new health resources over the last three decades. Governments have appeared, where they have spoken on the subject, to want to contain the growth of the hospital sector, and especially to develop 'community care' as an alternative. Recent government statements on the subject are *The Consultative Document on Priorities* in the National Health Service, and its successor, *The Way Forward* (DHSS, 1976a, 1977). They expound the trends and problems with admirable clarity. The practical results of resulting policies are simply not measurable – perhaps without them the trends would have been even more marked – but there is certainly no sign of governments succeeding in turning an extremely powerful tide.

Third, this trend has built-in mechanisms for perpetuating itself, and of these the medical school is paramount. Hospitals are the training grounds for all kinds of health workers and the teaching hospitals are the elite of these, the 'centres of excellence' in the practice of the most sophisticated medicine, where the emphasis is on the short-term care of people with acute episodes of illness. It is these hospitals which define for new health personnel what is the medical task and how it should be carried out. Their image is heavily imprinted on doctors and nurses who will have to do quite different kinds of work in quite different surroundings (McKeown, 1976a).

Fourth, it may be remarked that the very success of hospital technology is now being widely questioned. National statistics do not suggest that it is achieving improvements in health or life expectancy commensurate with the resources devoted to it (Cochrane, 1972; Powles, 1973). Some writers suggest that it has actual and potent dangers (Illich, 1975). The view taken here is that hospital technology is often useful – but is by no means an unmitigated triumph – and that its most significant failure is its highly partial view of the task of health care. There will be more discussion below of the incidence and pattern of health in the community. It is enough to suggest here that the trends of hospital medicine and the patterns of health and disease too often appear to have little to do with one another.

Finally, it seems highly likely that the way in which hospitals can attract resources for the high-technology end of medical care has implications for the rest of the health care world. It should already be clear that the community services have not joined very fully in the general economic growth of the last three decades; the main sufferers have been the chronic sick, for whom services at home and in hospital are often of poor quality. This, and the problem of resources in poorly served regions, will be looked at next in this section.

The chronic sector

Distinctions between chronic and acute illness and between the long- and short-term sick are not in fact clear-cut ones. However blurred the line, though, it is worth distinguishing between these categories, because the distinction helps us to understand better what the health services really do, and because, at least at the extremes, the problems and the services for the two groups are very different. A very large part of the work of the health services in general is concerned with people who have conditions which will never go away, though they may be relieved (rheumatism, bronchitis, incontinence) and a very large part of the hospital sector is devoted to caring for the very long term sick, especially the elderly and mentally sick. The emphasis in many cases is on care and relief more than it is on complete cure. This section concerns itself particularly with the hospital care of the chronically ill, since it is in hospitals that the deprivation of the chronic sick is most apparent.

The figures below summarize the shape of the hospital service: the first is a description of patient flow, of how many patients used the various services in a given year; the second shows the pattern of hospital places on an average day.

The contrast between the two diagrams is marked. Diagram 1 shows that the great majority of patients who use the hospital service as in-patients go into surgical, medical or obstetric wards. However, they stay there for very short periods, often only a matter of days. Patients in mental or geriatric wards or units for the younger disabled are likely to stay very much longer. The result shows in Diagram 2. Almost two-thirds of the beds in use at any one time are in these latter categories. Not all the patients here will be very long stay, but many will be. If the task of the hospital service is seen in the light of Diagram 2, it will be realized how much of its work concerns the long-term sick. Furthermore, many of these patients are wholly dependent on their hospitals for their way of life; hospital conditions may be of overwhelming significance for them.

The small interest shown by clinical medicine in the long-term sick has a long history. Abel-Smith (1964) describes how in the nineteenth century the voluntary hospitals founded as a free service to the poor became the centres of medical interest and prestige. For the sake of medical interest and medical training they developed a practice of preventing beds becoming 'blocked' by people who would be ill for a long time with little chance of cure. Thus they excluded the very people for whom they had been founded, and the 'real work' of caring for the sick, and especially the sick poor, was carried out in general workhouses, with scant medical help. The story has a modern parallel in the descendants of these same voluntary hospitals, now often the elite teaching hospitals. These, too, concentrate on short-term 'interesting', cases and longer-term ones find themselves in quite different institutions where conditions are much less attractive.

Conditions in the worst of these long-stay hospitals have been highlighted in recent years by a series of reports. The most graphic, and famous, of these is Barbara Robb's *Sans Everything* (1967). But a series of government enquiries followed, and confirmed the picture in more sober language. Two features stand out – the very poor level of resources, especially of higher grade staff, and the low interest and morale of some workers. Even the resources available have been shown to be most unevenly used: at one hospital investigated there were five consultants (equivalent to three full-time

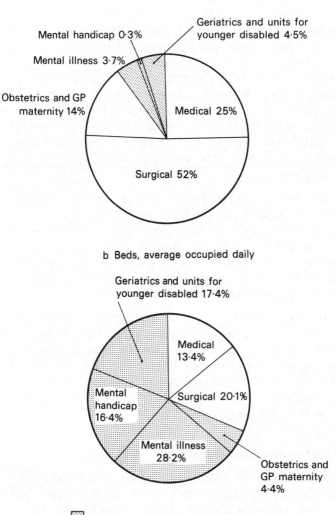

a Discharges and deaths

b Beds, average occupied daily

 Specialities containing most long-stay patients

Figure 1   Hospital: number of beds and patient flow by broad speciality, England 1976
(a) Discharges and deaths
(b) Beds, average occupied daily
Source: Health and Personal Social Service Statistics for England,
1977, Table 4.6

consultants) for 2,000 patients. This is small enough, but only one of these was left with responsibility for the great majority of patients (86 per cent) who were long-stay – the others worked in special units (HMSO, 1972). The situation exemplifies both features of the problem – poor staffing and low interest in the great bulk of long-stay patients.

In response to these problems the government established a Hospital Advisory Service to keep a watch on the chronic hospitals, and some money was set aside to improve them. But the money was little and the succession of scandals and inquiries has not dried up. In 1974 a committee of inquiry into South Ockenden Hospital, a mental handicap institution, commented (HMSO, 1974, p. 3) on the sorry history:

> Declarations of policy and recommendations to improve the subnormality services have gone out from the Department of Health during these years. They are admirable documents with admirable aims and well thought out recommendations as to how they should be put into practice. But the gulf between the admirable goal and the money provided has seemed to the staff, and others, to be very wide.

The committee also remarked that the report on the hospital by the hospital advisory service had been very critical but was virtually ignored – underlining the purely advisory capacity of this service. The long-stay hospitals and their patients are still the 'under-privileged part of the hospital service' described by the advisory service (HMSO, 1971, p. 30) and they show no signs of imminent escape from their deprivation.

The regional distribution of services

It was one of the more telling criticisms of health services before the NHS that they were very badly distributed. London and the south coast were well enough served, but other regions, especially northern ones, lacked decent standards of service. Bevan's hope of 'universalizing the best' has already been quoted: the NHS was established in the clear hope and intention of transforming the very unequal geographical spread of services. To aid this policy, finance was to be through central government taxation – avoiding the inequalities of local rates – the hospital system was to be regionalized, and there was to be a system of encouraging GPs to disperse themselves more equally. Only if resources could thus be geographically matched to the population could the principle of universalism be fully implemented. As we have seen earlier, real resources in the NHS have multiplied – an increase quite enough to have lifted the worst to the standard of the best, without lowering standards in the latter. This section therefore examines what has happened to the regional distribution of services as a key element in describing a 'universal' service in practice.

As a preliminary it is well to look briefly at the distribution of sickness. Services can only be equally available to the sick if they are matched to the rates of illness in different areas. To deal with this issue fully raises complex problems, but one can report a simplified picture. All sources of information agree in their broad pattern, if not in every detail. Northern regions and Wales have worse than average health, midland regions about average, and southern regions better than average (DHSS, 1976b, pp. 18–19). The differences are considerable: standardized mortality ratios (see below for an explanation of these) in 1972 were 10 per cent above average in the northern region, while for the outer south east they were 11 per cent below.

For health services to be matched, even very broadly, to need, the NHS would have had to redistribute health services very markedly since 1948. In fact, it has maintained generally the same regional pattern of services that existed before. Thus northern regions not only lack the extra resources to match their extra ill health, they do not even reach the level of resources spent in the south. This pattern is so marked that one writer has formulated an 'inverse care law', that 'The availability of good medical care tends to vary inversely with the need for it in the population served' (Tudor Hart, 1971). It is a pattern repeated in the distribution of teaching hospitals (which are concentrated in London), and the distribution of general practitioners (who prefer and are permitted to work in middle-class areas) and domiciliary services (Butler, 1973). In 1975 the government established a 'Resources Allocation Working Party' to consider the distribution of government funds 'with a view to establishing a method of securing, as soon as practicable, a pattern of distribution responsive objectively, equitably and efficiently to relative need' (DHSS, 1976b, p. 5). The task of implementing proposals, however, is a major one, and is meeting powerful opposition. The forces which have for so long maintained unequal provision, despite a universal service, are clearly powerful.

In order to link this section more closely with concerns elsewhere in this chapter it is important to underline the social character of this apparently geographical problem. The NHS, it has been suggested, sought to detach the provision of health services from market principles, from the principle of ability to pay. One arm of this policy was open access to services without financial barriers, but the other arm was their relocation to places where services had been impoverished. Before the NHS, the places impoverished in health terms were likely to be the places which were socially and economically deprived – where people had money to pay, the services were likely to be better. To the extent that the NHS has not altered the pattern, then, the geographical spread of services has a social base. The greatest amount of sickness and the worst services are in regions with the highest proportion of manual workers.

Political control — administrative structure and professional influence

Some main features of the health services provided to the community have now been outlined. The final part of this review of the NHS in practice concerns its internal political structure, questions of who controls its resources, who determines the directions in which it moves. This discussion can go only part of the way to explaining developments in the NHS, because of the importance of the wider social, political and economic context within which any welfare service operates. But to show the internal political structure is to show at least one part of the mechanism through which health services in Britain are related to the wider social world.

The administrative structure of the NHS is one part that has undergone substantial change since the 1946 Act, change embodied in legislation of 1973. As has already been noted, the 1946 Act adopted three administrative structures: separate control for hospitals, general practitioner and related domiciliary services, and local authority preventive services. Of these, the two last were adopted from much earlier services. This tripartite structure was much criticized for its problems of co-ordination, and especially of proper assessment of priorities as between one kind of care and another.

General agreement about these difficulties finally resulted in legislation for a reorganized service with a single administrative structure. The reformed structure had perhaps three key features: first the transfer of all services to the care of independent authorities, outside the structure of local and central government machinery; second the hierarchical placing of these authorities in a line of management from the Department of Health and Social Security; and third the probably increased role in these authorities allowed to the doctors, as the most powerful professional group in the service.

On the first point, the legislation rejected the use of existing elected local authorities in favour of three specially appointed tiers of management – Regional Health Authorities, Area Health Authorities and districts. Local authorities had been given only a small part of the NHS in 1946, partly because of professional objections, but also partly because of their unwieldy structure. The year 1974 presented a new situation, as local authorities too were due for reorganization, but again their claims were rejected. Local participation was limited to some local authority appointments to area health authorities, and the newly constituted community health councils (see below).

The three management tiers were designed to provide a strict line of authority and accountability from the DHSS to the lowest level. Community participation in decisions was explicitly precluded by this arrangement, in favour of criticism from the outside by Community Health Councils. These councils operate at the district level and consist of representatives from local interested organizations. Their main function is to monitor services, and consider management proposals from the consumer's point of view. Their powers are very restricted and they are supposed to function by publicity and influence. The extent of this influence is still an open question.

Professional influence, especially doctor influence, has always been strong in the NHS. Doctors have influenced the development of the services through their professional organizations (Eckstein, 1960; Willcocks, 1967) to such an extent that they have provided a model of the successful pressure group in academic studies: doctors take decisions about patients and thus, direct resources at the lowest level – a potent influence for consultants in view of the quantity of resources at their command; further, they develop the technology and pass it on by teaching – a powerful influence over the direction of new medical and health service effort; and finally doctors have always had strong positions on the official governing bodies of the

NHS. The new structure gave doctors their strongest voice at the district level, districts being managed by professional teams in which the medical voice dominates. These professional teams are new in the reorganized service, and arguably have entrenched medical influence more strongly than ever before.

Thus key features of the internal political structure of the NHS are its relative independence of central and local democratic authorities and the influence of its medical personnel. This combination of features largely excludes local community involvement. The power of the professional voice has clear connections with the trends described earlier in this section.

Conclusion

It may be as well at this point to draw together the strands of this chapter so far. As a distribution system based on welfare rather than market principles, the NHS has had obvious success in practice. Its success in catering for the whole population is partly indicated by the small size of the private sector. Though the principle of a wholly free service has been breached by charges for prescriptions, glasses and dental treatment, most costs are borne through taxes, and everyone has free access to primary care and expensive hospital treatment where needed. Thus the financial barriers to care are minimal. The NHS is without any of the discriminatory rules which distinguish the eligible from the non-eligible, the claimant from the non-claimant in other social service areas. However, freedom from discriminatory rules is not all. There may be no law or rule preventing, say, the elderly confused patient in Bury from receiving optimum health care, but if the facilities do not exist locally, he will probably fail to receive it. To study the NHS principles in practice, therefore, we have looked at the provision and distribution of services, and have highlighted some of the failures, especially with respect to the chronic sick and the poorer regions.

These failures may be seen to have strong links with the recent developments in medical technology outlined. At the simplest level, resources used in one area are not available to meet problems in other areas. But medical technology also has a major role in defining the task of health services and moulding the people who work in them. It thus has a very direct influence on the determination of NHS priorities, as well as the strong political voice described.

Health and the National Health Service

Introduction

The previous section has focused on the way the National Health Service is used to meet people's needs for health services and on some of the ways in which it has failed to meet those needs. Meeting needs for health services, and producing health, however, are not the same thing; people who are sick in our culture are recognized to require health services, even when those services cannot make them well again. Services, in other words, provide quite other things than health; health may be one of the products, but it may well not be.

However, clearly the originators of the NHS hoped to provide both health and health services; they hoped that health could be produced in at least some of those who used the service, and they believed that the strategy of provision would result in a healthier population. Bevan's much-quoted faith in the decreasing cost of the NHS is some evidence of this. In studying the impact of the NHS, then, it is important to look more directly at the nature of health than we have done so far. The social pattern of health in Britain can then be examined, both as the problem which the NHS is supposed to be tackling and as evidence of the success or otherwise of NHS strategy so far.

Health and the environment

Modern medicine focuses on health and illness as conditions intrinsic to individuals. It has been said that it treats bodies as if they were machines: it is assumed that there is no problem until they go wrong; when they do go wrong medical diagnosis and research look for clues within the body mechanism, and treatment is the manipulation of the body by surgery and drugs (McKeown, 1976a).

This contrasts with a view of bodies as organisms interacting with their environment, as organisms which can adapt according to circumstances, and which operate more or less well partly according to the conditions which they have to tolerate (Dubos, 1968). In this view individual variations are recognized, but are only partial as explanations of why some people are sick and others healthy; the treatment of sick individuals, again, is seen to be highly partial as a response to the problem of illness in the community.

The contrast between these two views is a caricature. Medicine does recognize environmental assaults on human beings, and environmentalists occasionally remember that sick people want help with their bodies when they go wrong, and sometimes find it in medical knowledge. However exaggerated these contrasting views may appear to be they do have a profound impact on the way people think about improving health, and on the strategies adopted to that end. It is the first model which underpins the whole western medical enterprise, which guides its research and technology, and which encourages massive spending on sophisticated machines and buildings.

It is also largely this model which informs the strategy of the NHS in meeting Britain's health problem. We have already seen the extent to which the NHS subscribes to medical technology, but even in its preventive activities the view of health projected through the NHS is an individualistic one. Preventive health is seen as health education to encourage people to live healthier lives, as personal supervision (maternity and child welfare) and to a small extent as industrial medical services (Navarro, 1976). In neither its preventative nor its curative aspects, then, does the environmental model of health and disease play much part; the NHS concerns itself very much with bodies as machines rather than with people in their social and economic environment.

There is, however, a great deal of evidence which indicates the value of viewing health within the social and economic environment. McKeown has written extensively, for example, about the improvement in health over the last 250 years in Britain, and has argued convincingly that almost the whole of a very dramatic improvement can be attributed to environmental changes, in particular food supplies, and almost none to medical treatment (McKeown, 1976b). Other researchers have looked at the incidence of particular diseases. Doll, for instance, studied the incidence of various cancers and demonstrated dramatic variations in their geographical scatter which can only be explained by social, cultural and economic factors; in principle, he concluded, all cancers are preventable (Doll, 1967 p. 91). The contrast in health and life expectancy between the developed and the under-developed world provides further evidence of the value of the environmental approach: the same diseases in different environments – measles, for example – produce widely different effects; other diseases which scourge poorer countries are easily eliminated from areas with better living conditions. Finally, such social patterning in the incidence of disease is easily traceable – as will be shown below – even in a comparatively homogeneous, industrialized country such as Britain.

To see health and disease as very largely rooted in social, cultural and economic factors is not to deny that the medical approach sometimes has its uses. Such a view, though, does call in question our faith in medical, individualistic solutions to essentially social problems, and it does lead towards an explanation of some of the more basic failures of the strategy for health adopted by the NHS.

The social pattern of health in Britain

As has already been suggested, the fact that one can trace social patterns in the incidence of health and disease is itself powerful evidence of the value of a 'social' approach to the subject. But to look at the social pattern of health in Britain is also a basis for examining the success or otherwise of the NHS in providing health for everyone in the population, rather than just health services, and it is a starting point for considering the value of different strategies in tackling the health problem in Britain.

It would be possible to study health in relation to a range of 'social' variables – income, family composition, race and so on. Indeed such studies do yield interesting and valuable results. However, this section takes as its theme the relationship of health and social class, using occupational categories to stand for the latter. The reasons for this are several: the practical ones of the availability of information and the fact that the information yields very striking social patterns; general theoretical ones of the significance of social class as a category in social analysis; and historical reasons, concerning social class and health in particular. The latter point may be developed in two ways: first, the links between sickness and poverty, and sickness and occupation, have been recognized as extremely important in Britain since at least the beginning of the nineteenth century; second, the NHS, in its policy of universal provision may be presumed to be fundamentally concerned with the advantage and disadvantage in health and health services that is reflected in social class statistics.

The following information is of two kinds: mortality statistics from the Registrar General and morbidity statistics from the *General Household Survey*. Neither of these is in itself an ideal measure of what we want to look at (and their disadvantages will be mentioned), but in combination they are more impressive. Their advantages and disadvantages complement one another, and their conclusions are highly consistent. If we were to add data from other sources on, for example, absence from work through sickness, or infant mortality, the pattern would be repeated, and it amounts to powerful evidence for the continued importance of social class in the pattern of health and sickness in Britain (Townsend, 1974).

Clearly, death rates are not an ideal indicator of health and sickness patterns, since not all illnesses lead to death – many quite disabling ones such as rheumatism do not kill. On the other hand, it seems unlikely that one group in the population have healthy short lives while another group have unhealthy long ones. And the figures below have an advantage over most others in the certainty of death in contrast to the social and cultural definitions of illness. The figures are standardized mortality ratios: these are death rates, standardized for age, to eliminate the effect of different age structures in different social classes, and they are based on an 'expected' or average value of 100 – i.e. if all social classes had the same rate, each value would be 100.

Table 4   Standardized mortality ratios for adult males, by social class, 1970–2 England and Wales

Social class	I	II	III N	III M	IV	V	All men
SMR	77	81	99	106	114	137	100

Source: Occupational Mortality 1970–2, HMSO, 1978

It will be seen from Table 4 that Social Class I had a mortality ratio only 77 per cent of the average, while Social Class V had one 37 per cent above the average; the gradient shows a steadily worsening picture with decreasing social class.

The *General Household Survey* investigates sickness and disability in the home population, and thus shows us more directly what we are looking for than do the mortality statistics; on the other hand it relies on self-assessment of illness and thus contains a strong subjective and cultural element. However, the results parallel one another remarkably. The amount of limiting long-standing illness suffered by the highest socio-economic group is less than half that suffered by the lowest.

Table 5 Chronic sickness: persons reporting limiting long-standing illness by sex and socio-economic group: rates per 1000 GB 1974

Socio-economic group	Males	Females
Professional	82	93
Employers and managers	113	115
Intermediate and junior non-manual	147	143
Skilled manual (including foremen and supervisors) and own account non-professional	132	124
Semi-skilled manual and personal service	147	198
Unskilled manual	225	229
Rate for all persons in each sex	134	150

Source: General Household Survey 1974 Table 5.8 (modified)

Again the gradient (with one exception) shows a steadily worsening picture as one descends the column through the socio-economic groups.

Data from various sources, then, combine to show how very highly patterned is the incidence of sickness and death in the community, and in particular, how strongly advantage and disadvantage in health are linked with advantage and disadvantage in the social and economic system at large. Two conclusions may be drawn for present purposes: first, that the strategy of universal provision of medical services has not succeeded in producing a more equal standard of health throughout the community; and second, that it is rather unlikely to do so. It has already been suggested that despite apparent policy the services have not in fact been provided very equally; but even if they were, the evidence seems to point to a social and economic foundation for health and thus a rather poor prospect for the kind of medical services provided for individual needs under the NHS.

Conclusion

At first sight the last section may appear to overwhelm the concerns of its predecessors. If health and health services seem to have less to do with one another than often thought, why should we concern ourselves with the distribution of health services and the direction of health policy?

There are, perhaps, three main reasons: first, some medical services do give health and prolong life; second, health services provide things other than health and long life – they provide care as well as, indeed much more than, cure, and they help sustain people at higher levels of activity than they might otherwise enjoy; third, though the products of health services may be less dramatic than they seem, their financing and distribution still involve questions of justice. Legislation seems to promise health services in the community according to need rather than according to social class or other criterion, and it is a concern of social policy study to measure the reality against the objectives.

The reformers who struggled to provide a health service that would reach all the people were not misguided in their objectives; even if health services have not transformed the health of the mass of the population, their existence, use and distribution are important issues. The evidence presented in this chapter points to some of the questions that may be asked about that use and distribution; even the negative conclusions of part three can liberate us from preconceived ideas about the functions that health services perform and the value of their various aspects.

Finally, however, it is worth looking more closely at the NHS's concern with medical services rather than with health. It was remarked at the beginning of this chapter that State involvement in health care had produced a system of distribution more detached from market criteria than in other social services. On the other hand, health itself is still fundamentally related to people's economic position. Because it does not confront the latter fact, the NHS may now seem a less radical organization than it did at first. The provision of individualized medical services – however equally – may actually serve to obscure the social and economic roots of health, and may thereby help to justify and maintain the social and economic conditions which produce sickness.

References

Abel-Smith, B. (1964), *The Hospitals 1800–1948*, Heinemann.

Beveridge, W. (1942), *Report on Social Insurance and Allied Services*, Cmd 6404.

Butler, J. R. (1973), *Family Doctors and Public Policy*, Routledge & Kegan Paul.

Cochrane, A. L. (1972), *Effectiveness and Efficiency: Random Reflections on Health Services*, NPHT.

DHSS (1976a), *Priorities for Health and Personal Social Services in England*.

DHSS (1976b), *Sharing Resources for Health in England*, Resources Allocation Working Party.

DHSS (1977), *The Way Forward: Priorities in Health and Social Services*.

Doll, R. (1967), *Prevention of Cancer: Pointers from Epidemiology*, NPHT.

Dubos, R. (1968), *Man, Medicine and Environment*, Pall Mall Press.

Eckstein, H. H. (1959), *The English Health Service*, Oxford University Press.

Eckstein, H. H. (1960), *Pressure Group Politics*, Allen & Unwin.

Field, F., Meacher, M. and Pond, C. (1977), *To Him Who Hath. A Study of Poverty and Taxation*, Penguin.

HMSO (1969), *Digest of Health Statistics*.

HMSO (1971), *Hospital Advisory Service, Annual Report for 1969/70*.

HMSO (1972), *Report of the Committee of Inquiry into Whittingham Hospital*, Cmnd 4861.

HMSO (1974), *Report of the Committee of Inquiry into South Ockenden Hospital*.

HMSO (1976/7), *Fit for the Future*, Report of the Committee on Child Health Services, Cmnd 6684.

HMSO (1977a), *Health and Personal Social Service Statistics for England*.

HMSO (1977b), *General Household Survey 1974*.

Illich, I. (1975), *Medical Nemesis*, Calder & Boyars.

McKeown, T. (1976a), *The Role of Medicine: Dream, Mirage or Nemesis?*, NPHT.

McKeown, T. (1976b), *The Modern Rise in Population*, Arnold.

Navarro, V. (1976), *Medicine under Capitalism*, Croom Helm.

Powles, J. (1973), On the limitations of modern medicine, *Science, Medicine and Man*, vol. I, pp 1–30.

Robb, B. (1967), *Aid for the Elderly in Government Institutions. Sans Everything: a Case to Answer*, Nelson.

Titmuss, R. (1950), *Problems of Social Policy*, HMSO, and Longmans.

Titmuss, R. (1970), *The Gift Relationship: from Human Blood to Social Policy*, Allen & Unwin.

Townsend, P. (1974), 'Inequality and the health service', *Lancet*, vol. 1, pp. 1179–90.

Tudor Hart, J. (1971), 'The inverse care law', *Lancet*, vol. 1, pp. 405–12.

Willcocks, A. J. (1967), *The Creation of the National Health Service*, Routledge & Kegan Paul.

7

'Social Security'

Stewart MacPherson

Social security is concerned with financial support – it attempts to deal with problems of financial hardship and income maintenance. If our fundamental concern is with inequality, then social security is concerned with inequality of income. As a field of study its range must be wide, embracing the distribution of income, the taxation system, private insurance provision and the system of income transfers organized by the State. It is this last area which concerns us primarily here; the nature and effectiveness of this part of the State's involvement in social welfare.

In any society, the nature and scope of social welfare depends upon the state of development of that society as well as on the socio-cultural framework, historical origin of services, perception of needs and priority given to social welfare services. As with social welfare in general, social security must be seen in context.

In traditional societies small, scattered, local communities are basically self-sufficient and self-reliant; community solidarity and mutual aid are a feature of communities of people marked by a relatively high degree of equality and cohesiveness. Subsistence agricultural production predominates, ensuring, in the absence of natural disaster, a basic minimum level of living. There is equality and a network of reciprocal obligations at a low level of resources. Solidarity and service from people to people is the outcome of the low level of development of production and productivity; faced with common problems, people support each other. With the breakdown of traditional society, economic, social and political inequalities emerge and reinforce each other; poverty develops together with the process of concentration of wealth and political and economic power. The generation of poverty is inherent in the growth of feudal society and later in the development of industrial society. Social values and mechanisms develop to serve the needs of society. Thus we find the belief that poverty is inevitable, that resignation to the will of God is a virtue and that it is the duty of the rich to have compassion and to help the poor when poverty becomes manifest in ways which seriously threaten family and community life. Welfare is entrusted to the Church and organizations inspired by it. As the economic system increasingly emphasizes individual freedom and initiative the privatization of social welfare grows as ideas of individual responsibility are espoused. Thus social welfare is increasingly perceived, not as the responsibility of the organized community as a whole, but as the task of private groups of citizens.

The development of the monetary economy in capitalism modernizes the nature of dependence. The patron/client relationships required by feudal social and economic dominance are replaced by the impersonal mechanistic relationships of industrial capitalism.

With the aggravation of poverty and the further decline of the possibilities of mutual support in an increasingly privatized money economy, the State gradually takes over the social welfare functions of private groups and agencies. The functional necessity of social welfare is to alleviate to some degree the effects of the economic system.

Thus the actual function of social welfare is closely related to changes in the objective conditions which prevail in the pattern of production, distribution and consumption of goods and services in the society. Both poverty and wealth are the results of social arrangements which in turn are an outcome of an historical process of formation of social and institutional relations which have benefited a minority. The perception of poverty as resulting from individual characteristics of individual people or groups of people, namely the poor, represents the dominant values, and corresponds to dominant class interests.

A crucial point is that dominant values have been pervasively internalized by the subordinate classes. Thus poverty is attributed to the poor themselves and not to the social arrangements of which they are a part. This internalization of dominant values serves to ensure the stability of the prevailing structure of social relations.

The social security system, our concern here, must be seen in this context; government action is such as to sustain existing social arrangements and social processes – to ensure the maintenance of prevailing economic relations and the ideology that secures them in the minds of the population.

Social Security Provision

The Beveridge Report of 1942 (HMSO 1942) embodied the reforms of social security which followed the Second World War and has yet to be replaced as the basis of contemporary social security. By 1939, four funds existed in Britain to provide social security benefits: health insurance, unemployment insurance, agricultural unemployment insurance and pensions for widows and orphans. The coverage given by these schemes was far from comprehensive, benefits were limited, and administration was complex and expensive. The underlying concept was that of making special provision for the minimum income requirements of identified groups with particular needs. As a safety net below this provision the Poor Law continued, until 1948, in the form of public assistance (Marsh, 1950).

Beveridge proposed a new scheme which would be comprehensive and which had as its fundamental principle the notion of contributory social insurance. Thus the insurance scheme would provide benefits to adults where there was an interruption or loss of earning power. All the major contingencies were to be covered. In addition, the needs of families were to be met by 'a general system of children's allowances, sufficient to meet the subsistence needs of all dependent children when the responsible parent is in receipt of any insurance benefit or pension, and of all such children except one in other cases' (Beveridge Report, para. 11). There were also intended to be free school meals for all children and free welfare milk and foods for all infants. Heavy emphasis was put on the prevention of subsistence poverty by the development of a comprehensive health and rehabilitation service by a Keynesian full employment policy (Beveridge, 1944).

The social insurance benefits were set at subsistence levels; Beveridge envisaged the development of private insurance schemes to supplement the basic subsistence benefits. As an insurance scheme, benefits were to be closely related to employment-linked contributions. This, it was argued, would ensure that benefits would be clearly seen as a matter of right, earned by the recipient. The stigma of public charity and the indignity of the means test, powerfully felt in the pre-war period, would thus be avoided.

Social insurance then, was seen as being 'designed of itself when in full operation to guarantee the income needed for subsistence in all normal cases.'

There remained the problem of those with other than normal needs and those who, though in need, failed to qualify for full or any insurance benefit.

The national assistance scheme was to be the safety net for those who failed to satisfy the requirements of the insurance system (Marsh, 1950; George, 1968). Benefits under *this* scheme, which replaced the remnants of the Poor Law in 1948, would not be subject to any contribution test but on a means test. Arguing that such benefits were different from National Insurance in which the insured must get something for their contributions, Beveridge stressed that a basic assumption here was that national assistance would be 'residual'. It would be of minor significance in the whole plan for social security and would diminish in importance as time moved the younger generations through to full comprehensive insurance coverage.

In summary then, Beveridge produced a plan for social security which was intended to ensure that no one in the population would fall below a subsistence income level. This was to be done by a comprehensive system of insurance, with flat-rate contributions linked closely to employment, and flat-rate benefits at subsistence level. There was heavy emphasis on adequate children's allowances and strong encouragement of supplementation by private insurance. The national assistance scheme was to be 'less desirable' and seen as increasingly residual as the insurance scheme became fully operational.

The National Insurance Scheme

In principle, the national insurance scheme provides benefits in return for contributions on the model of private insurance.

When a particular risk, covered by the scheme, materializes, a claimant may not necessarily be paid benefit. First a number of specified conditions of entitlement must be satisfied including, for most benefits, payment of the appropriate contributions. The principal statute now is the Social Security Act 1975, which consolidated earlier legislation dating effectively from 1946. Under this Act, the level of contributions and benefits must be reviewed annually with reference to changes in the general level of earnings. Contributions may also be changed in the light of the state of the national insurance fund.

Different amounts and types of contribution must be paid to the scheme by different categories of person. The principal differences flow from the contributor's employment status: employed, self-employed, non-employed. Employers also contribute to the fund. There are four classes of contribution, and for the employed and self-employed the contributions are graduated according to earnings within a specified range. Changes in contribution requirements are frequent and current regulations can be found in the appropriate leaflets issued by the Department of Health and Social Security.

The claimant's contribution record is crucial to benefit entitlement in a number of ways. Certain benefits are restricted to those with contributions in a certain class: the self-employed, for example, are not entitled to unemployment benefit. Benefits vary also in their requirements as to the number of contributions and the timing of these contributions relative to the claim for benefit. For certain benefits, a defective contribution record means that no benefit at all will be paid, for others there may be benefit at a reduced rate. To confuse the picture still further there are now several benefits which, although administered through the national insurance scheme, have no contribution conditions; of these, attendance allowance and non-contributory invalidity pension are the most important (see below).

National insurance benefits are extremely complex in detail and we can only attempt here an outline of the most important aspects of the scheme.

Most insurance benefits consist of a flat-rate weekly amount, which may be supplemented by additional amounts for dependants and in some cases by earnings-related supplements.

To establish entitlement to unemployment benefit a claimant must be unemployed, available for employment and must satisfy the contribution conditions. There are a number of rules which may disqualify the claimant: for example, leaving employment 'voluntarily' without 'just cause', losing employment through 'misconduct', and refusing suitable employment without 'good cause'. If the claimant can satisfy the various conditions and avoid the disqualifications, flat-rate benefit will be paid, with additions for dependants, for up to one year. In addition, assuming an appropriate contribution record, earnings-related supplement will be paid in addition to the flat-rate benefit. This begins after two weeks and lasts up to six months. It is based on the claimant's previous earnings and the total amount of benefit, flat-rate and earnings-related supplement is limited to 85 per cent of the claimant's average weekly earnings.

Thus, assuming contribution conditions are satisfied and there is no disqualification, a claimant should receive both flat-rate and earnings-related benefit in the first six months, flat-rate benefit only in the next six months and after one year will cease to be entitled to unemployment insurance benefit.

Sickness benefit is similar in operation to unemployment benefit but with the major difference that it effectively continues for as long as the incapacity continues. A claimant must satisfy the contribution conditions and must be incapable of work because of illness or disablement. Again there are a number of ways in which a claimant may be disqualified from receiving benefit. Flat-rate sickness benefit with additions for dependants is paid for six months. If the incapacity continues, it is replaced by invalidity benefit for as long as the incapacity lasts. Those who do not satisfy the contribution conditions for invalidity benefit should, after six months' incapacity, qualify for a non-contributory invalidity pension, for which there are no contribution conditions, and it is in effect parallel to invalidity benefit for those not qualifying for that benefit. It was introduced by the Social Security Benefits Act 1975. As an addition to these long-term sickness benefits, invalidity allowance is paid at three rates according to the claimant's age, and earnings-related supplement is paid in addition to sickness benefit on the same basis as for unemployment benefit.

Thus the effect of these provisions is that there is now entitlement to flat-rate benefit plus earnings-related supplement in the first six months of sickness for those who satisfy the contribution conditions. After six months, entitlement to 'insurance' benefit exists regardless of contribution record for as long as incapacity lasts. Invalidity allowance is additional to the invalidity benefits but the loss of earnings-related supplement after six months generally means a significant reduction in benefit. The rates of flat-rate benefit for sickness are the same as for unemployment, as is the earnings-related supplement. The non-contributory invalidity pension is paid at a lower rate than the parallel contributory invalidity pension. Clearly the most significant difference between benefits for unemployment and sickness is that the former ceases after one year whereas the latter continue for as long as the incapacity remains.

Attendance allowance, instituted in 1970, and since widened in coverage, demonstrates clearly how the original Beveridge scheme failed to cover comprehensively the needs brought about by chronic sickness and incapacity. Although described in the legislation as part of the national insurance scheme this benefit has no contribution conditions and its separation from the contributory principles of the scheme as a whole is demonstrated by its funding, which is not from the national insurance fund but from a separate appropriation by Parliament. The benefit is paid to a person requiring, for reasons of physical or mental incapacity, frequent attention or supervision. There are two rates: a higher rate if attention or supervision is required day and night and a lower one if either is required only by day or night.

Another non-contributory benefit, introduced in 1975, is the invalid care allowance. This is paid to a person who is engaged in caring for someone receiving an attendance allowance. It is intended for 'those of working age who would be breadwinners in paid employment but for the need to stay at home and act as unpaid attendants to people who are severely disabled and need care'. It is not paid to married women on the grounds that they 'might be at home in any event'. It is paid at the same rate as the non-contributory invalidity pension. Thus it is restricted in its coverage and paid at a low rate. It is again interesting to note how another gap in the Beveridge cover has been, at least partially, filled by the use of a 'national insurance' benefit which has no contribution conditions.

The national insurance scheme provides two forms of maternity benefit: a lump sum maternity grant and weekly maternity allowance. The maternity grant is paid on the basis of the claimant's contributions or her husband's contributions, as a small fixed payment for each child born. The maternity allowance is a weekly benefit paid for eighteen weeks around the date of the child's birth, with the possibility of an earnings-related supplement. It can only be claimed by women who have paid full contributions and is paid only when the claimant is not working. It is essentially sickness benefit for childbirth and is paid at the same rate. Pregnancy as such is not recognized as a specific disease or disablement for sickness benefit purposes and so for women in employment, who have paid full contributions, maternity allowance provides similar benefits.

There are three forms of widow's benefit, all related to the deceased husband's contribution record. Widow's allowance is paid for the first six months after widowhood with additions for dependent children and an earnings-related supplement – widow's supplementary allowance – based on the husband's earnings. After six months this higher rate of benefit is replaced by widowed mother's allowance in the case of a widow with children, or widow's pension if the widow was over forty when her husband died. Widowed mother's allowance continues as long as the children remain with her, and are under nineteen years of age. The age-related widow's pension continues until the claimant reaches sixty-five. Remarriage or cohabitation disqualify the claimant from receiving widow's benefits. Thus widows' benefits may be quite high in the first six months, provide benefit for as long as there are dependent children, and allow for the difficulties of older widows. They are all dependent on adequate contributions having been made by the deceased husband.

There have been a great many changes in the legislation affecting retirement pensions in recent years. The Social Security (Pensions) Act 1975 changes the contribution system from April 1978 and the benefits from April 1979.

At present, when a man over sixty-five retires from full-time work, he is entitled to a flat-rate pension provided he satisfies the contribution conditions. If he has a dependent wife aged less than sixty he will be entitled to a dependant's addition for her, subject, if she is working, to the amount of her earnings. The age-limit for a woman is sixty, and if she retires she will be entitled to a pension in her own right if she satisfies the contribution conditions. If she is married she can qualify on the basis of her husband's contributions for a pension up to the amount of the dependant's addition.

From 1961 until 1975 graduated contributions were paid on earnings above a certain figure. This scheme has now ended but present pensioners may receive some graduated pension in addition to their flat-rate pension. The numbers entitled and the amounts of extra benefit are small.

Increments to the basic pension are paid if retirement is deferred for up to five years after the normal pensionable age. Again, the numbers affected and the amounts of extra benefit are small.

The national insurance pension is only an old-age pension after age seventy for a man and sixty-five for a woman. In the five years before these ages it is a *retirement* pension and thus the crucial test for entitlement is that the claimant must have retired from regular employment. After the age of seventy for a man and sixty-five for a woman the claimant is deemed to have retired even though he or she may be employed full-time. However, in the five years prior to these ages any earnings the claimant has will affect his other pension.

There is also a non-contributory pension, first introduced in 1970. It was at first applied to those excluded from the national insurance scheme because they were over pension age when the scheme began in 1948. The old person's pension has since been extended to any person reaching eighty years of age who failed to qualify for a contributory retirement pension or qualified for one at a lower rate than the old person's pension.

Thus, in summary, the present pension provision depends critically on the claimant's contribution record. For the first five years after pensionable age, retirement is the crucial test and earnings will reduce the pension. After that the pension is paid by virtue of old age, and for any elderly person who does not qualify under the insurance schemes there is the supplementary pension under the supplementary benefits scheme (see below).

The industrial injuries scheme is now based on the Social Security Act 1975 and its contribution, administration and appeals provisions have been merged with the main national insurance scheme. Only employed contributors are covered by the industrial injuries scheme and there are some very distinctive differences between this and the main scheme. There are no complex contribution conditions – insurance begins on the first day of employment. All benefits under the scheme have common conditions of entitlement, and the rates of benefit are higher than the comparable national insurance benefits. Benefits are paid for incapacity for work, or disablement, or death caused by personal injury by accident arising out of and in the course of employment, or caused by a prescribed industrial disease. Industrial diseases are listed in regulations and are related to specific occupations, but accidents and injuries arising out of and in the course of employment have been the subject of more dispute than perhaps any other provisions of social security law. Given the more generous provisions of the industrial injuries scheme both in the level of benefits, their duration and the range of needs covered, the question of entitlement to benefits under this scheme, rather than reliance on the benefits of the main national insurance scheme, is usually of profound significance for the claimant and his dependants.

Injury benefit is a weekly benefit paid for six months where a person is incapable of work. It is thus analogous to sickness benefit, but the rate is higher and the conditions less stringent.

Industrial disablement benefit is paid according to the degree of disability and is paid either as a lump sum or, for disabilities over 20 per cent, as a weekly benefit. The payment continues for as long as the disability remains, regardless of employment status or earnings. It is thus a compensation for loss caused by industrial injury. A number of increases may be made to the basic disablement benefit in addition to those paid for dependants. Hospital treatment allowance brings the benefit up to 100 per cent during hospital treatment for the injury or disease. A constant attendance allowance is payable and an exceptionally severe disablement allowance in extreme cases. The scheme pays an unemployability supplement where the claimant remains incapable of work, on conditions similar to those for national insurance invalidity benefit. Of particular importance, the scheme pays a special hardship allowance, in certain cases, to claimants who return to work but are unable to follow their regular occupation or one of an equivalent standard. This makes up the difference, subject to a specified maximum, between what the claimant would have been earning in his regular occupation and that which he is able to earn following the injury or disease.

With this last provision particularly, it can be seen that the industrial injuries scheme has much more far-reaching cover than the main national insurance scheme. It compensates on a long-term basis for the results of sickness and injury. Death benefits under this scheme also vary from those of the main scheme. The widow's benefit is for life or until remarriage; a remarriage gratuity is paid;

widower's pension is paid to a man dependent on his wife; benefit may be paid to parents who were maintained by the deceased; a woman living with the deceased at the time of his death who had the care of one or more of his children is entitled to a weekly allowance. This last provision is in marked contrast to the widow's benefit provision of the main scheme, which allows nothing less than legal marriage.

In summary then, the industrial injuries scheme provides better rates of benefit, a far wider coverage of need, more generous interpretation and more realistic assessment of the effects of sickness and injury. This is in no way to suggest that the scheme is without faults – it has very many, principally related to its exclusion of claimants from benefits under it – it is rather to point out the significant differences between it and the main national insurance scheme. Some of the deficiencies and differences in the original scheme were discussed in earlier books (Marsh, 1950; George, 1968 and 1973).

Child benefits, previously family allowances, are a weekly benefit paid to all families with dependent children. It is now paid for all children, and not, as before, only for second and subsequent children. The benefit is effectively 'clawed back' from many recipients through income tax, but the child benefits payments are made directly to the mother as a universal grant with no contribution conditions and no means test. Child benefits are financed out of general taxation.

To complete the picture of current social security benefits, there are two schemes which provide means-tested benefits – supplementary benefits and family income supplement. The former, which replaced national assistance in 1966, has assumed a major role in social security provision. The latter has a minor but significant role. Supplementary benefits are paid to those not in full-time work, in order to bring their resources up to a specified minimum. The current supplementary benefits rate is the one most usually regarded as the 'official' poverty line. Supplementary benefits have developed not as the ultimate residual benefit that Beveridge intended, but as a substitute for and supplement to national insurance benefits, thus whenever a person fails to qualify for national insurance benefit, either because of gaps in insurance coverage, failure to meet the conditions, or when the amount of insurance benefit falls below the supplementary benefit rate, then supplementary benefits acts as a substitute or as a 'topping up' addition. This was not the role envisaged for such a scheme in the original Beveridge conception and the vast increase in numbers of claimants is given by those administering the scheme as a major reason for the problems in its administration. The fundamental principles of entitlement to supplementary benefit are extremely simple, but as a scheme intended to respond to individual need, which began with the guiding principle of being 'less desirable' than national insurance, the practice is far from simple. The scheme is subject to widespread criticism, both in terms of the level of benefits and their administration. Any contact with this part of the social security system will reveal the myriad possibilities for unpleasantness, arbitrariness and stigma which mark these benefits off from those of the 'insurance side'. As a means-tested benefit depending on individual application, one of the major problems is that very many of those who are eligible for benefits fail to claim them. This is compounded by the stigma associated with this benefit and the operation of rules and administrative practices to control 'abuse'. What needs to be stressed is that the supplementary benefits and insurance schemes are not separate income maintenance devices with separate clienteles and separate functions. They are now subsystems that interact with each other.

The scheme is one which was designed to deal with short-term needs and exceptional, individual needs, at a subsistence level. The massive increase in the number of claimants, a huge number of long-term claimants and the impossibility of administering a discretionary system of such size are the major factors which lie behind the current difficulties of this part of the social security system.

Family income supplement, introduced in 1970, is another means-tested benefit, akin to supplementary benefit. The two are mutually exclusive, FIS being paid only to families where the head is in full-time, low-paid work. The principle is simple. The FIS Act, as amended, prescribes certain amounts related to family size and provides for a family to receive benefit if its gross income is below the prescribed amount. The scheme is administered by the Supplementary Benefits Commission but unlike the position for supplementary benefits, little is left to the commission's discretion. Because the income levels are set very low the number of families which benefit is small and smaller than it could be because the take-up is far from complete. As single-parent families are treated in the same way as two-parent families and because of the generally lower levels of women's earnings FIS has a very high proportion of single-parent families headed by women among its claimants. The scale and impact of the benefit is very small in terms of the income needs of families, though it can be significant for individuals. The principle it embodies is, however, of great significance: not since the early nineteenth century has there been supplementation of earnings in this way. That it should be necessary reflects on the inadequacy of both wages and child benefits.

This then is the current system of social security benefits. A full treatment would demand both greater detail of benefits and their administration together with an examination of the array of means-tested benefits administered by central and local government. Further, to comprehend the overall pattern of social security, non-State provision, particularly of pensions, and the system of tax reliefs and allowances must be seen in intimate relation to the more obvious system of social security benefits and allowances.

This chapter is concerned with only one part of the total picture – the major social security benefits. Before discussing their effectiveness, we must look briefly at poverty: how it is viewed and how it is measured, as one of the major expressed purposes of social security is the prevention of financial poverty.

The concept of poverty has been the subject of a considerable debate in recent years. As defined by Booth and Rowntree at the end of the nineteenth century, poverty is the financial inability to live at subsistence level (Booth, 1892; Rowntree, 1901). Thus it was concerned above all with physical efficiency, with food, clothing and shelter. It embodied the view that so long as a given list of basic necessities could be satisfied a person was not poor. To draw up and price such a list in some 'scientific' way, was gradually recognized to be impracticable. It was accepted that poverty could only be meaningfully discussed in relation to the society in which people lived. There developed then what might be called a 'social subsistence' concept; necessities were seen as having social referents as well as physical ones. Tea is a commonly used example. Of no nutritional value, it would not be included in a pure subsistence list of necessities. However, its social significance is such that it must be included in any list which is to have practical application. Once this notion is conceded, of course, any list of goods will be constantly revised to take into account the changing life styles of the population concerned. It remains, for all that, a subsistence view. The current supplementary benefits rate, based on Rowntree through Beveridge, continues to express it. Put simply, this concept looks for the minimum acceptable level at which people can be expected to live.

The development of the concept of 'relative' poverty is linked with this extension of the subsistence concept but has, in a number of formulations, broken with it completely. The point is essentially this – if the living conditions of the poor are to be judged against the standards of the society in which they live what should be used as a measure? Should it be the standard of the 'nearly poor', the 'average', 'the majority', or should it be the whole society including the rich? Whatever comparison is made implies that significant value judgments have already been made. When poverty is seen as relative to the conditions in the whole society it becomes essentially a concept of inequality, concerned with the unequal distribution of resources, status and power; seen in this way it demands that attention be paid to the whole distribution and to the mechanisms which produce and maintain that distribution. Ultimately, then, poverty will be seen in terms of unacceptable inequality, and a solution to poverty will be seen as possible only when inequality is reduced to an extent regarded as acceptable.

Social security, as we have seen, is concerned with subsistence poverty; the emphasis on subsistence poverty represents the ideological considerations which underlie the social security system. The most important of these is that the poverty line must not be much higher than the wages of the lowest paid worker. Anything else undermines the operation of the labour market. The insistence on maintaining the myth of an objectively determined poverty line minimizes the problem and draws attention away from inequality as an issue. There is no doubt whatever that resources are more than sufficient to abolish subsistence poverty without any major upheavals in the economy or society. The current social security provisions are based on expressed intentions to do just that. How effective are they in achieving this limited goal?

The search for 'poverty numbers' has employed very many people for quite some time. In 1965 Abel-Smith and Townsend demonstrated that widespread subsistence poverty still existed and was growing, thus denting the complacency of those who believed that it had been abolished by the welfare state (Abel-Smith and Townsend, 1965).

Since then, there has been a steady stream of figures, constantly adjusted and revised, which have attempted to quantify the 'poverty problem'. Even when the same yardstick is used – the supplementary benefits rate for example – the results are estimates which rarely agree and are subject to wide margins of error. Such figures as are available give a snapshot picture, often on a given day of the year, and indicate very little about the numbers who are at one time or another in subsistence poverty. Current estimates would suggest over 5 million people are dependent in whole or part on supplementary benefit itself, over 2 million dependent on incomes below supplementary benefit levels, and over 1 million dependent on incomes at supplementary benefit level.

Thus a very large number of people are living on incomes at or below the 'official poverty line'. If we look at the various groups living at this level, we see how the social security system has failed to deal with subsistence poverty. Retirement pensioners are by far the largest group: the old constitute two-thirds of all those dependent on supplementary benefits. The reasons are clear. First and foremost, the basic national insurance pension is lower than the supplementary benefit rate, allowing for rent. Any pensioner without additional income will be below the poverty line, and thus eligible for supplementary benefit. The effect of graduated pension and increments for deferred retirement is minimal. A number of pensioners receive an even lower national insurance pension because their contribution record is deficient. Thus the inadequacy of the national insurance pension is a major cause, made worse for many by the contribution test. Occupational or private pensions lift the incomes of some pensioners above the poverty line but the numbers benefiting from such provision are relatively few. Occupational pensions reflect the distribution of rewards from employment and their benefits are weighted heavily in favour of men rather than women, non-manual rather than manual workers. The inequalities of working life are perpetuated into old age. That the old should live at subsistence poverty levels is shocking enough; the situation is much worse because there is massive non-take-up of supplementary benefit by old people. Recent estimates suggest that as many as a million pensioners are eligible for supplementary pension but do not claim it.

Thus the national insurance scheme fails to give adequate income in retirement and the 'safety net' of supplementary benefits fails because it is a means-tested benefit demanding individual application. The reasons for non-claiming are complex and there have been no satisfactory explanations. There is undoubtedly dislike of means tests as such, with memories of 'assistance' exacerbated by frequently harsh administration and, perhaps more important, a climate of opinion hostile to claimants of supplementary benefits. Against all the evidence, abuse of claimants is common in the media and heavily exploited by politicians. Despite attempts to distinguish benefits for the old, supplementary pensions, from benefits for those under pension age, supplementary allowance, large numbers do not claim. Lack of knowledge and the complexity of the benefits system may be relevant, but the failure of the social security system to keep old people out of subsistence poverty stands as an indictment of social security and society as a whole.

As we have seen, provision for the sick and disabled is fragmented and demonstrates the extensive inequality *within* the social security scheme. Those who qualify for both sickness benefit and earnings-related supplement may have adequate income for the first six months; after that the rates of sickness benefit are below the poverty line, demanding recourse to supplementary benefit. As we have seen, industrial injuries benefits are both higher and cover a wider range of needs without contribution conditions. For the long-term sick and those suffering from recurrent sickness, national insurance fails; benefits are inadequate and the contribution conditions prevent very many people from receiving even these inadequate benefits. The non-contributory invalidity pension is set at a rate so far below the supplementary benefit level that its effect for most claimants is simply to alter the proportions of their total benefit from different sources; there is no financial gain.

For the chronic sick and disabled, the social security system fails miserably. The contribution conditions prevent those without a sustained employment record from getting insurance benefit; the non-contributory invalidity pension is inadequate; attendance allowance applies only to very few of the most severely disabled; the only provisions for the additional financial hardship caused by disability are the discretionary additions to supplementary benefit. Very few claimants are paid these and the amounts are small. For families not entitled to supplementary benefit there is no provision for the needs of a disabled family's members, apart from the family fund which makes lump-sum grants for the special needs of handicapped children. Social security fails to meet the special needs of chronic sickness and disability and condemns hundreds of thousands to a life-time of poverty.

We can clearly see here that social security deals reasonably well with short breaks from employment. The weaker the link with employment, either in terms of previous contributions or potential capacity, the worse provision becomes. For the unemployed, the benefits again protect a number but not all from financial poverty in the short term, namely those who can qualify for earnings-related supplement. After six months, flat-rate benefits alone are inadequate and after a year only supplementary benefit is available. Again, the benefits are adequate only in the short term for those with good contribution records. Long-term unemployment is increasing, particularly among older workers. The most vulnerable in the employment market are the worst provided for by social security, both the control procedures and the structure of benefits act against those who fail to remain in employment; the longer they do so the more harshly they are treated.

There are two groups of one-parent families in relation to social security – widows and others. National insurance only provides benefit for widowed mothers, but although this group is much better off than other single parents, the level of benefits and the contribution test means that they must rely on supplementary benefits.

For the other groups of one-parent families – the unmarried, separated and divorced, the only non-means-tested benefit is child benefit. Those in low-paid full-time work may qualify for FIS, those not in full-time work have only supplementary benefit, and child benefit is taken into account before these are paid. One-parent families headed by women have been the fastest growing group on supplementary benefit. The social security system, with its very heavy emphasis on the assumption that women shall be dependent on men, denies adequate benefits as of right to those who, for whatever reason, are in circumstances which alter this relationship. Only widowhood is seen as involuntary and even then it is the contribution record of the husband which decides the woman's entitlement to benefit. The unmarried, separated and divorced are thus held to be at least partly responsible for their condition. Further-more, their conduct may be seen as threatening to the institutions of marriage and the family. The harsh treatment of single mothers by the supplementary benefits scheme, associated essentially with a determination to enforce the responsibilities of husbands and fathers, exemplifies attitudes to this group. Dominant social values placed on marriage and the family result in continued inequality in the treatment of one-parent families.

Finally, as we have seen, benefits for those in full-time work are minimal. Child benefit has now been extended but would need massive increases if it were to provide anything like realistic financial support for families bringing up children. Family income supplement has little impact and embodies a concept of sub-sistence poverty which undermines any role social security may have in bringing about greater equality. The question of inequality in income and wealth is the crucial one, not just for those in work, but for those dependent on benefits also. The system of benefits both reflects and reinforces the inequalities in society at large.

Social security is failing to deal with subsistence poverty; the means-tested supplementary benefits scheme, seen as residual in the Beveridge plan, is assuming a greater and greater significance as the national insurance scheme fails to deliver adequate benefits. The benefits system is marked by inequalities within itself which reflect dominant social values related to work, social class, marriage and the family. There has been no attempt to reduce inequality and the attempt to alleviate subsistence poverty with little vertical redis-tribution of income and wealth has failed.

Proposals for the reform of social security abound. There are numerous suggestions for the improvement of benefits for specific groups; the piecemeal approach has been used for thirty years. On a grander scale there are those who argue that what is needed is a 'return to Beveridge', that is, a scheme which would achieve his objectives – comprehensive, adequate benefits as of right. The Child Poverty Action Group suggests this approach, but would use earnings-related contributions to finance flat-rate benefits, thus achieving some redistribution. They attempt to retain the contribu-tion principle but with so many qualifications as to make it essen-tially meaningless except as a potent myth to buttress the notion of the 'right to benefit'.

Others, Kincaid and George particularly, argue against any contributions which link benefits to employment (Kincaid, 1973; George, 1973). They support a system based simply on citizenship and financed from taxation. Both these approaches recognize that poverty and inequality are closely linked and that social security must be seen in the context of the total distribution of income and wealth, both State and private. They differ in that CPAG has subsistence poverty as its focus of concern, as did Beveridge, whereas Kincaid and George are concerned with inequality and with subsistence poverty as an extreme form of that wider phenomenon. In effect, however, their proposals come together at a number of points, with CPAG clearly being more cautious in its approach and less ambitious in its goals.

Finally, what of schemes which would apparently avoid the myriad complexities we have at present by merging benefits and taxes into one system which would both collect taxes from some and distribute benefits to others? The principles are straight forward and may be seen in 'negative income tax' plans, 'guaranteed income' plans and other schemes which have been proposed. There are three components to any scheme of this kind: a minimum level, a tax rate, and a break-even point where neither benefits are paid nor taxes collected. Settling the first involves either decisions about subsistence poverty or about the acceptable lower limit of the range of final incomes. Setting the second raises questions of incentives and the relationship between benefits and earnings. The third determines the extent to which benefits 'spread' upwards through the income distribution or are restricted to the poorest. As a device it is neutral; the criticisms of previous proposals have essentially been of the choices made in setting these parameters and the values implicit in those choices. Thus, such a device can be used to limit benefits to the very poorest, using a low minimum-income level and thus minimizing vertical redistribution. But it can also be used to produce considerable redistribution.

Above all else, such schemes make explicit the goals and effects of social security and personal taxation in relation to income distribution. Radical change in social security is, however, unlikely. What is more likely is that the system of benefits will continue to be adjusted to deal with only the most conspicuous inequalities; that the trend to non-contributory 'insurance' benefits will continue at a modest level; that the discretionary element in supplementary benefits will be eroded and that the net impact of social security and taxation in the pattern of inequality will continue to be small.

The dominant classes support social security because it ensures that the lower classes bear the costs of their own old age, disability, sickness and unemployment. It also tends to lessen political pressure for genuine interclass transfers of wealth. The political acceptability of attempts to reduce inequality depends on whether or not they bring some advantage to the dominant classes, or important sections of them. Reforms concerned with subsistence poverty among 'deserving' groups may do so, but genuinely egalitarian reforms designed to change the rules of distribution and ownership do not. Even an attack on subsistence poverty will meet considerable opposition since it is clear that poverty persists because it functions to uphold the stratified nature of society. The existence of the poor demonstrates, by negative example, the values of a competitive society rooted in possessive individualism. We have seen throughout the social security system the imperatives of the economic system take precedence over financial need or social rights.

This does not mean that improvement cannot be sought, and gained, but it does mean that any real solution to the problem of financial hardship must alter the pattern of distribution between classes, rather than between individuals, and to do that social security must be transformed not revised.

Some indication of the scope and source of statistical data on social security is given in the following tables:

Table 6 Families and persons with low net resources* in Great Britain

	Families	Persons
December 1974	4,740,000	7,300,000
December 1975	5,250,000	8,880,000

Source: Social Trends No. 7, 1976, Table 5.29.
*Supplementary benefit rates plus 20%.

Table 7 Families (A), normally with low net resources, (B) Great Britain, December 1974 (thousands)

	Below SB not receiving SB	On SB	Below SB + 20%	Total
Married couples with children	(C)			
families	90 (1)	80 (1)	120 (2)	290 (4)
persons	390 (2)	390 (2)	580 (2)	1360 (6)
Single persons with children				
families	20 (4)	260 (41)	20 (3)	399 (48)
persons	70 (4)	760 (44)	60 (3)	890 (51)

Source: Social Trends No. 7, 1976, Table 5.31.
A Head under pension age.
B SB to 20%.
C Figures in brackets show percentage of families and persons of type.

Table 8 Supplementary benefit ordinary scale rates as a percentage of average weekly earnings of male manual workers (including rent and family allowances)

		Married persons		
	Single household	Without children	With 2 children under 5	With 4 children, 2 under 5 2 aged 5–10
1948 (Oct)	17·4	29·0	39·9	52·9
1958 (Oct)	17·5	29·6	40·9	54·2
1968 (Oct)	19·8	32·4	44·1	58·0
1971 (Oct)	18·8	30·6	41·5	54·5
1972 (Oct)	18·3	29·7	40·3	52·9
1973 (Oct)	17·5	28·5	38·5	50·5
1974 (Oct)	17·1	27·8	37·6	48·6
1975 (Apr)	17·5	28·5	38·5	50·5
1976 (Apr)*	17·2	28·0	37·8	49·7

Source: based on Table 3.3, p. 27, Field, F. Poverty the Facts, CPAG, 1975.
*Computed from SB rates April 1976 and average weekly earnings April 1976 63.3 (New Earnings Survey, 1976, Department of Employment). See also SBC Annual Report, 1975 onwards.

Table 9   Recipients of national assistance and supplementary benefit (not including dependants) (thousands) Great Britain 1948, 1974, 1975

	1948	1974	1975
Retirement pensioners and NI widows over 60	495	1,712	1,679
Others over pension age	143	96	
Unemployed with benefit	19	73	135
Unemployed without NI benefit	34	228	406
Sick and disabled with NI benefit	80	95	109
Sick and disabled without NI benefit	64	165	133
Women under 60 with dependent children	32	245	283
NI widows under 60	81	42	55
Others	63	24	
Total persons	1,011	2,680	2,800
Total claimants and dependants	1,465	4,092	4,500
Claimants and dependants as percentage of population	3·0%	7·5%	8%

Source: 1948 and 1974 figures from Table 1, p. 9. Lister, R. *Social Security: The case for reform,* CPAG 1975. 1975 figures from SBC *Annual Report,* 1975 (HMSO 1976).

Table 10   Registered unemployed* by benefit entitlement, May 1976

National insurance only	37·2%
National insurance and SB	11·7%
SB only	34·4%
No benefit	16·6%

Source: Department of Employment Gazette, January 1977.
*There is an additional group of unemployed not registered as unemployed and hence not counted here.

References

Abel-Smith, B. and Townsend, P. (1965), *The Poor and the Poorest*, G. Bell & Sons.

Beveridge, W. H. (1944), *Full Employment in a Free Society*, Allen & Unwin.

Booth, C. (1892), *Life and Labour of the People of London*, Macmillan.

George, V. N. (1968), *Social Security; Beveridge and after*, Routledge & Kegan Paul.

George, V. N. (1973), *Social Security and Society*, Routledge & Kegan Paul.

HMSO (1942), *Social Insurance and Allied Services*, Cmd 6404, (Beveridge report).

Kincaid, J. (1973), *Poverty and Equality in Britain*, Penguin.

Marsh, D. C. (1950), *National Insurance and Assistance in Great Britain*, Pitman.

Rowntree, S. (1901), *Poverty, a Study of Town Life*, Nelson.

Policies Designed to Deal with
Social Problems

8

The Personal Social Services

Joan L. M. Eyden

Introduction

The services that have been considered so far have been those which most citizens use at some time during their lives – as school children, as patients, as retirement pensioners, etc. Some members of the community, however, have needs which they and their families are unable to meet without additional forms of help. Others, because of their difficult or anti-social behaviour, are brought to the notice of the authorities for special care, treatment or control. That some groups have special claims on the community, because of handicap or infirmity, has been recognized for many centuries, but recently in this and many other countries there has been increasing emphasis on their individual needs as *persons* with physical, mental or social handicaps, rather than on the problems they may have in supporting themselves in an industrial society.

Because of this emphasis on the individual, personal and social aspects of these handicaps, the services which have been developing over the last half century to meet the special needs of these groups have become known as the 'personal social services'. In many ways this label becomes more questionable the more one examines it. Nevertheless it has become part of current usage to apply this term to those services which are mainly the responsibility of the local authority social service departments.

The Local Authority (Social Services) Act (1970) provided for the establishment of one new department to replace the children's and welfare departments of the major local authorities and to take over certain powers and duties in relation to mental health and to mothers and young children previously the responsibility of the local authority health departments. The services thus incorporated into the new department presented a most confusing picture over the country as a whole and to many interested observers appeared totally inadequate to meet established need, quite apart from the existence of suspected but hidden problems. The inadequacy of these services may be partly accounted for by the difficulty the ordinary ratepayer and taxpayer may have in understanding some of the more subtle needs of those who suffer a handicap; partly because the rapid increase in scientific knowledge and technology has only recently begun to show ways in which some people can be helped through, for instance, sophisticated hearing devices and aids to greater mobility and self-help; partly because problems affecting only a very small number of people are not always recognized by the rest of the community unless the imagination of the general public is caught as in the case of the 'thalidomide babies'; partly because unconventional or anti-social behaviour associated with certain forms of physical, mental or social handicap tend to arouse antagonism and social ostracism. Perhaps even more important, the clients of the personal social services tend to be those with least economic and political power and their claim to scarce resources has therefore been unrecognized and unacknowledged.

Before considering further the current position with regard to the work of the local authority social service departments, it may be helpful if we look briefly at the development of collective provision for people suffering from physical handicap, from mental disorder, for deprived children and socially vulnerable families and for the elderly.

The Needs of Physically Handicapped People

One of the basic problems in the provision of adequate services for persons with physical handicap has been that of terminology and definition and the consequent difficulty of establishing the size and nature of the services required. The most important comprehensive survey of the extent of disability in this country so far undertaken was that by the social survey division of the Office of Population Censuses and Surveys in the late 1960s. Its results were published in

1971, *The Handicapped and Impaired in Britain* (Harris, 1971). Some authorities use the term 'handicap' to indicate any form of activity curtailment, including difficulty over self-care, to the inability to find employment or form adequate social contacts. Other authorities regard the latter only as a handicap and the former as disability. A further complicating factor is the variety of causes of handicap, which includes sensory defects, strokes, arthritis, multiple sclerosis and so on, as well as loss of limbs due to accidents. This means that handicapped individuals may need very different help, particularly from the medical and educational services. Nevertheless the personal and social effects of handicap may lead to social needs, for income, for special housing, for aids to mobility, for training, for sheltered employment, for opportunities for social contacts which are common to many of those with physical handicap no matter what the cause. Harris's survey suggests that there are some three million people with physical impairments, of which over a million are significantly disadvantaged in their lives because of physical disability.

Social Policy and Physical Handicap

In the earlier paragraph, the difficulty of establishing the size and nature of the services required by handicapped people was mentioned. Perhaps the word 'required' here was inappropriate for it is ambiguous. Are the services provided those which handicapped people themselves desire? Are they those which other people think should be provided as some compensation for the 'diswelfares' – in Titmuss's (1968) terminology – the handicapped suffer? Or are they those services which will enable handicapped citizens to live as full lives as possible, integrated into the community in which they live? It can be argued (Sainsbury, 1968), that disability sets in train psychological and social processes similar to ageing, which leads the handicapped to 'disengage' from much of the normal social activity of everyday life. Because they are not thought able to play the roles typical for persons of their age and sex, they reconcile themselves to roles which are, from the viewpoint of society, both limited and marginal. They therefore seek to hide their disabilities from the gaze of other people and prefer formal associations outside the mainstream of social life, tending to develop specialized forms of social relationship which emphasize their 'apartness'. Such a view has seemed to dominate much of the provision for the disabled in the past, both by the many specialist voluntary organizations devoted to the welfare of the disabled and by statutory bodies. Yet as Sainsbury (1968) found as a result of her survey of a group of disabled people in the London area, this view is contrary to the wishes of many of the recipients themselves.

> The most important problem to emerge from the study is the difficulty of reconciling the expressed needs of the disabled and the provisions made for them. Most disabled persons required help to enable them to participate as fully as possible with others in daily life. But the provisions made for them tended to segregate them from the rest of the community. Thus the aspirations of many of the persons interviewed and the objectives of social policy were in conflict.

This survey was undertaken in the 1960s and there have been considerable developments both in the stated aims of social policy by the government and voluntary organizations and in the actual services now being provided. In particular, there has been a growing emphasis on the needs of the younger disabled and the channelling of more resources into efforts to increase their independence and mobility. Yet by far the largest group of the disabled needing special help are those aged between fifty and the mid-seventies suffering a chronic illness. There is thus no simple solution to the provision of services which will meet the very varied needs of the whole group of handicapped people.

The acceptance by the State of some responsibility for those who are physically handicapped goes back at least to the Act of 1531, Concerning Punishment of Beggars and Vagabonds, which sought to distinguish between the deserving and undeserving poor and gave JPs the power of granting licences to beg to 'all aged poor and impotent Persons'. This was extended in the famous Poor Law of 1601, which was concerned only with the destitute. Special provision by religious foundations certainly goes back many centuries earlier, but again was primarily concerned with the material needs of those they sought to help. The establishment of a School for the Blind in Liverpool in 1790 for instruction and industrial training was perhaps the first institution of a more modern character to be founded.

Throughout the nineteenth century local societies for the blind, the deaf and the crippled continued to develop, providing a wide variety of services according to the particular interests and concern of the founders. With the provision of universal elementary education in the last decades of the century the State was forced to consider the special educational needs of the handicapped child. A Royal Commission on the Blind was set up in 1885 with the duty of investigating 'the conditions of the blind, the various systems of education existing at home and abroad, the employments open to them, and the means by which education might be extended and the number of persons qualified for suitable employment increased'. In 1886 its terms of reference were widened to include the deaf and dumb and its report issued in 1889 led to the Elementary Education (Blind and Deaf Children) Act, 1893. Under this Act the duty of providing for the education of these children passed from the Poor Law authorities to the local education authorities, and parents had a duty to see that their handicapped children received education between the ages of five and fifteen.

Apart from education, perhaps the most important step in providing a universal and comprehensive system of welfare for any group of the handicapped in this country was taken in 1919 when, after the report of a departmental committee set up in 1914, the newly established Ministry of Health issued a circular which required local authorities to compile a register of blind persons in their area if they wished to benefit from certain grants-in-aid. This was followed in 1920 by the Blind Persons Act – the first statute concerned with the general welfare of a specific group of physically handicapped persons. This Act imposed on local authorities the duty of framing and implementing at least a minimum scheme for the blind, including the care of children under school age, the education and training of children, young people and adults; employment in workshops or through home-worker schemes; the augmentation of wages; the provision of hostels, homes and home teaching; and the giving of financial assistance to the necessitous blind. An important feature of the Act, and of that of 1938, was that local authorities could discharge their responsibility for all or any part of their schemes through voluntary organizations which they could reimburse from public funds. By 1939 at least a minimum nationwide service had been built up for all members of this handicapped group, but in seeking to provide a service capable of giving or restoring the maximum amount of 'contributive' citizenship to all members, local authorities were only partially successful, differing strikingly in quality from area to area. In spite of this inequality, blind welfare services were considerably in advance of comparable provision for any other physically handicapped group.

Wartime conditions brought an impetus to the development of services for other groups of the handicapped from another quarter. The conditions of severe unemployment characteristic of the 1920s and 1930s gave way to an unprecedented demand for labour of every kind. Many handicapped people had the opportunity for the first time of proving what they could do as industrial workers. Not only was there a rapid development of medical rehabilitation, particularly after the introduction of the Emergency Hospital Service, but in 1941 the Minister of Labour introduced a pilot scheme for the training and resettlement of disabled persons. This and the recommendations of an interdepartmental committee led directly to the passing of the Disabled Persons (Employment) Act, 1944. The Act marked a most important stage in the development of a comprehensive service for all the disabled as its aim was to help men and women who were substantially handicapped by some kind of disability to obtain suitable employment – preferably in open industry. Although it covered only those capable of productive work of some kind, it applied to people with all types of disability who 'on account of injury, disease or congenital deformity' were substantially handicapped in getting or keeping employment or work which would otherwise be suitable (see Chapter 2).

Good medical and industrial rehabilitation and settlement in employment solves many of the problems – personal and social as well as economic – of the handicapped and their families. The implementation of the Disabled Persons (Employment) Act, and the nationwide provision of rehabilitation incorporated into the National Health Service, however, still left many needs unmet. More adequate provision for financial aid was made by the National Insurance and National Insurance (Industrial Injuries) Acts of 1946 and Part II of the National Assistance Act, 1948. The replacement of national assistance by supplementary benefit in 1966, the introduction of a non-contributory invalidity pension in 1975, of a mobility allowance in 1976, an attendance allowance in 1971 and an invalid care allowance in 1976 have all extended the amount and range of financial support for handicapped individuals and their families. The fact that the last three benefits are non-contributory and non-means-tested is some recognition that handicapped persons usually have extra expenses because of their disability and also that many are unable to benefit from an insurance scheme geared to the needs of working men and women. In 1977 some disabled housewives became eligible for a non-contributory invalidity pension after years of campaigning by DIG (the Disablement Income Group) but the financial situation of many disabled people and their families is still far from satisfactory and they remain some of the most financially disadvantaged in our society.

It was the National Assistance Act, 1948, which first made statutory provision for general welfare services for all groups of the handicapped, extending to the deaf and crippled, and others the possibility of the same kinds of help which had been developed for the blind under the Acts of 1920–38. These Acts were repealed by the 1948 Act, but the duty of providing services for the blind continued under it. Section 29 of the Act empowered county councils and county boroughs to make arrangements for promoting the welfare of persons who were blind, deaf or dumb, and others substantially and permanently handicapped by illness, injury or congenital deformity. Schemes could include an information service, the provision of social and occupation centres, workshops, hostels, home-worker schemes and 'giving such persons instruction in their own homes or elsewhere in methods of overcoming the effects of their disabilities'. Unfortunately the submission of schemes and their subsequent implementation were not made compulsory until 1960. Moreover, such phrases as 'methods of overcoming the effects of their disabilities' were liable to very different interpretations. As a result the development of services for the deaf and the so-called 'general' classes of handicapped persons in the 1950s and the 1960s was patchy and inadequate.

The Younghusband Report of 1959 on the employment and training of social workers in the local authority health and welfare services (HMSO, 1959) emphasized among other things the importance of adequate professional social work support for the handicapped and their families and the 1960s saw a considerable increase in the number of trained workers in the welfare departments of local authorites.

The Chronically Sick and Disabled Persons Act, 1970, passed as a result of much pressure from organizations of the disabled themselves as well as others concerned with their welfare, spelled out in much greater detail than in previous legislation, the powers and duties of local authorities for the care and support of physically handicapped persons. These include responsibility for providing telephones, TV licences, parking schemes, housing adaptations, aids for daily living, holiday accommodation and transport services as well as social work support and home help.

Although there is much criticism of the continued inadequacy of the services and of the uneven way in which the Act has been implemented by different local authorities, nevertheless there has been a marked increase in the services of all kinds which have been provided for the disabled and it is estimated that local authority expenditure on these amounted to some £15 million in 1975/6. Expenditure on aids, adaptations and telephones alone reached nearly £9 million (Ennals, 1977).

Social Aspects of Mental Health and Mental Disorder

The term mental disorder is currently used to cover mental illness and mental subnormality (or mental handicap or retardation). There is, and has been for many years – indeed centuries – considerable controversy over definitions of mental illness and handicap and even more over the meaning of psychopathy. Mental disorder at times manifests itself in behaviour thought to be in some way 'abnormal' and what constitutes deviant or abnormal behaviour tends to vary from society to society. Moreover the medical or pathological model of mental disorder leads in some instances to the concept of 'diminished responsibility' for one's actions and consequent problems for those responsible for law enforcement. Although there has been a considerable development of research in the mental health field in the last few decades the results have often been apparently contradictory and capable of various interpretations. In an introductory article in a discussion paper of the British Association of Social Workers, *Aspects of the Social Care of the Mentally Ill* (1975), F. M. Martin suggests that

in spite of a vast accumulation of clinical experience, a
proliferation of theoretical schemata and not inconsiderable
international investment in research, our collective
understanding of the factors which contribute to the causation

of psychiatric disorder remains fragmentary and tentative. Indeed, even quite basic questions as to the very nature of psychiatric disorder are now in dispute – in some respects more sharply than ever, since a number of very influential contemporary writers argue in rather persuasive terms that the whole notion of illness as conventionally understood in medical contexts cannot be appropriately applied to those aberrations of thought, emotion, relationship and behaviour which in advanced societies tend to be recognized as the province of the psychiatrist.

The debate will no doubt continue, but without necessarily accepting those models of mental illness which identify the patient – especially the schizophrenic – with the radical critic of a constricting and dehumanizing society, his family with the oppressive forces of the established order and the collusive psychiatrist as an agent of control and coercion, there is much evidence to suggest that social factors play an important part in the aetiology of much mental illness. Any consideration of the prevention, care and treatment of mental illness must, therefore, give due weight to family and social conditions.

A definition of mental handicap, retardation or subnormality suggested by the American Association on Mental Deficiency and quoted in Pamphlet No. 5 of the National Development Group for the Mentally Handicapped considers that 'Mental retardation refers to significantly subaverage general intellectual functioning, existing concurrently with deficits in adaptive behaviour and manifested during the development period.' It continues, 'It is generally agreed that *both* intellectual and adoptive functioning, must be shown to be impaired before a person can be classified as mentally handicapped. Neither low intelligence nor impaired adaptive behaviour alone is sufficient.' It thus follows that social education, care and support are crucial in the provision of services for the mentally handicapped. This is why there has been considerable emphasis in recent years on the contribution of local authorities rather than on that of hospital-based health services. In *Better Services for the Mentally Handicapped* (HMSO, 1971) the DHSS states that research findings have demonstrated that an appropriately stimulating environment leads to positive improvement in the abilities of mentally handicapped children. Children living with their own families have been shown to be much less backward in social development than children of similar intelligence in institutional care. Official policy is based on the view that mentally handicapped children and adults should not be segregated unnecessarily from other people of similar age, nor from the general life of the community. Each handicapped person should live with his own family as long as this does not impose an undue burden on them or him; he and his family should receive full advice and support and the opportunity to develop to his maximum capacity and to exercise all the skills he acquires however limited they may be. It is emphasized that understanding and help from friends and neighbours as well as from the local authority are needed to assist the family to maintain a normal social life and to give the handicapped member as nearly a normal life as his handicap permits.

The Development of Social Policy in the Mental Health Field

The history of provisions for the mentally disordered is a long and complicated one, and one in which the State has been interested for many centuries – unlike its almost complete disregard for the fortunes of the physically handicapped. The Act De Praerogativa Regis (c. 1324) differentiated between the 'lunatic' – 'one who aforetime hath had his wit and memory but happen to fail of his wit', and the 'natural fool' – 'one that hath no understanding from his nativity and so is, by law, presumed never likely to attain any'. This attempt at differentiating between the mentally ill and the mentally handicapped related only to their capacity to hold and administer land and in subsequent centuries there continued to be considerable confusion – legal, social and medical – between lunacy and idiocy.

The main concern of the public, and therefore of the State, was with the potential danger to the community of those who were sometimes thought of as being possessed by devils. Although it is true that by the eighteenth century public concern was beginning to be felt for the treatment of the lunatic, custody and restraint were still the time-honoured methods of dealing with the insane whether in public institutions or private asylums. Destitute lunatics could be sent to the workhouse under the Poor Law, while others could be sent to gaols or houses of correction under the Vagrancy Acts. The nineteenth century saw a series of inquiries and acts which sought to meet the urgent need of safeguarding the interests of patients and was primarily concerned with the removal of flagrant abuses and the improvement of madhouses, asylums and workhouses. The emphasis on custody made it imperative that procedures for the detention and protection of patients should be carefully regulated. Jones points out that the enlightened interest of doctors and philanthropists might have resulted in the establishment of a new and constructive attitude towards the whole problem of the care and treatment of the mentally disordered in the middle of the nineteenth century (Jones, 1960). Yet this promise was not fulfilled. The latter part of the century continued to be dominated by two public fears – the fear of the insane and the fear of illegal detention of the sane.

The Lunacy Act (1890) was mainly a consolidation of former Acts concerned primarily with the prevention of ill-treatment and of illegal detention. Its provisions emphasized the legal aspects of insanity and confirmed the rigid structure of institutional care based on legal certification, which had been established and which tended to inhibit the development of a more constructive attitude during the first decades of the twentieth century.

Meanwhile, there was an increasing interest in the problems of the mentally defective. The Idiots Act (1886) made it possible for local authorities to make separate provision for idiots by building special institutions, but little was done as the measure was a permissive one only. Local authorities were also given powers to provide education in special schools or classes for feeble-minded children by the Elementary Education (Defective and Epileptic Children) Act (1899) some six years after powers had been given for the provision of special education for blind and deaf children.

This interest in the mentally defective was part of an increasing general concern about the growth of 'a social problem' group. The study of eugenics was attracting considerable interest at the beginning of the twentieth century and the importance of the hereditary and natural factors in mental defect and disease, coupled with limited recognition of environmental factors, led to a demand for the provision of institutions for the segregation of mental defectives and the supervision of those remaining in the community to prevent them from becoming parents. The outcome was the Mental Deficiency Act (1913) which gave local authorities, working through mental deficiency committees, the duty of ascertaining all persons 'subject to be dealt with', to provide institutional care and guardianship; and to provide for the supervision of mental defectives in the community. The social repercussions of mental deficiency were recognized in that the definition of those 'subject to be dealt with' involved an attempted estimate of social functioning. The classification of those affected – idiots, imbeciles and feeble-minded – was based on the extent of mental defect and the need for care and supervision; a fourth category, labelled the moral imbecile, was added as an attempt to bring within the scope of statutory regulation a number of those who were deemed members of the 'social problem group' and who might otherwise not prove able to be dealt with. This category led to much controversy among doctors, lawyers and members of the general public, because of difficulties of definition – the same controversy as today centres round the term psychopath. Another important innovation in the Act of 1913 was the setting up of a board of control which took over all the powers and duties of the existing Lunacy Commissioners and became responsible for the supervision of local authorities in the exercise of their powers under the Act and for the protection of all defectives. This Act, amended in 1927, remained the basis of provision for mental defectives until the National Health Service Act revolutionized the machinery of administration.

Jones (1960) points out that between the wars parallel movements took place in the care of the mentally ill and of the mental defective.

> In both cases, there was a swing away from the concept of permanent detention, and a desire to find means of integrating patients more closely with the society which had been previously concerned only to reject them; but they were distinct movements, and there was comparatively little contact between them up to 1939.

The Mental Treatment Act (1930) by creating categories of voluntary and temporary patients made it possible for the local authority asylums, in future to be called mental hospitals, to make progress in the treatment as well as the care of the mentally ill. The authorities were also given permissive powers to provide psychiatric outpatient clinics at general as well as mental hospitals, and to make arrangements for after-care. The Act was hailed as a break-through, but although progress was made during the 1930s and 1940s, the stigma of certification and indeed the stigma attached to mental illness itself remained very strong and continued to work against the early treatment and hospitalization of mental patients. Few local authorities used their powers to provide a care service for patients in the community and those that did tended to work through voluntary organizations.

The National Health Service Act (1946) – discussed in Chapter 7 – affected the development of provisions for both the mentally ill and the mentally defective, because for the first time it brought the institutional care of both these groups under the same administration as other hospitals, thus giving recognition to a movement towards integration which had been gathering momentum. A report, *The Future Organization of the Psychiatric Services*, published jointly by the Royal Medico-Psychological Assocation, the Psychological Medicine Section of the BMA and the Royal College of Physicians, in June 1945, stressed (Jones, 1960) that 'the argument for treating psychiatry in all essential respects like other branches of medicine' was 'strong and conclusive . . . there is everything to be said for making the administrative structure of psychiatry exactly the same in principle and even in major detail as that of other branches of the health service.' As the Minister of Health became the central authority for mental health the Board of Control retained only its quasi-judicial interest in protecting the liberty of the subject. Local authorities lost all their hospitals and mental deficiency institutions but were given wide powers – capable of very varied interpretation – for the prevention, care and after-care of patients.

In spite of the administrative changes brought about by the National Health Service Act, it became increasingly obvious that the existing law relating to mental illness and mental deficiency was out of date and needed revision. Accordingly a Royal Commission was set up in 1954 and its report, published in 1957, recommended far-reaching reforms (HMSO, 1957). It advocated the repeal of the existing Lunacy, Mental Treatment and Mental Deficiency Acts and their replacement by a single legal code embracing all forms of mental disorder. The commission hoped that in most instances those suffering from mental disorder would have access to treatment, both as out-patients and in-patients, in exactly the same way as those suffering from any other illness, and that the practice of the formal designation of certain hospitals for the reception of mentally disordered patients would be discontinued. The report, however, recognized that some provision had to be made for the compulsory admission of patients to hospital for care and treatment in certain circumstances, but it advocated that this should be primarily an administrative procedure on medical recommendation instead of legal certification, with the safeguard of a right of appeal to a specially constituted tribunal. The categories of patients who in certain circumstances could become subject to compulsory powers, it was suggested, should be mentally ill patients, psychopathic patients or patients with a psychopathic personality, and patients of severely subnormal personality.

The recommendations were welcomed by most professional and lay opinions, although there was considerable controversy over some points of detail – notably the responsibility to be placed on the medical profession to recommend compulsory admission and the definition of the categories of patients subject to compulsory powers. There was also discussion, particularly in Parliament, about the suggested extended responsibility of local authorities and how far these should be mandatory. The report strongly endorsed the recommendations of many witnesses that there should be a shift of emphasis from hospital to community care and that 'the local authorities should be responsible for preventive services and for all types of care for patients who do not require in-patient hospital treatment or training or who have had a period of treatment or training and are ready to return to the community' (HMSO, 1957).

The Mental Health Act (1959) implemented most of the recommendations of the commission. It repealed almost all of the existing legislation in this field, including the complicated arrangement for certification. Administratively, the Act completed the change already initiated by the National Health Service Act and abolished any legal or administrative distinction between mental hospitals, in the future to be called psychiatric hospitals, and any other hospital. The only exceptions were the 'special' hospitals providing maximum security conditions for specially dangerous patients which were to be administered centrally by the Minister of Health. The Act ensured that the normal method of admission should be completely informal. However, it provided for two forms of compulsory admission – for observation (for a maximum of twenty-eight days) and for treatment. Except in an emergency the application for admission had to be founded on the written recommendations of two medical practitioners and made either by the nearest relative of the patient or by a mental welfare officer. In all cases the patient had to be suffering from a mental disorder that was of a nature or degree warranting detention and that it was necessary in the interests of his health or safety or for the protection of other persons that the patient should be so detained.

The definitions and classification of mental disorder in the Act differed in a number of important respects from those in the report of the Royal Commission. Thus, in Section 4, psychopathic disorder was defined as 'a persistent disorder or disability of mind (whether or not including subnormality of intelligence) which results in abnormally aggressive or seriously irresponsible conduct on the part of the patient, and requires or is susceptible to medical treatment'. A new category was added – that of subnormality – which was defined as a state of arrested or incomplete development of mind (not amounting to severe subnormality) which required or was susceptible to medical treatment or other special care or training of the patient. The Act made a number of provisions for the easy discharge of patients subject to compulsory powers and the possibility of appeal to a mental health review tribunal. Part V of the Act was concerned with the admission of patients involved in criminal proceedings and the transfer of patients under sentence, and gave the courts power to provide for the more flexible treatment of offenders suffering from mental disorder.

Local health authorities, the county and county borough councils, were given wide powers to provide residential accommodation, day centres for training and occupation, and other ancillary services and for the appointment of mental welfare officers, thus defining in greater detail the powers given to authorities under the National Health Service Act (1946).

In the 1960s there was considerable progress in the mental health field, modernization of many more hospitals, the use of informal procedures for more than 80 per cent of in-patients, the provision of more occupation and training centres for the mentally subnormal, hostels for all groups of the mentally disordered and an energetic policy for the recruitment of mental welfare officers. These developments have continued in the 1970s but the reorganization of the personal social services, of the National Health Service and of local government has, at least in the short term, caused problems of continuity, co-operation and co-ordination which have been to the disadvantage of many patients. Moreover, the policy of early discharge from hospital and the attempts to settle long stay and chronic patients in the community, which have been energetically pursued by most hospitals since the Act, has often had adverse effects on patients, their families and on public opinion because of the inadequacy of alternative care and supporting services in the community. One result of this concern was the setting up in 1975 by the Secretary of State for Social Services of an independent advisory body, the National Development Group for the Mentally Handicapped.

There is also increasing concern over certain basic assumptions of the Act. Some organizations are pressing for the removal of the mentally handicapped from the coverage of the Mental Health Act, because their problem, it is argued, is primarily social and educational not medical. Perhaps the most heated discussions concern the sections in the Act relating to compulsory admission to hospital for treatment and to mentally abnormal offenders (Gostin, 1977). Because of the mounting criticisms of the Act and of its implementation, the Department of Health and Social Security has initiated a study of present practice and the possibility of a new Mental Health Act (HMSO, 1976).

The Elderly

Although the needs of the elderly, unable to support themselves because of increasing illness and frailty, have long been recognized, it was not until the last decade of the nineteenth century that public attention began to be directed towards the urgent necessity of providing more adequate assistance for old people. Friendly societies, savings banks and charity were insufficient to meet the need and the only means of subsistence for many was through poor relief. After much public agitation and concern, the Old Age Pension Act (1908) was finally passed. Thus a first major step was taken to make a more adequate provision for the elderly outside the Poor Law.

In recent years the social problems connected with the ageing have attracted more and more attention. There are a number of factors involved – the greater number of people living into their seventies and eighties, the greater affluence of society, which has led to the expectations of higher standards for all members, the increase in mobility which has often led to the isolation of the older generation from the younger members of the family. Moreover, the rapid development of industrialization and the pace of social and economic change has meant that flexibility, enterprise and new ideas are more highly prized in modern society than experience, tradition and stability, with a consequent denigration of the contribution which elderly people can make to the community. Thus not only has the economic and material dependency of the elderly increased quantitatively, but greater social and personal insecurity and lack of status has led to a new quality of need.

The 'problems of old people' are sometimes talked of as though all elderly people were alike and had the same requirements instead of being a category of unique persons differentiated from the rest of the population only by their age. Moreover the rate and effects of ageing vary greatly from person to person, and although there has been an increasing interest in geriatrics by the medical profession in recent years, there is still too little known about the factors involved. In the preceding chapters reference has already been made to a number of ways in which general social provision endeavours to meet some of the needs of elderly people. For example the chronic and degenerative conditions associated with ageing occupy a considerable proportion of the resources of the health service. Private superannuation schemes encouraged by fiscal policy, national insurance retirement pensions and supplementary pensions are designed to help the elderly to obtain at least the necessities of life. The development of a conventional retirement age of sixty-five for men and sixty for women, however, poses problems for many active elderly people able and willing to work either full or part-time. Not only does the tempo of modern industrial life not permit the easy absorption of elderly people into suitable employment, but superannuation and insurance schemes do not give much encouragement to delayed retirement, especially in times of high unemployment. Some firms, local authority welfare departments (now social service departments) and voluntary organizations have undertaken experimental projects for the employment or occupation of elderly people, but these are on a very limited scale.

The provision of housing for the elderly has been an important responsibility of local housing authorities in recent years and specially designed flats and bungalows are part of the building programme of all authorities. The charitable provision of almshouses and homes for the aged antedate statutory provision by many centuries and there are innumerable trusts today, some dating back to the Middle Ages, some of recent foundation, which assist elderly people able to live independently. There is increasing concern that supporting domiciliary services should be available to enable elderly people to live in their own homes for as long as possible. 'Sheltered housing' units, wherein elderly tenants can live independently but have the help and supervision of a warden when necessary, are increasingly being provided either by voluntary trusts or jointly by housing and social service departments. Some old people, however, do not wish to live alone and for others this is impossible or unwise because of increasing infirmity. Since 1948 the responsibility of local authorities under Part III of the National Assistance Act to provide residential accommodation for those who 'by reason of age, infirmity or any other circumstance are in need of care and attention which is not otherwise available to them', has resulted in the provision of many small homes for elderly people. In 1948, when local authorities were faced with discharging this responsibility, they had to make use of many large ex-Poor Law institutions as these were the only buildings available to them. Some of these have been successfully adapted to meet modern requirements, most have now been closed and replaced but for many years some old people have had to live in substandard accommodation. In spite of the policy of keeping old people in their homes for as long as possible, there is a growing demand for residential accommodation for the frail elderly, partly because of the total increase in the numbers of people in the upper age groups, partly because of the increasing practice of active treatment and rehabilitation for patients in hospital geriatric units and partly because of the difficulties which many families experience in looking after their elderly relatives in all social groups. The numbers of those in the population aged over seventy-five went up by 10 per cent between 1971 and 1976 and it is estimated that there will be a further increase of 45 per cent over the next fifteen years (HMSO, 1977).

As with the provision for income maintenance and housing, almost all statutory domiciliary services through which the needs of the elderly may be met come under general legislation – the National Health Service Acts, the Public Health Act (1968) the Chronically Sick and Disabled Persons Act (1970) etc. General practitioners, home nurses, home helps, health visitors, social workers, all contribute to these supporting services. Local authority social service departments may provide day centres, clubs, meals on wheels, aids and adaptations for the infirm, all of which help the elderly to continue to lead an active life in the community for as long as possible and take some of the strain from family and neighbours giving care and support to them. It is estimated that one in eight of the retired population is in contact with either the NHS or a social service department. There is still considerable need for the expansion of the domiciliary services, although, for instance, the numbers receiving home help went up by 20 per cent between 1974 and 1976 (HMSO, 1977).

In the voluntary sphere there has been a great deal of specific provision for elderly people, much of it grant-aided by the local authority. Clubs, social and occupation centres, holidays, outings, friendly visiting, help with shopping and the care of gardens and other forms of assistance are organized in most areas, and many schemes show considerable imagination, understanding and enterprise. Much of this work is carried out by or with the collaboration of Age Concern (formerly Old People's Welfare Committees), but there are many organizations taking part, the Churches, Toc. H, the WRVS, the Red Cross to name only a few. Interestingly enough, much of the impetus for the development of Old People's Welfare Committees came from the Assistance Board in 1940, when the Board took over responsibility for the provision of supplementary assistance to pensioners from the public assistance committees. Until that time many elderly people had a regular weekly contact with the relieving officer through whom they received assistance under the Poor Law, and who was able to keep a friendly eye on their welfare, especially of those living alone. He was able to arrange for medical care, hospitalization or the provision of other services which might be needed. The introduction of supplementary pensions paid through the Post Office and subject only to half-yearly review, meant that a number of old people were left friendless and thus the organization of a friendly visiting service was encouraged. The National Old People's Welfare Committee (now Age Concern), established in 1940, became a national focal point for information and advice on all aspects of the care of the elderly and acted as a pressure group in the interests of old people. The National Corporation for the Care of Old People, set up in 1947 by the trustees of the Nuffield Foundation, has undertaken and grant-aided a variety of experiments for the welfare of the aged and assisted the carrying out of research. Such studies as *Social Welfare for the Elderly* (Harris *et al.*, 1968), *Old People in Three Industrial Societies* (Shanas *et al.*, 1968), as well as numerous publications from Age Concern and the National Corporation, document the needs and provisions for the elderly. All tend to highlight the need for better co-ordination of services and a more efficient deployment of resources. Ideally the elderly person should have a realistic choice of alternatives – for accommodation, for occupation and for social activities. This can only be obtained through a genuine partnership between voluntary and statutory agencies and only if neighbourly services are undertaken not just out of pity, but as the expression of a greater respect for the old as individual people and regarded as full members of the local community, welcomed to all the activities going on *in* the community. We shall then perhaps both individually and collectively cease to think of old age as a problem.

Children and the Family

Statutory authorities and voluntary organizations have for long been interested in the welfare of children. Charities from the Middle Ages onwards provided for the care and education of poor children, while the Poor Law made particular reference to the need to apprentice pauper children so that 'they may get their living when they shall be of age'. In the nineteenth century the Factory Acts developed from attempts to prevent the ill-treatment and abuse of pauper apprentices.

Provision for children in our society has developed partly from a philanthropic concern for the welfare of those who are helpless and so obviously unable to fend for themselves, partly from concern for the workers and citizens of tomorrow upon whom the future safety, prosperity and well-being of the community depends. Linked with this concern was the desire to minimize the cost to the public of deprived and delinquent children and a fear that the young offender of today could become the hardened criminal of tomorrow. These motives gradually offset concern lest State intervention should weaken the responsibility of the family for its members. The idea that children have rights has gradually gained ground. The report of the National Children's Homes in 1884, stated, 'It is quite time that the doctrine of parental rights should not be allowed any longer to be a doctrine of children's wrongs.'

During the past hundred years society has demanded higher and higher standards of education and child care and social, fiscal and industrial policy has increasingly recognized that children are no longer an asset but a social and economic liability to a family. Thus two main trends can be distinguished. First, there is the provision of special services for those children who are neglected, deprived of a normal home life or specially underprivileged in some way. Second, there are those services which have developed to help families to meet the normal needs of the child and adolescent in a rapidly changing industrial society. Many of the latter began as services for the deprived and under-privileged, as attempts to do something to modify the educational, economic and social inequalities of the poorest sections of the population, but have gradually been incor-porated into present-day health, education and welfare services available for all citizens on like terms. The school health service, the provision of school meals, of nursery schools, of holiday homes and school camps and the like began as attempts to improve the physical condition of children in the elementary schools, first by voluntary effort and later by education authorities. They have become increasingly accepted as ancillary education and health services and used by a large proportion of families. In spite of the development of the major services, it seems likely that some children will always need special services and care. It has been the neglected and home-less child who has attracted particular attention and concern.

The Development of the Child Care Service

To cope with a growing problem of deprived and abandoned chil-dren during the nineteenth century, many schools and orphanages were founded, often small and local in character, but towards the end of the century the great national children's organizations began to develop: the National Children's Homes and Orphanages (1869); Dr Barnardo's Homes (1870); the Waifs and Strays (1881); and perhaps most significantly, the National Society for the Prevention of Cruelty to Children, founded in 1884 as a result of pioneer work in America and in Liverpool. Legislation initiated by Lord Shaftesbury and other like minded philanthropists succeeded in establishing some protection of children through the Factory and

Mines Act and the Education Acts. Successive Poor Law enact-
ments endeavoured to improve the lot of the pauper child, particularly after the vigorous criticisms of current practice contained in
the report of the departmental committee 1894.

These developments reflected a growing interest and concern for
children, but it was not until 1889 that the first Act was passed
specifically for the prevention of cruelty to, and the better protection of, children and began the long line of Acts of which the
Children Act (1975) is but the latest. The Act of 1889, although
limited in scope by modern standards, was referred to in Parliament
as the Children's Charter. Subsequent Acts in 1894, 1904, 1908 and
1933, besides liberalizing the treatment of youthful offenders and
setting up juvenile courts, widened the powers of the courts in
regard to children and young people neglected, ill-treated, or in
moral danger, and made it possible for children 'in need of care or
protection' to be committed to the care of a 'fit person' which, under
the Children and Young Persons Act (1933) could be the education
department of a local authority. The year 1926 saw the first legal
recognition of adoption by the Adoption Act of that year and the
protection of children fostered privately for reward, which had
developed from the Infant Life Protection Act (1872) was incorporated in the Public Health Act (1936).

As in other areas of social welfare, two world wars led to the
acceptance of an increase in responsibility by the State for children.
For instance, the First World War led to the Maternity and Child
Welfare Act (1918) and to the institution of a special welfare
service by the Ministry of Pensions for war orphans, and the Second
World War saw an extension of care by the local authorities and the
Ministry of Health through the operation of the evacuation scheme
and all that that implied. The general disruption of family life
caused by wartime conditions led to a much greater need for substitute care for children by voluntary societies as well as by public
authorities. The subsequent quantity and quality of alternative care
gave rise to mounting public anxiety, leading in 1945 to the
setting-up of an inter-departmental committee under the chairmanship of Miss Myra Curtis (HMSO, 1946)

> to inquire into existing methods of providing for children who
> from loss of parents or from any cause whatever are deprived
> of a normal home life with their own parents or relatives; and

to consider what further measures should be taken to ensure that these children are brought up under conditions best calculated to compensate them for the lack of parental care.

The report of the committee the following year showed the multiplicity of authorities, both voluntary and statutory, responsible for the care of deprived children; the startling variations in methods and quality of care; and the almost complete lack of trained social workers and residential staffs in the whole of this important field. The committee recommended a simplification of administration and a clear-cut responsibility for any child deprived of a normal home life, the adoption of a policy of boarding out as a more acceptable method of alternative care than the children's home or institution, and the urgent necessity for providing professional training of a high standard for child-care workers. The committee urged the necessity for a special local authority committee to be set up to take responsibility

> based in part on the need we feel for emphasizing the function of home-finding as something separate and distinct from the education and health services given to all children; but in part also on our desire that it should have its own executive officer with the standing of an important official of the council, in direct touch with the responsible committee. . . . Throughout our investigation we have been increasingly impressed by the need for the personal element in the care of children.

Most of the recommendations of the committee were accepted by the government and embodied in the Children Act (1948), which made it the duty of the major authorities to appoint a children's committee with a special department headed by a children's officer. It was the responsibility of the authority

> to receive into their care, where it appears to the Local Authority that their intervention is necessary in the interests of the welfare of the child, any child in their area under the age of 17 years who has no parents or guardians or has been abandoned or lost or whose parents or guardians are prevented, for the time being or permanently, from providing for his proper accommodation, maintenance and upbringing.

After the Children Act (1948) the child care service developed
rapidly. According to Heywood (1959)

> The new Children Act, 1948 provided a framework based on
> principles of administrative unity, individual need and the
> value of the natural family which were new in the legislation
> for deprived children. These principles themselves, and the
> insight of the new administration, stimulated a development
> in the service which led very quickly to change, to awareness
> of the best form of treatment for the child and later to an
> emphasis on the conditions leading to the deprivation, and
> the prevention of them.

This is perhaps too optimistic a view of the development of
the service in the 1950s and 1960s, but the rapid growth and
subsequent publication of research into the physical, emotional
and social growth of infants typified by the work of John Bowlby,
had a considerable effect on the aims and methods of work of
children's departments. Dr Bowlby's publications (Bowlby and
Fry, 1955) came at a time when the new service was still very
much in a formative stage and affected its development in a number
of ways.

Thus in the attempt to give children the best substitute family
care, following the recommendations of the Curtis Committee,
child care workers stressed the advantages of fostering in a 'normal'
home. Because, however, the impossibility and indeed the unde-
sirability of providing for all children in this way necessitated the
continuation of some form of group care, children's departments
developed the small residential family unit scattered through the
area and usually in charge of a married couple as house parents, as
the typical pattern of residential care. But, even more significant for
future developments, increasing recognition of the importance to a
child of his own parents, inadequate though they might be, led to
renewed efforts to care for neglected children within their own
families, and thus prevent family break-up whenever possible. Even
in the late 1940s the work of the Pacifist Service Units (later the
Family Service Units) with 'problem families' and the investigation of
the Women's Group on Public Welfare and subsequent report *The
Neglected Child and His Family* (WGPW, 1948) had helped to focus
attention on the possibility of preventative measures and of working
with the family to enable it to stay together. During the 1950s there

was increasing emphasis on work with families primarily through a more co-ordinated and intensive use of existing services such as the work of health visitors, school welfare officers, the NSPCC, and other problem family workers as well as the child care officers. Experience, however, suggested that further provision was needed and so the departmental committee set up in 1957, under the chairmanship of Viscount Ingleby, to inquire into the working of the law relating to juvenile courts and the care and treatment of young delinquents, was asked in its terms of reference (HMSO, 1960) to consider

> whether local authorities responsible for the child under the Children Act, 1948, in England and Wales should, taking into account action by voluntary organizations and the responsibilities of existing services, be given new powers and duties to prevent or forestall the suffering of children through neglect in their own homes.

In their report in 1960, the committee examined the existing provisions and discussed the factors involved, suggesting that

> much of the difficulty which at present exists, apart from that attributable to the shortage of skilled casework staff, is due to inter-service rivalries and above all to failure to analyse the different processes involved . . . it is most important too that arrangements should be made for making the services known to the public and for giving advice so that individuals know where they can apply for help.

The Children and Young Persons Act (1963), which implemented the main recommendations of the committee, confirmed and extended the power of local authorities to take action to prevent or remove conditions that might result in children coming into or remaining in care or being brought before a juvenile court whether as offenders or as in need of care or protection. Under Section 1 it became the duty of the local authority to ensure that the necessary advice, guidance or assistance (which could be in kind or exceptionally in cash) was provided either directly through one or other of their own services or indirectly through a voluntary organization. Although neither the report nor the Act went nearly as far as some child care and other workers hoped – indeed not nearly as far as the much more radical Kilbrandon report on services in Scotland in

1964 – the local authorities in England and Wales were given clear powers for extending their work with children and families.

However, in tracing these developments in social policy, it is important to note the implied connection between child neglect and deprivation on the one hand and juvenile delinquency on the other. Although the child care service set up in 1948 was at first only peripherally concerned with delinquents, experience of working with families and a steady spate of research reports seemed to suggest that delinquent children were 'no different' from deprived children who had not been in trouble with the law. They, too, were victims of family and environmental circumstances and suffered from broken, neglectful or unhappy homes. The rising incidence of juvenile crime in the late 1950s and 1960s caused considerable public concern and, as discussed in Chapter 10, a number of reports were issued attempting to analyse and suggest remedies for the problem. Thus two government White Papers, *The Child, the Family and the Young Offender* (HMSO, 1965) and *Children in Trouble* (HMSO, 1968) were both based on the assumption that there was a strong causal connection between juvenile delinquency and unsatisfactory home conditions. However, both aroused considerable debate, a debate which still continues based on different assumptions about the main cause of juvenile crime and best methods to deal with young offenders. One of the points at issue was the extent of the involvement of the child care service as opposed, for instance, to the probation service in both the prevention of delinquency and the 'treatment' of juvenile offenders. The Children and Young Persons Act (1969) which closely followed the philosophy and recommendations of *Children in Trouble* was largely a compromise between opposing points of view. The Act retained the juvenile court system of dealing with both criminal and care cases, but its provisions sought to prevent as many children as possible from appearing in the courts and blurred the distinction between offenders and non-offenders by instituting common court procedures and requiring common care and treatment facilities.

The emphasis upon the family origins of juvenile delinquency current in the 1960s 'had highlighted the inadequacies of the personal social services, divided by their specialisms and hence often unable to help the family as a whole' (Packman, 1975). Hence one of the most fruitful ways of bringing down the level of juvenile crime as well as preventing the necessity of taking as many children into care because of deprivation or neglect was seen to be the creation of a real 'family service'. Thus, the 1969 Act depended for its success upon the basic restructuring of the personal social services, as recommended by the Seebohm Committee.

In spite of the re-organization of the personal social services under the Local Government (Social Services) Act (1970), there is much criticism of the 1969 Act, particularly in view of the fact that juvenile delinquency appears to be increasing rather than diminishing. Part of the difficulty arises because the Act has not yet been fully implemented, partly because of the shortage of trained social workers; partly because of the lack of adequate residential accommodation – particularly of facilities for seriously disturbed and aggressive youngsters; and perhaps because of poor communications between magistrates and social workers.

It is perhaps ironic, as Packman has pointed out, that 'Developments in prevention and work with delinquency not only strained, modified and redefined the original aims and methods of the child care service; they also contributed to its demise' (Packman, 1975). A department which was primarily set up to provide good alternative care for children deprived of a normal home life, was absorbed less than twenty-five years later into a social service department whose powers and responsibilities went beyond those even of a comprehensive family service.

Yet at the same time as the new social service departments were being set up, concern was mounting as some children seemed to be suffering because bonds with parents appeared to be too tenaciously preserved. Scandals concerning children ill-treated or killed by parents and well-publicized 'tug-of-love' cases in fostering, adoption, divorce and custody proceedings suggested that the rights of the child over parental 'wrongs' should once more be asserted and new legislation brought in to redress the balance. The report of the Houghton Committee (HMSO, 1972) reflected much of the disquiet over the existing law and practice, and the Children Act (1975) was the outcome of much discussion and controversy. It is concerned with integrating adoption services within the mainstream of child care provision, with more stringent requirements for the registration of voluntary agencies, and with measures designed to protect the welfare of children in care, providing them with greater security. The new clauses should make it possible to make long-term plans for at least some of the children in care, despite parental opposition or indifference. In spite of the remedial and preventive work done by social workers in the new departments there were in 1976 more than 100,000 in the care of local authorities in England, an increase of 13,000 since 1971. There were fewer admissions to care because of the death or illness of a parent, and fewer admissions because of homelessness, but an increased number of admissions following court appearances, apparently a direct result of the new responsibilities of the local authorities as a result of the Children and Young Persons Act (1969) (HMSO, 1977).

Working with children and families illustrates, perhaps more acutely than any other area of need, the dilemmas facing the social service departments of local authorities. Public opinion tends to put the blame on the departments and their workers whenever a child is injured or dies from neglect or ill-treatment. Yet the same public opinion is quick to resent any so-called 'interference' by officials and social workers in the personal affairs of individuals and families, and reluctant to provide adequate resources for the help and support of those who are often the most vulnerable in the community. During the past thirty years a considerable amount of knowledge and experience has been gained in the whole field of child care and there are some, including many social workers, who feel that this expertise is in danger of being lost with the manifold responsibilities of the new departments. But as Packman points out (1975) the task set the children's departments in 1948 was clear cut and circumscribed.

> Children deprived of a normal home life were to be provided with good substitute care by a new professional, personal service. . . .Experience and training taught social workers that the needs of deprived children were subtle, complex and difficult to assess and that provision to meet these needs must necessarily be flexible and varied. There were no simple problems nor simple answers . . . what is expected of services for deprived children today and of the social worker who staffs them, is much more ambitious and difficult than was the case in 1948.

The creation of social service departments provides an opportunity for a much more comprehensive and flexible approach to the support and help of families in need, whether or not that need arises from, or is exacerbated by, material deprivation.

Seebohm and After

This necessarily brief account of the development of services for certain vulnerable groups in society may perhaps indicate the piecemeal way in which legislation has been passed and implemented. By the mid-1960s there was growing dissatisfaction with the inadequacies of the various services and particularly with the overlapping and inefficiency of the existing organization of these services. The administrative specialization which existed did not appear to be based on any clear and coherent principle and took little account of the family unit as a whole. The proliferation of field workers within the different departments meant that a number of workers might all be concerned with the welfare of one family but co-ordinating machinery and co-operation between services did not seem to be effective. Contact between worker and client too often centred on the necessity of establishing eligibility for the service by that particular department rather than on a constructive and helpful exploration of the needs of the individual or family.

In 1965 the government appointed an inter-departmental committee under the chairmanship of Sir Frederick Seebohm. Its brief (HMSO, 1968b) was 'to review the organization and responsibilities of the local authority personal social services in England and Wales, and to consider what changes are desirable to secure an effective family service'. After more than two years of investigation, including taking evidence from some 450 to 500 individuals and bodies, the committee findings were published in 1968 and provoked a wide-ranging debate which eventually led to the passing of the Local Authority (Social Services) Act (1970).

The committee's recommendation that radical organizational change was necessary was based on a number of factors: that personal needs must be met on the overall requirements of the individual or family rather than on the basis of a limited set of symptoms; that there must be a clear pattern of responsibility and accountability; that fragmented services were not in a strong position for bargaining for scarce resources and that a comprehensive service could use resources more effectively to meet need and could provide more efficient machinery for the collection and dissemination of information and for monitoring the service provided. The committee emphasized that help from the new service must be both accessible and acceptable to those in need and must be community based.

The committee therefore advocated the establishment of a new unified and comprehensive social service department to meet the social needs of individuals, families and communities. This would incorporate the existing functions of children's and welfare departments, together with certain responsibilities of the local authority health departments – notably those covering community provision for the mentally ill and handicapped, home helps and day care for young children. The new departments should be the responsibility of a statutory social services committee of the major local authorities. Generally the response to the proposals of the committee was favourable, although there was some disquiet at a possible re-organization in advance of the radical reform of local government and of the national health service, both of which were under discussion. Some of the severest criticism of the recommendations came from the local medical officers of health, who stood to lose a considerable number of their responsibilities in advance of any new function which might be given them in a re-organized national health service. Although some social workers were apprehensive at the wider responsibilities that might come their way if the recommendations were implemented, most welcomed the proposals. Indeed the Seebohm Report has been called 'a Social Workers' charter' for it recommended a much better career structure for social workers, who were seen as the key occupational group in the new departments from whom the chief officers would be drawn whenever possible. Many social workers, therefore, who had been irked by the widespread view of social work as a 'supplementary' or 'ancillary' occupation, subordinate to other professions, now felt that the time had come for them to be accepted as a full and independent profession.

As already mentioned, the main recommendations for re-organization were implemented by the Local Authority (Social Services) Act (1970) and came into effect a year later. Unlike the Social Work (Scotland) Act (1968), it gave no additional general powers or duties to the local authorities, concentrating as it did on the actual amalgamation of the existing services. The structure of the new department, its methods of work and procedures were left to the initiative of the new committees of the local authorities themselves. The Act did, however, make it possible for the responsibility for the promotion, monitoring and accreditation of professional social work training courses to be in the hands of one body in the future – the Central Council for the Education and Training of Social Workers – and for the setting-up of an advisory Personal Social Services Council, established in 1973.

Those responsible for the creation of the new departments had a formidable task. They not only had to devise a new organizational structure to meet the demands of a service now providing a wide range of facilities – residential establishments, day care and social centres, fieldwork teams, etc., but to reconcile differing administrative procedures and regulations, eligibility rules and philosophies. What for instance was to be the role of social workers in the new department? What methods were they to be encouraged to use – mainly traditional case work or should they be helped to acquire skills in group and community work? What was to be the place of residential provision in the total service to be provided? How far should the department be involved in community development, committed as it was to a policy of community care for the groups of vulnerable people for whom it was responsible?

Moreover, the new departments had to assume new responsibilities under the Children and Young Persons Act (1969) and the Chronically Sick and Disabled Persons Act (1970) at a time when senior officers, social workers, residential and clerical staff were coming to terms with the new organization. The difficulties of the departments were further aggravated by the re-organization of local government brought about by the Local Government Act (1972) and radical changes in the structure of the National Health Service by the National Health Service (Re-organization) Act (1973). It is not surprising that there have been considerable criticisms levelled against the departments involving charges of low standards, inadequate service, delay in meeting established need or the slow implementation of new legislation. It is easy to criticize but more difficult to know how far these charges are justified, and, if they are, whether inadequacies are in fact due to fundamental weaknesses inherent in the re-organization itself or to temporary difficulties which will disappear with more stable conditions. Inflation and the economic depression of the mid-1970s have not made the task of the local authority any easier.

References

Bowlby, J. and Fry, M. (1955), *Child Care and the Growth of Love*, Penguin.

Ennals, D. (1977), *Hansard*, 933 122.

Gostin, L. O. (1977), *A Human Condition MIND* special report.

Harris, A. (1971), *The Handicapped and Impaired in Britain,* Social Survey Division of the Office of Population Census and Surveys, HMSO.

HMSO (1946), *Report of the Care of Children Committee*, Cmd 6922.

HMSO (1957), *Report of the Royal Commission on the Law relating to Mental Illness and Mental Deficiency*, Cmnd 169.

HMSO (1959), *Report of the Working Party on Social Workers in the Local Authority Health and Welfare Services*.

HMSO (1960), *Report of the Committee on Children and Young Persons*, Cmnd 1191.

HMSO (1965), *The Child, the Family and the Young Offender*, Cmnd 2742.

HMSO (1968a), *Children in Trouble*, Cmnd 3601.

HMSO (1968b), *Report of the Committee on Local Authority and Allied Personal Social Services*, Cmnd 3703 (Seebohm Report).

HMSO (1971), *Better Services for the Mentally Handicapped*, Cmnd 4683.

HMSO (1972), *Report of the Departmental Committee on the Adoption of Children*, Cmnd 5107.

HMSO (1976), *A Review of the Mental Health Act, 1959*.

HMSO (1976), *Social Trends*.

Heywood, J. S. (1959), *Children in Care*, Routledge & Kegan Paul.

Jones, K. (1960), *Mental Health and Social Policy*, Routledge & Kegan Paul.

Martin, F. M. (1975), 'Social factors in the aetiology of mental illness', in a discussion paper *Aspects of the Social Care of the Mentally Ill*, British Association of Social Workers.

Packman, J. (1975), *The Child's Generation*, Basil Blackwell and Martin Robertson.

Sainsbury, S. (1968), *Registered Disabled*, G. Bell & Sons.

Titmuss, R. M. (1968), *Commitment to Welfare*, Allen & Unwin.

Women's Group on Public Welfare (1948), *The Neglected Child and his Family*, Oxford University Press.

9

Social Policy in Relation to Crime

Philip T. Bean

Crime, Social Policy and the Penal System

The link between criminology, and social policy and administration (and criminology for these purposes means the study of crime and the penal system), has existed since social administration became a recognized academic discipline. The link at one level is obvious, for whilst social administration is primarily concerned with the study of social problems, criminology itself is concerned with one of the major social problems of our age. All modern industrial societies have high levels of crime, and it seems that this will remain so, at least in the foreseeable future. In so far as a solution appears to be possible, the aim is not to eradicate crime, but to strive for a more acceptable level. Whether an acceptable level can be realistically achieved, or indeed whether it is possible to decide what actually constitutes an acceptable level must be a matter for public debate. At this stage, crime appears as one of those intractable problems which has no immediate solution.

The link between social problems and crime, and between social administration and criminology should not, however, be taken too far. Crime may be a social problem but it is a social problem with a difference. There are two reasons for saying this. First, that individual crimes may be regarded as a social problem but it is the level of crime which really constitutes the problem. Emile Durkheim (1964) once observed that crime was normal in so far as it was to be expected in all societies. He said it was abnormal if it was too high and it was also abnormal if too low – both conditions he regarded as pathological. Unfortunately he nowhere gave any indication as to what could be regarded as a normal or healthy level of crime, although presumably he would regard the current level as too high. Now Durkheim was not saying that criminals were normal, he was merely drawing attention to the presence of crime in all societies. Notice that Durkheim regarded a low level of crime as equally pathological, for he thought that under those conditions people would be bound too tightly to the existing social order. Society would then be stagnant. Normal crime was functional to a healthy society for it demonstrated that social change was possible.

The second reason is more pertinent. Everyone who breaks legal rules is likely to be prosecuted and likely to be sentenced by the courts and punished. This feature introduces a different component and adds a new dimension which is absent from all other social problems. Legal rules are unique social rules in our society, they are backed by a coercive apparatus rendering persons who break them liable to judicial control. Built into a study of crime, therefore, must be a recognition that there is an institutional response which would involve the full powers of the State – even to the extent of detaining offenders for long periods in prisons or in some rare instances involving capital punishment. These institutional responses vary with each society, and within each society over a period of time. The response to crime in Britain differs from the response elsewhere, and the modern response differs from that of earlier periods. These earlier responses would now be regarded as inhuman although nineteenth-century penologists would doubtless find features of our modern penal system open to criticism; they would regard many aspects as wasteful in terms of time and resources. They may even criticize the current lack of concern shown to the criminals' victim. We may criticize many of the earlier responses, but it is as well to recognize that our own is not above censure.

These two special features of crime will be considered, sometimes obliquely, throughout this chapter, particularly in those sections related to the penal system. In the early part of the chapter consideration will be given to examining the extent of crime; this will be followed by a brief examination of the sentencing practices, and then some of the major philosophies of the penal system will be considered. The final section will be devoted to the juvenile offender. In order to understand the influence or effect that crime has on modern society we need to ask about the nature and extent of crime. The central question is, therefore, 'How much crime exists within a given society or social group?' and, following from this, is the trend towards an increase or decrease? What is equally important for our purposes is to ask about the type of offenders being convicted. Or, to put the question another way, will the penal system be able to cope with a possible increase in offenders? All these questions are basic to any study of crime.

How Much Crime?

The major source of information available is the criminal statistics for England and Wales which are published annually and provide data on the crimes known to the police and those which are cleared up, i.e. generally speaking, those which lead to a successful prosecution.[1] In the criminal statistics a distinction is made between indictable and non-indictable offences, the latter being regarded as the least serious, e.g. minor motoring offences, drunkenness, etc. We shall be concerned mainly with the more serious, i.e. the indictable offences. In 1975 there was a total of 2,105,631 indictable offences known to the police in England and Wales, and of these, 44 per cent were cleared up (HMSO, 1975). In that year the number of indictable offences known to the police exceeded 2 million for the first time. The criminal statistics now classify indictable offences into eight separate categories. Table 11 shows the number of indictable offences known to the police according to each category for the years 1971 and 1975 respectively, and also shows the percentage cleared up.

Three general points can be made from this table. First the number of indictable *offences* should not be confused with the number of *offenders* convicted on indictable offences. This table refers to the former, which are likely to be the most numerous. Second there was an increase in the number of offences involving violence and robbery. This general increase is a continuation of the trend which began in 1954 and which has produced an annual increase of about 6 per cent. (There were exceptions: 1972 and 1973 showed a small percentage decrease but the upward trend was resumed in 1974.) The third point concerns the figures for criminal damage, which appeared to reflect a 300 per cent increase from 1971 to 1974. These figures should be interpreted with some reser-

Table 11   Number of indictable offences in England and Wales known to the police, according to category for 1971 and 1975, and percentage cleared up

Offence category	No. indictable offences 1971	% cleared up in 1971	No. indictable offences 1975	% cleared up in 1975
Violence against the person	47,036	82	71,002	81
Sexual offences	23,621	76	23,731	78
Burglary	451,537	37	521,867	34
Robbery	7,465	42	11,311	40
Theft and handling stolen goods	1,003,645	43	1,267,674	41
Fraud and forgery	99,789	83	123,055	85
Criminal damage	26,995	34	78,546	37
Other indictable offences	5,575	92	8,445	92
Total:	1,665,663	45	2,105,631	44

Source: Criminal Statistics, 1975, Tables 2.1 and 2.4.

vations, for the increase is almost certainly the result in part of changes in the legal definition of criminal damage, thereby automatically increasing the numbers of indictable criminal damage offences.

A more substantial feature of the table concerns the clear-up rate. The percentage of indictable offences cleared up in 1971 was 45 per cent compared with 44 per cent in 1975. Or put another way, more than half the indictable offences known to the police remained undetected. In spite of the large increase in crimes the clear-up rate remained steady, a result in part, perhaps of the efficiency of the police. However, the percentage of crimes cleared up varied within each category, being as high as 92 per cent for 'other indictable offences,' i.e. blackmail, perjury, etc., to 34 per cent for burglary. (In London the clear-up rate for burglary is down to 26 per cent, whilst the clear-up rate for murder in England and Wales, which is included in this category of violence against the person, is 93 per cent.)

Variations in the clear-up rate reflect numerous factors. Some relate to the high priority given by the police to certain crimes: murder for example, whereas minor thefts have low priority. Other factors relate to the comparative ease of detection: violence against the person has a high clear-up rate, for the victim and assailant invariably had an established relationship prior to the offence being committed. This feature also helps explain the high clear-up rate for murder: about 65 per cent of all murders occur within the family. Conversely, burglary has a low clear-up rate where the difficulties of detection are immense and often depend on chance happenings or the willingness of others to assist the police.

With an overall clear-up rate of 44 per cent theories derived from studies of convicted offenders should be treated with caution, since those arrested may produce an unrepresentative sample. One criminologist, David Matza (1964), regards the convicted criminal as suffering from bad timing, in that those convicted are simply unlucky or perhaps less intelligent than those who do not get arrested. One need not wholly accept Matza's argument to see some validity in his statement. Offences which are spontaneous and have a high visibility – i.e. committed in a public place – are much more likely to be detected or reported than those requiring careful planning and have low visibility – fraud, for example. Areas with high crime rates tend to be patrolled more regularly than those with lower rates, whilst children who come from unfavourable backgrounds are more likely to be prosecuted than their more favourable located counterparts.[2] 'Bad timing' means more than being unlucky, it becomes more related to factors such as the visibility and the nature of the offence, the area in which the person lives and the person's social background.

The number of crimes known to the police does not, of course, provide an answer to the question about the extent of crime in a society. Crimes known to the police are merely crimes which the police have reported to them or they discover themselves. Many crimes are never reported. Sir Leon Radzinowicz (1964) has suggested that only about 15 per cent of all indictable crimes committed in England and Wales are known to the police, whilst Howard Jones (1965) puts the figure at 25 per cent. This dark figure, or hidden figure of crime – as it is sometimes called – varies according to the offence.

Radzinowicz says in respect of sexual offences that offences such as indecent assault are rarely reported, and neither are some of the more serious such as rape. Shoplifting is probably grossly underreported as is domestic violence and perhaps even burglary (Hood and Sparks, 1970).

There are a number of reasons why crimes remain hidden. First, there are those instances where the victim may choose not to report the offence, perhaps because he does not wish to be involved in the court proceedings, or he may wish to avoid any likely publicity. Alternatively he may not report because he does not regard the matter as part of his duty to report offenders, or he may simply feel sympathy for the offender, particularly if the offender was a child or an elderly person. These reasons would equally apply to those who were not victims, but who nevertheless know that an offence had been committed.

Secondly, there are those types of offences where there is no recognized victim. These victimless crimes, which are defined as those involving a willing exchange of prohibited goods and services, involve criminal acts where the persons concerned are both intent on avoiding detection (Schur, 1965). The sale of prohibited drugs, certain forms of gross indecency, or homosexual practice are examples of victimless crimes. So too are blackmail, or handling stolen goods. Detection of these types of crimes are often too difficult and yet paradoxically they have a high clear-up rate because it is only at the point of detection that the crimes actually become known to the police.

Finally there are those crimes which are not victimless, but occur where only the criminal knows that the offence has been committed. Shoplifting is an obvious example, but so too is murder, particularly when the victim is a member of a family suffering from, say, a terminal disease. Motoring offences, and particularly drunken-driving offences are further examples of crime being committed where the criminal may be the only person who knows of the existence of the offence. In addition there are special cases where the police themselves decide not to prosecute if the information provided leads to the arrest of more serious offenders. This involves a sophisticated form of plea bargaining where one offence is traded off against others regarded as more worthy of prosecution. Also there are cases where the Director of Public Prosecutions decides not to prosecute if prosecution is adjudged not to be in the public interest.[3]

These examples are not intended to be exhaustive, merely to demonstrate why hidden crime remains high. It is possible that every adult over the prosecutable age in our society has, or will at some stage, commit a crime, perhaps even an indictable crime, and will almost certainly do so if he is a motorist. Hence Matza's comment about 'bad timing' and the difficulty of ever establishing the nature and extent of criminality in our society. Instead of asking who are the criminals, it sometimes seems more worthwhile to ask who are not, for the latter appear to be in the minority. In social terms, the high crime rate has certain important repercussions. 'Living with crime' becomes a feature of our lives, for so much of what we do is aimed at avoiding being a victim. In the obvious and personal sense women and young children always regard themselves as vulnerable, but for others too, private possessions need to be guarded and areas of cities with high levels of violence have to be avoided or carefully negotiated. Yet paradoxically there are high social gains. An industry of crime prevention has developed which includes professional security guards, store detectives, as well as police and criminal lawyers, all depending for their existence on the threat posed by the criminal. Crime may be a social problem, but it involves large vested interests. Some criminologists talk of a trade in crime and note that it is lucrative. This argument is not new: Marx observed that the police and the locksmith are dependent on the exploits of the criminal, and if he were alive today, he would doubtless have included the probation officer, the prison officer, a variety of social workers and the criminologist.

The Method of Sentencing Offenders

All offenders over the age of ten (the prosecutable age, or the age of criminal responsibility as it is often called) are likely to appear before a court to be tried or sentenced.[4] Briefly there are two main kinds of courts in England and Wales: the magistrates' courts, which for these purposes include the juvenile courts who deal with offenders under the age of seventeen; and the higher courts such as the crown courts, as they are now called, which deal with all serious offenders. These higher courts also deal with appeals from the lower courts, and all offenders who could be dealt with by a magistrate's court but who exercise their right to be tried by a judge and jury. The new crown courts replaced the older quarter sessions and assizes.

In England and Wales there are more than 1,000 magistrates' courts, most presided over by unpaid justices whose office dates back to the fourteenth century. In some larger cities, particularly London, the magistrates are stipendiary – full-time salaried lawyers – who owe their office to a public enquiry in Middlesex in the nineteenth century which found that many of the lay justices were corrupt![5] The magistrates' courts deal with all the non-indictable offences – there were 1,652,825 non-indictable offences dealt with in 1976, together with many indictable offences (HMSO, 1976a). In fact almost 90 per cent of all offenders appearing at courts are sentenced by the magistrates. In terms of offenders, as opposed to offences, in 1970 for example, 350,705 persons appeared in magistrates' courts, facing one or more charges for indictable offences, and only 42,852 or about 10 per cent were committed to the high courts (Bottomley, 1973). The magistrates' courts, therefore, have a key role to play in the sentencing process.

There are no national surveys of the proportions of defendants who plead guilty in cases tried by the magistrates' courts, although numerous estimates, sometimes based on small research studies, indicate that the proportion is about 90 per cent. More certain information is available for the higher courts, where about 75 per cent plead guilty. The figures vary according to different areas of the country, being much lower in London (about 52 per cent) but higher in Liverpool, Leeds and Birmingham. The figures also vary according to the type of offence; about 96 per cent of those charged with burglary plead guilty, compared with about 45 per cent of those charged with malicious woundings and about 25 per cent of those charged with indecent assault on young girls (Bottomley, 1973). It needs to be emphasized, therefore, that changes in the numbers of persons pleading guilty would seriously affect the criminal justice system in England and Wales, for if the percentage of not guilty pleas were to increase, the courts would face a long backlog of cases resulting in lengthy delays for defendants awaiting trial.

Many features of the modern penal system have been introduced since the end of the Second World War, although others, such as the prisons, have their origins in the Middle Ages. Jury trial was introduced by Henry II (Devlin, 1966), whilst the police and probation systems are by comparison of recent origin, the police force being established in 1845 and the probation service was officially created by the 1908 Probation and Offenders Act, although the equivalent of the modern probation officers had practised in the courts since about 1870 as court missionaries. Conversely detention centres were provided much later under the 1948 Criminal Justice Act, whilst deferred sentences and community service orders were introduced in 1972. The modern penal system is, therefore, an amalgam of institutions which developed at different points in time and as a result of different responses to crime. Below is a table which provides information on the various sentences available and compares the numbers sentenced for 1950 and 1975, and shows the pattern of sentencing for 1976.

Attempts to understand the modern penal system must, therefore, be related to the historical antecedents of the various institutions concerned. The range and the diversity of these institutions makes it difficult to comprehend them, and difficult enough to do so within their historical frameworks – the precise origins of the jury system and the numbers of jurors involved, for example, are still open to speculation. Yet the greatest difficulty is to interpret the present-day aims of the various institutions. Is imprisonment meant to be a deterrent, an opportunity for reforming the individual, or simply a form of removing the offenders for the protection of the public? Is probation simply a method of supervision for an offender in the community, or is it a means of providing help or therapy, or

Table 12 Types of sentence, availability, and numbers sentenced for indictable offences, England and Wales, 1950 and 1975

Type of sentence	For whom available in 1975 (age groups)	When introduced	Nos. sentenced (for indictable offenders only)	
			1950	1975
Absolute/conditional discharge	All offenders	Criminal Justice Act 1948 (Section 7(1))	16,112	54,813
Attendance centre order	All offenders under the age of 21	Criminal Justice Act 1948 (Section 19)	No facilities available by 1950	8,061
Borstal training	Offenders between ages of 15 and 21	Prevention of Crime Act 1908, but largely amended by the Criminal Justice Act 1961	1,418	8,978
Care order	Offenders up to the age of 17	Children and Young Persons Act 1969, (Section 7 and 20)	–	7,187
Community service order	Offenders over the age of 17	Criminal Act 1972 (Section 15)	–	3,126
Detention centre	Offenders aged 14 to 21 years	Criminal Justice Act 1948 (Section 20)	No detention centres available until 1952	10,119

Fine	All offenders	Origins in antiquity but substantially extended by Criminal Justice Act 1948 (Section 13)	35,716	206,771
Hospital order	All offenders	Mental Health Act 1959 (Sections 60 and 65)	—	865
Prison (immediate)	All offenders over the age of 17	Origins in antiquity, various amendments, but main changes in 19th century, particularly from 1877	20,977	32,558
Prison (suspended)	All offenders over the age of 17	Criminal Justice Act 1967 (Section 39)	—	27,274
Probation order	All offenders over the age of 17	Probation of First Offenders Act 1887, but substantially altered by the Criminal Justice Act 1948 (Section 3)	27,619	25,483
Supervision order	All offenders under the age of 17	Children and Young Persons Act 1969 (Section 13)	—	17,429
Deferred sentence	All offenders	Criminal Justice Act 1972 (Section 22)	—	10,244
Suspended sentences with supervision order	All offenders over the age of 17	Criminal Justice Act 1972 (Section 12)	—	2,381

Source: *Criminal Statistics 1950*, Cmd 8301 and *Criminal Statistics 1975*, Cmnd 6566.

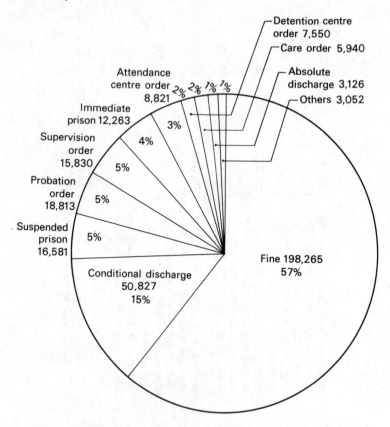

Figure 2   Sentencing by magistrates' courts for indictable offences, 1976, for England and Wales
Source: Adapted from *Criminal Statistics*, 1976

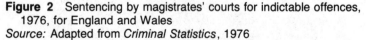

just a system of punishment? An examination of the judiciary's reasons for sentencing offenders may not provide answers to these questions, for numerous aims seem to exist in sentencing: some may operate together, so that, for example, a sentence of imprisonment may involve deterrence, retribution and an opportunity to provide treatment.

A further complication surrounds the official aims of the institutions, which appear at one level to be contradictory or at least capable of revision. Consider, for example, Rule 1 of the Prison Rules (1964) for England and Wales which states 'the purpose of

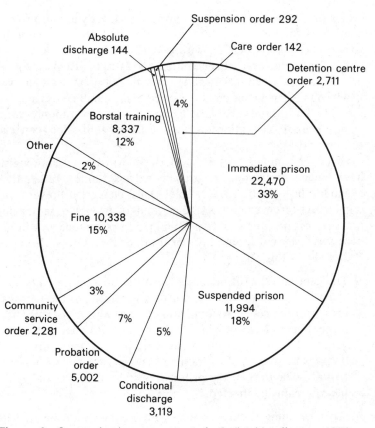

Figure 3   Sentencing by crown courts for indictable offences, 1976,
   for England and Wales
Source: Adapted from *Criminal Statistics*, 1976

the training and treatment of convicted offenders shall be to
encourage and assist them to lead a good and useful life.' Such an
aim is not only ambitious but confusing also, for it avoids consideration of the basic feature of all custodial sentences: simply to detain
offenders for defined periods. In more realistic tones, the Home
Office publication (HMSO, 1969) *People in Prison* says 'few large
organizations have only one aim and it often obscures the real
situation to try to bring all the activities of any one of them within
one simple formula or slogan'. It than summarizes the aims of
imprisonment as follows: 'first it is the task of the [prison] service

under the law to hold those committed to custody and to provide conditions for their detention which are currently acceptable to society. Second, in dealing with convicted offenders there is an obligation on the service to encourage and assist them to lead a good and useful life.' Even so, this statement still fails to indicate the way in which these two aims could be successfully combined, if at all. It merely demonstrates the varied nature of the institutions, warns against over-simplification and shows that generalizations can lead to obscurity.

Given the complexity of the modern penal system, criminologists have tended to examine separate penal institutions, rather than examine the system as a whole. This does not prevent the criminologist from examining the methods of disposal or sentencing practices of the courts, but an examination of sentencing will not necessarily say much about the institutions themselves. *People in Prison* shows this clearly:

> The general aims [of prison] govern the treatment of *all* convicted offenders and do not vary according to the reasons for which the courts send any one to custody. A court may properly pass a custodial sentence on one offender to act as a general deterrent . . . and on another because the court believes he is in need of training that can be given to him in custody. The duty of the prison service in respect of each of them remains unaffected.

In short, the aims of those passing sentence may not coincide with the aims of the institutions to which the offenders are sent.

The sentencing practices in respect of persons sentenced for indictable offences by the magistrates and crown courts in England and Wales for 1976, are shown in Figs 2 and 3. These are for persons sentenced for indictable offences and again should not be confused with the number of indictable offences mentioned earlier.

There are differences in the percentages sentenced to imprisonment between the magistrates' and crown courts. These differences certainly reflect the severity of the offences, and even with the crown courts, the upper band crown courts would sentence fewer offenders to a fine than the lower band.[6] Even so, the modal penalty – that which occurs most often – is clearly shown in both figures to be the fine, with 198,265 offenders with indictable offences being fined by the magistrates' courts and 10,338 in the crown courts in

1976, making 208,603 out of a total of 414,856, or about 50 per cent. For offenders convicted of indictable offences, the percentage fined in the magistrates' courts is about 96 per cent. If an aggregate is taken of the offenders with non-indictable offences and those with indictable offences the fine emerges as the most common penalty. This percentage has remained relatively steady, at least since 1964, when detailed records began to be collected on sentencing patterns.

This general stability is the most common feature of our sentencing practices. Linked with the predominance of the fine, these two factors provide the most important generalizations that can be made about sentencing. Where new sentences are introduced, as with the community service orders, the numbers sentenced to that order remain small – partly of course, as a result of the lack of facilities generally available – and from the figures it can be seen that only 2 per cent of those sentenced for indictable offences received such an order. However, in spite of the general stability of sentencing patterns, certain new trends are emerging, which if they continue, will affect future patterns. One important trend has been the proportionate decrease in the use the courts made of the probation order. This trend began in 1972 and has continued throughout, particularly in those offenders in the 17–20 year age group. To some extent the decrease can be accounted for by the increased facilities available to the courts in the form of new sentences such as deferred sentences, or even community service orders, but it has to be recognized that we may be witnessing a change in attitudes towards probation. The radical image of the probation service, which fostered so many new ideas in sentencing, is being lost, and courts, it seems, are seeking alternative sentences outside the probation framework.[7]

Yet the most controversial aspect of sentencing concerns those offenders sentenced to imprisonment. In October 1976 the number of offenders held in prison service establishments (which includes borstals and detention centres), reached a record level in excess of 42,000. the average daily population for the year was 41,443 (HMSO, 1976b). The population and the average daily population was the highest recorded this century. The controversy centres around two main areas: first whether it is necessary to send so many offenders to prison and second the extent of overcrowding created by these large numbers of offenders sentenced. The first area is a complex one and slightly beyond the scope of this chapter, except to add that in spite of numerous alternatives, particularly the introduction of suspended sentences, courts are still sending large numbers to prison. All the available evidence seems to suggest that many offenders sentenced to prison, and particularly those on short-term sentences, could have been given alternative sentences, probation, for example (Wilkins, 1958; Babst and Mannering, 1965; Hood and Sparks, 1970).

The other main area concerning overcrowding poses acute problems. In 1969 it was considered that a crisis level would be reached whenever the total prison population reached 40,000, and it is now 2,000 more than that and rising steadily. In 1950, for example, there were about 20,000 offenders in prison and about 2,000 were sleeping two or three to a cell. By 1968 these numbers had increased to about 35,000, of whom about 9,000 were sleeping two or three to a cell: By 1976 there were 42,000 offenders in prisons with probably 15,000 sleeping two or three to a cell. The extent of overcrowding is greatest at the local prisons,[8] which contained about 43 per cent of the total male population of prisons. As shown in Table 13, the local prisons had more than 17,000 prisoners, with a certified normal accommodation of 11,678. The problem of how to reduce the overcrowding must, of course, be linked to the increase in crime generally. At the present time, no solution seems to be available, although constant attempts are made to find alternative sentences and reduce the courts' powers to impose prison sentences. There

Table 13   Prison population and accommodation, 1976, in England and Wales

Type of establishment	Average population	Certified normal accommodation
Remand	1,774	1,877
Local prisons	17,251	11,678
Open training prisons	3,180	3,494
Closed training prisons	10,418	10,705
Open borstals	1,772	1,927
Closed borstals	4,010	3,784
Senior detention centres	1,171	1,393
Junior detention centres	585	657
Establishments for females	1,282	1,160

Source: HMSO *Report of the work of the prison department*, 1976, p. 3.

are limits to what can be achieved here, and limits to what can be politically and socially tolerated, so that the size of the prison population is beginning to be the key issue within the general problem of crime.

Some Aspects of Philosophy of the Penal System

Up to this point some of the most important features of crime and sentencing have been considered. Yet it needs to be recognized that the courts and the penal system are institutions which operate within certain philosophical frameworks. It is now necessary to examine some features of the framework, and particularly those concerned with treatment. The study of legal rules and the justification for those rules belongs to the area of jurisprudence, where questions such as the nature of law or the justifications for punishments are central areas for debate. Criminologists, sociologists, social administrators and social workers have all contributed to that debate, but it must be admitted that their contributions have often been marginal and more often have failed to confront the basic questions about the nature of punishment. Nowhere is this more clearly demonstrated than in the current vogue for 'treatment', the implication being that treatment is somehow helpful to the offender whilst punishment is not, or that treatment and punishment are opposed to each other.

The social scientists' involvement in the penal system has been a slow process. Initially the social scientists' theories of deviancy were disregarded by the courts and the penal system, for the judiciary in particular retained its traditional views and retained a sense of lofty isolation. Members of the judiciary, and for that matter members of the legal profession, operated and still operate, according to classical and neo-classical theory (Taylor, Walton and Young, 1973). Briefly, the early classical theory emphasized the rational nature of man, who, before committing offences, apparently weighed up the expected advantages and disadvantages of his individual acts. Punishments were therefore devised, and justified according to principles of deterrence. If offenders rationally decided that the advantages of committing a crime outweighed the disadvantages then deterrence would operate by increasing the punishments. However, defects in classical theory were soon apparent. Rationality appeared to be a variable component closely allied to age, personality, and social background. Once this criticism became accepted, classical theory required basic amendments.

The neo-classicists made the necessary amendments. They modified classical principles by grafting on to classical theory their own special views of the nature of man and the nature of crime. They retained the concept of rationality, with some exceptions, as far as the trial was concerned, but introduced the concept of 'mitigating circumstances', which allowed individual differences to be considered prior to the sentence. As Ian Taylor, Paul Walton and Jock Young say, 'Man was still accountable for his actions, albeit with certain minor reservations, but was no longer the automatic rational man of pure classicism.' The result, they say, was as follows:

> At the centre are adult sane individuals seen to be fully responsible for their actions. They are identical to their ideal type action of pure classical theory except that some cognizance is taken of their particular circumstances. These allowances are relevant only to mitigation – they do not form the basis of excusing the actor his responsibility.
>
> Children and often the aged are seen to be less capable of making accountable decisions.
>
> A small group of individuals, the insane and grossly feeble minded are seen to be incapable of adult freedom of action. With these groups actions are determined, there is no question of the actors being responsible for what they do.

The shift towards neo-classicism was not an isolated movement favoured only by nineteenth-century lawyers, but a movement developed in Britain which has dominated thinking throughout the Western world. It has, and still does, provide the basis of modern thinking and although sentences may still be passed on retributive principles – because the offender has deserved punishment by his criminal actions – retribution has easily fitted into the neo-classical framework. The notion of how much punishment is deserved can be adjudged by the offence and then softened by the mitigating circumstances.

The importance of neo-classicism for the social scientist was that it provided the opening through which they entered an arena traditionally reserved for lawyers. Once descriptive accounts of the offenders' backgrounds were permitted, and indeed had become an area of legal interest also, the role of the social scientist became more clearly defined. The social scientist, and particularly the probation officer and social worker, were in a position to provide those mitigating circumstances by presenting their reports to the courts about the offender's background and personality. The point here is that, however eager social scientists might have been to influence the courts, they could not have achieved an influence without the structural requirements provided by neo-classicism. It was not enough to want to achieve a level of influence; there had to be a recognized entrée through which the social scientists could pass (Hardiker, 1977 and 1978).

Historically the influence of the social scientists in the courts was confined to presenting an account of the offender's background and personality. This account was often a sentimental one, which emphasized the unhappiness and paucity of so many of the offenders' lives. Gradually a more specific theory developed, largely reinforced by the more academic interests of criminologists, and which for convenience will be called the treatment model. In general terms supporters of the treatment model view criminals as maladjusted individuals and they view the function of the courts and the entire penal system as institutions which provide a diagnosis of the offender's personality, and also provide the necessary treatment to cure that condition. The treatment model, however, was never as simple as this, and never fitted into that single unitary approach. In fact it is difficult to give a precise definition. However, David May (1971) has provided perhaps one of the clearest expositions and his definition will be used here. In his terms the treatment model consists of four inter-related assumptions.

First, that supporters of the treatment model would argue that the explanation of crime was to be found in the behaviour and motivation of the criminals and not in the law or its administration. In other words the 'causes' of crime could be found in the study of the individual criminal, and it follows, therefore, that to remove or reduce crime these 'causes' must be identified and treated. In the treatment model the legal system was relegated to an inferior position, and studies about laws, and how laws are implemented became regarded as secondary. The criminal provided the major and overriding focus.

Second, supporters would argue that in some identifiable way criminals (or delinquents) are different from non-criminals. This second proposition follows logically from the first, for if the aim is to identify the 'causes' of crime, then it would seem that those causes exist only in the criminals. Conversely they would be absent in non-criminals. The aim of research, therefore, was to distinguish those features which were special or exclusive to criminals. The area to be covered was wide, for these 'causes' may be psychological or social. Once identified, however, it became a short step to treat the offenders and thereby remove the necessity to commit crime. Technically the diagnosis of the condition has to take place prior to sentence, and treatment takes place during the sentence – although the treatment and the sentence are really indivisible.

Third, the criminal and delinquent would be seen as constrained and so unable ultimately to be held responsible for their actions. This third proposition stands in direct conflict with neo-classical theory, where the assumption there is of the rational man able to make free independent decisions. Supporters of the treatment model see criminals either as subject to pressures, or unconscious drives, or as being products of a certain type of social background, all of which convey the image of the constrained man, who, if he has freedom to choose, has only limited freedom. To the supporters of the treatment model the modern criminal enjoys freedom only within a cage, the cage being his psycho-social world which restricts boundaries and external movement.

Finally, supporters would say that criminal and delinquent behaviour as such is not the real problem. They would regard this type of behaviour as possessing significance only as a pointer to the need for intervention, or, as David May says, it would be the presenting symptom that draws attention to the more intractable disease. A key argument used by supporters of the treatment model is that the origins of any criminal act could be traced to earlier personal developments. Crime then was the presenting problem – or the symptom whilst the earlier defects became the disease itself. Armed with this view, supporters would apply the treatment model to any existing social problem, whether it be attempted suicide, homelessness, or even unemployment. Joel Handler (1973) calls the treatment model the 'unified theory of deviance', for it encompasses all social problems and all solutions.

The four maxims must, of course, be recognized as a general exposition of the treatment model; individual supporters may emphasize different features or even add additional points. However, as a general set of propositions, these four maxims would probably include the most comprehensive general statement of the treatment model as it now operates. As far as the modern penal system is concerned, the influences of the treatment models have been profound, and the development or extension of that model has provided the largest single influence on penal development in this century. Some of the implications need to be examined, for they relate to social policy generally, and to the penal system in particular.

The first point to note is that the treatment model has had to be incorporated into the overall philosophy of the penal system and has, therefore, had to accommodate to the existing structure. From a relatively insignificant position granted by the neo-classical criminologists it has enlarged itself and become an important influence. Yet its flexibility is its greatest asset for it has to be shown to be capable of giving treatment to criminals on the one hand, and linking with certain fixed aims of the penal system on the other. One fixed aim is called reductivism or the attempt to reduce crime. For the treatment model to exist within the penal system it must demonstrate that it too is reductivist, and here of course, is the first major difficulty. Does treating criminals reduce their criminality? Without attempting to review the literature here, the answer must be taken as being not yet proven (Bean, 1976).

The most obvious implication of the treatment model is that the study of crime is based on the study of the criminal. The advantage is that this enables the criminal to give an explanation of himself in the courts and to society generally. This feature must be welcomed, if only on general humanitarian grounds. The courts are monolithic institutions where each person has a fixed role and persons not familiar with the setting are liable to be immobilized by its rigidity or inflexibility. In the sense that a report is prepared by a treatment official where the offender has been interviewed under less inflexible conditions, the offender at least is provided with an opportunity to present himself to the courts, even if it is by way of a report. Also the presence of a large number of treatment officials in the courts – inevitably members of the probation service – has produced a greater awareness of the difficulties under which many offenders operate their day-to-day lives.

The second advantage of the treatment model is that it offers help to offenders with personal difficulties. That many offenders have personal difficulties is well known and well documented, and any help offered to them, particularly on their release from prison, must again be welcomed on humanitarian grounds.

The third advantage is that treatment has led directly or indirectly to the development of many new forms of penal sanction. The probation order is the most obvious example, but so is parole, the community service order and the facilities for the treatment of mentally abnormal offenders under the Mental Health Act, 1959. Prison welfare officers are now firmly established within penal institutions, including borstals and detention centres. In short the treatment model has prevented the penal system from becoming static. Of course, not all these sentences or changes rely on a pure view of treatment. Parole for example, can appeal to strong economic motives, for it is a good deal less expensive to have a prisoner on parole than in prison, and the community service order is partly retributive for the sentence involves the offender repaying his debt to society in the form of social compensation. Even so, many of the ideas which led to the introduction of these sentences originally developed from the thinking behind the treatment model.

Conversely, it is now beginning to be recognized that there are disadvantages too, and some disadvantages pose problems of a political nature. Consider the problem of sentencing. In order to operate the treatment model effectively, information on the background of the offender needs to be collected and presented by officials of the court – the probation officers. Leaving aside the quality of that information, or even the way in which it is obtained or presented, which in itself raises serious doubts about the validity or utility of such reports (Perry, 1974; Bean, 1975), we have arrived at a position whereby agents of the State have acquired the right to enquire into the personal lives of the deviant members. It matters not whether those officials are probation officers, or any other type of social worker for the purpose of that information is to assist the court and this makes that report a report for a State agency. Contrast the present-day acceptance of reports with the views of the nineteenth-century liberals. Those penal philosophers did not think it was any business of the courts to make enquiries into the offenders' personal lives. In classical theory only the offence determined the nature of the punishment; in the treatment model the offence is less important, for it is the offence plus the character assessment of the offender that determines the sentence. In the pure view of treatment, character is regarded as the most important.

The other political implication is no less serious. Once it becomes established that treatment is required, then certain groups must be given the power to operate and implement the treatment. If the offender fails to respond, treatment has to be discontinued, as it has to be discontinued if the offender does exceptionally well. The point here is that certain selected groups have to be given powers to make those decisions. One can see this very clearly in the proposals of the Younger Committee, which considered alternatives to replace existing borstals and detention centres (HMSO, 1974). This committee proposed two new types of sentences: the custody and control order, and the supervision and control order. In the custody and control order, offenders would be released from institutions when they were considered ready for release, and the decision to release would depend, in less serious cases, on the findings of a local review committee composed of selected people, some of whom are experts in the field of crime. Roger Hood (1975) makes some telling criticisms of these proposals, which he calls a form of 'resentencing by experts', for the decision to release, or not to release an offender, must be theirs.

This is not all, for the proposals of the Younger Committee for a supervision and control order go even further in elevating treatment experts to a position of considerable power. The supervision and control order would permit the supervising officer – in this case the probation officer – to confine an offender for up to seventy-two hours in a penal institution, without trial and without that offender committing an offence, if the supervising officer considered this to be in the offender's best interests. Such power puts the treatment officials on a level with the courts and the police.

One advantage claimed for the treatment model is that it provides flexibility in sentencing, allowing an offender to be discharged from, say a prison, or from a probation order if improvement has occurred. Now in one sense this is obviously an important factor, for on the face of it, there seems little point in requiring an offender to stay in prison when no obvious benefit would accrue. The method of attempting to ensure this is through parole. This aspect, like so many others of the treatment model, is a mixed blessing, for it raises numerous questions which have not produced clear answers. First it assumes that some 'peak' of training can be identified. In the light of the evidence so far, the assumption is unwarranted, for as Roger Hood (1975) says, no one has yet been able to show the criteria to be used to identify that peak. Intuitively, perhaps officials can say a peak has been reached, but this is only a form of inspired guess. Furthermore, who is to be responsible for making that guess? Inevitably we are back to the power of the treatment officials again and all that is implied.

The problems surrounding the treatment model are, therefore, exceedingly complex, and I think it would be right to say that the implications are only just beginning to be realized. It may seem plausible that offenders should be helped or treated, and it may even be acceptable on humanitarian grounds that treatment is to be preferred to punishment, yet to commit oneself to this position at a superficial level means ignoring certain basic issues. In addition to those mentioned above, five other problems need consideration. First do we not need some groups to protect offenders from over-zealous treatment officials or, to put the matter in an older philosophical context, 'Who shall guard the guardians?' It seems dangerous to assume that because certain occupational groups say they are concerned with helping others, that they will in fact be of benefit to those whom they claim they wish to help. Some people may be damaged by the experience of being helped, and some, it must be admitted by the malevolence of a few of the officials. Secondly, to operate treatment programmes successfully the obvious extension of treatment philosophies is to provide indeterminate sentences so that offenders will be released when they are seen to be ready for release. Roger Hood argues that this view would produce a new elite of offenders who have good homes to go to and good jobs available on release, but those less fortunate would stay in custody longer. Thirdly can we be certain that treatment produces more humanitarian sentences? In one sense of course, nearly all offenders would prefer probation to prison, but the treatment model offers no guarantees that a non-custodial sentence will be granted, neither does it guarantee that shorter sentences will be given. Those viewing prisons as primarily therapeutic or helpful may have fewer qualms about committing offenders to custodial institutions and may pass longer sentences (Hogarth, 1971; Wheeler, 1968).

Fourthly, there is the perennial question about the nature of punishment. Although treatment is usually presented as an alternative to punishment this is much too simple. Once an offender is taken to a penal institution or has to report to a probation officer, he is being punished, irrespective of the intentions of the person passing sentence. The Italian criminologist Garofalo summed it up as when he said, 'The mere deprivation of liberty, however, benign, is a form of punishment.' The philosophical arguments surrounding the difference between treatment and punishment are complex; at this point it is important to note that arguments for treatment within the penal system inevitably lead to a demand for punishment, if only because treatment requires the offender to be deprived of his liberty in order for that treatment to be given.

Finally there is the divisive nature of treatment policies. Under all treatment regimes the officials directly involved in the treatment process tend to receive the highest status, those marginally involved receive less. The increase in treatment programmes has led to certain occupational groups gaining status and others losing status and being discriminated against; police and prison officers for example, become regarded as 'authoritarian' or 'punitive' which in treatment language represents unacceptable personal characteristics. This divisiveness has, in one sociologist's view (Lemert, 1967), produced a sense of certainty amongst treatment officials which is little short of the self-satisfaction granted by the Divine Rights of Kings. A harsh criticism but it may well be valid.

The treatment model, therefore, is not easily accommodated within the modern penal system. Criticism is beginning to grow and the defects that have remained hidden for so long are being openly examined. One of the earliest exponents of treatments were the American Friends Service Committee, a group of American Quakers who have supported the treatment model for at least a century. They have now (1971) publically recanted:

> [There is] compelling evidence that the individualized
> treatment model, the ideal towards which reformers have
> been urging us for at least a century is theoretically faulty,
> systematically discriminatory in administration and
> inconsistent with some of our most basic concepts of justice.

The devastating critique of treatment produced by some criminologists and particularly the American Friends Service Committee highlights many of the defects in the present system. Unhappily a vacuum has been produced where no clear ideas are emerging (Radzinowicz and Wolfgang, 1977). Some criminologists argue for humanistic deterrence as being the only justification for a penal system (Bean, 1977), where the emphasis is placed equally on the terms 'humanistic' and 'deterrence'. Others ask for fewer laws and less involvement in offenders' lives (Schur, 1973). Others adopting a Marxist-dominated perspective regard all judicial sanctions as demonstrations of the power of the bourgeoisie over the predominantly working class offenders (Taylor, Walton and Young, 1975). Whichever approach is finally adopted, care should be taken to avoid superficial change based on trendy theories. The penal system ought never to be an institution where enthusiasts are permitted to practise their pet ideologies. Those directly involved – the prisoners – would doubtless support this view, fearing most of all the ideologues who may only care for their own enthusiasm and visions.

The Special Problems of Juveniles

Juvenile offenders pose special problems for the penal system, the most obvious being that they contribute disproportionately to the numbers of prosecuted offenders. In 1975 for example, about 30 per cent of all males convicted for indictable offences were juveniles – i.e. between the ages of ten and seventeen. Out of 418,402 males convicted in 1975 for indictable offences, 148,865 were juveniles, and these juvenile offenders were grossly over-represented in offences such as burglary, theft and criminal damage.

The second reason is related to the notion that juveniles represent a reserve capital. Or to put the point another way, that attempts to prevent juvenile criminality would lead to a reduction in adult criminality. Dr David Owen, during the debate on the 1975 Children's Bill, said that, 'a nation's children represent a nation's future'. He was echoing a view expressed nearly seventy years earlier by the Earl of Lytton during a House of Lords debate on the 1908 Children's Bill. The Earl of Lytton said, referring to the proposed introduction of juvenile courts, that the Bill was not only conceived 'in a spirit of tenderness and affection for child life, but also with real interest in the future welfare of the State' (Bean, 1975). As about 70 per cent of all adult offenders had earlier been juvenile offenders, there is clearly some force in this argument. The 'reserve capital' argument has led to a wider range of penal facilities for juveniles than for adults, and justified on the grounds that in order to reduce adult crime greater attention needs to be given to juvenile crime.

Third, the juvenile criminal poses special problems in terms of assessing or assigning guilt. Juvenile offenders constitute one group delegated by the neo-classicists as being outside the demands of rationality, and this precept exists in law. If a juvenile commits an offence and is below the prosecutable age, there is a presumption that he cannot tell right from wrong; between the ages of ten and fourteen juveniles are in a twilight zone where as individuals they are deemed to be incapable of knowing their acts to be wrong. They are presumed to be in *doli incapax* or ignorant of the wrongfulness of the act. This presumption has to be refuted if the trial is to proceed.

These special features of juvenile offenders has not only led to special consideration but a special form of control. Some criminologists would see these controls as reflecting a humane and enlightened attitude towards juvenile offenders, others would see them as disastrous, removing from juveniles the protection of basic legal rights and producing two kinds of justice in Britain; that given to adults and an inferior kind given to juveniles.

The 1908 Children's Act set out for the first time the principle governing subsequent legislation. Juvenile courts were to be separate from adult courts. One reason for this was that juveniles were considered a vulnerable group and should not be contaminated by older more sophisticated criminals. However, in 1908, the basic principles of justice still prevailed or, as Henri Giller and Alison Morris (1977) say, 'The prevailing idea was that the child was a wrongdoer charged with an offence and the old procedures for dealing with adult offenders were thought to be appropriate in most respects for dealing with children.' In 1933 the Children and Young Persons Act added a significant proviso to this precept, saying that juvenile court magistrates 'should have regard to the welfare of the child in determining appropriate dispositions'. In other words the offence and the welfare of the child should both be considered prior to sentence; previously the offence was thought the more important.

By the middle 1960s, there was pressure for change. Two arguments were presented which led eventually to the Government White Paper (HMSO, 1968), *Children in Trouble*, and subsequently in the 1969 Children and Young Persons Act. The first argument said that it was wrong for children and young people to be 'criminalized' by a court appearance and retain that conviction, (or finding of guilt) for the remainder of their lives, when they may have only been involved in youthful misconduct. The second argument returns us to the basis of the model, and the unified theory of deviance. Offending was seen to be merely a symptom of some deeper disorder. Juvenile delinquency was to be viewed differently from adult criminality, being regarded as behaviour which was often no more than an isolated incident in the pattern of a child's normal development. Alternatively, there was another group of juveniles whose behaviour did not contravene the criminal law, but was related to some form of deprivation, i.e. the endangered child who was in need of care or protection. These offenders and non-offenders supposedly showed the same underlying disorders so that in Richard Sparks's (1969) phrase 'There was no difference between the depraved and the deprived.' Both had needs which could be commonly identified and met. With regard to both groups, protecting society from the children's behavioural disorders and helping their development were seen as complementary concepts.

The Children and Young Persons Act (1969) which stemmed from the White Paper, placed emphasis on welfare provisions and also increased the role of local authority social workers to the exclusion of probation officers. The latter were said to have become too tarnished by their work with adult criminals. Extensive provisions were made for consultation between recognized groups prior to the offender being brought to court, and considerable power was also granted to social workers to provide flexible treatment programmes. The old approved schools were to be abolished, to be replaced by community homes which social workers would control, and where children on a care order could be treated as required. Early recognition of delinquency, full assessment of the child's needs and flexibility of treatment were the basic tenets of the new approach.

Many of the more radical sections of the 1969 Act have still not been implemented (particularly those relating to Sections 4, 5 and 7). However, many have, to the obvious consternation of the Magistrates' Association and similar bodies. Their consternation stems from a view that the 1969 Act is no longer concerned with providing justice. Tony Bottoms (1974) regards the 1969 Act as a decriminalizing Act, but one which substitutes one kind of control for another – the magistrates have lost power, but the social workers have gained it, for the Act has extended the influence of professional social workers and increased their discretionary powers at the pre- and post-court stage.

The Act has been controversial ever since its inception. A variety of criticisms have been directed at it: the British Association of Social Workers regard the principles of the Act as correct, but are critical that many of the more important sections have not been implemented. They regard it as 'a non-act'. BASW also regard criticisms of the increasing level of juvenile crime as being due to a lack of financial resources. In other words BASW believe that with a greater level of commitment from the government, financial or otherwise, a number of significant improvements could be made.

Others, such as Giller and Morris (1977), 'feel that a major reason for the supposed failure of the Act lies in the assumption that those asked to participate in the operation of the Act, share a common view of the appropriate way of handling children who offend'. Giller and Morris note that the basic premise underlying the Act was that groups such as police, school teachers, magistrates, and social workers could work together. Yet whilst these groups may share the same long-term goals – the prevention of crime – there is little agreement about the method of achieving that objective. One group emphasizes deterrence and the protection of the public, another emphasizes the offender's personal needs. The result is often acrimony and hostility between the parties, particularly as the strength of their respective arguments, more often than not, hides a wider dispute about the nature of power.

More cogent criticisms centre around the assumption that there are no differences between the depraved and the deprived. Richard Sparks (1969) finds this assumption unacceptable: 'The fact remains that one group steals and the other does not.' Sparks suggests that the difference is not one about a different degree of protection required for the community, but one where persistent delinquency is a different condition from, say, parental neglect. Persistent delinquency involves a different set of attitudes. Rod Ryall (1974) takes the issue further and his research shows that the behaviour of the delinquent is 'determined by his predisposition to view authority in a hostile light, by the central importance of development behaviour as a self image, and by the adequacy of control exerted to impede the continuance of the delinquent behaviour pattern'. In short, delinquents *are* different from non-delinquents, and changes in the nature of court orders and in the improvement in the quality of the treatment facilities will not affect the nature of the delinquent's behaviour.

Most critics would see the problem stemming from the euphemism 'Children in Trouble', which fosters the assumption that misbehaviour is linked to unhappiness. It also provides justification for treatment rather than punishment. Yet in line with the previous criticisms of the treatment model, we should not be misled by the humanistic overtones implicit in the view that offenders are 'Children in Trouble'. Under the 1969 Act, it is possible for a child to remain in care, and be subject to control, for nine years, whereas an adult, may have received a lesser penalty. The children themselves are, of course, not misled by the euphemism of approved schools being renamed 'community homes'. To them it is still a form of imprisonment, and they resent the lengthy time period under which they are controlled. As with all recipients of semi-indeterminate sentences, they bitterly resent not knowing when they are to be released.[9] Yet there is clearly another side to the argument. Children *are* vulnerable; some *are* deprived as well as depraved, and some certainly require special protection, particularly those who may be the recipients of severe physical injuries. These children have to be taken away from home if they are to be protected and they will always see this as punishment. Sandford Fox (1974) has raised the important question when he discusses 'a matter of the meaning of justice in the context of childhood'. He argues that a child has a right not to be treated, and conversely, that a child has a right to be punished. This is a curious way of using the term 'right', for rights do not usually involve a right to unpleasantness, unless, of course, that right to punishment is seen as less unpleasant for the child than the right to treatment. On more traditional lines David Matza (1964) insists that justice should be equated with fairness, and so uses a much older argument originally formulated by Aristotle, who saw justice in terms of equality of consideration. Aristotle believed that equals should be treated equally and unequals unequally, the difficulty being that there has to be specified criteria to decide on the nature of the inequality. What should that be? The offence, the child's background; or a combination of both? Traditionally the offence has been the major consideration, for in neo-classical theory, the offence remains the sole justification for meting out punishment. The treatment model, of course, leads to the use of different criteria, namely the offender's background.

The problem, however still remains, at least at the practical level of sentencing in the juvenile court. What happens if two children appear at court for the first time convicted of the same offence, but one comes from a severely deprived home and the other from a 'good' home? Should they receive different sentences? What happens also if a juvenile has been severely maltreated and in his own interests cannot return home, whilst the other, who has committed a relatively serious offence, is allowed to remain? It matters not whether a juvenile court, or any other court for that matter, sends the non-offender away, that will still be seen as a punishment and compared unfavourably with the other decision to allow an offender to be at home. These are some of the problems likely to occur when we attempt to answer Sandford Fox's pertinent question about the meaning of justice in the context of childhood. David Matza (1964) says 'the precise point at which justice ends and injustice begins cannot be definitely stated. It is in some measure a matter of perspective and this is eternally problematic.' This does not mean we abandon the quest, but merely evaluate the 1969 Children and Young Persons Act from that standpoint. In Valerie Bean's (1976) terms, we need to be clear about the treatment/punishment anomaly first, and then consider whether our definitions of the child's interests do not become part of a new problem.

Conclusion

No attempt has been made in this chapter to be comprehensive and cover the whole area of criminology. Some of the major issues have been raised which impinge directly on the relationship between social policy and the penal system, but the field is, of course, much wider and much deeper than could be dealt with here. The three major areas that have been covered – the extent of crime, sentencing and juvenile justice – have been selected as being key elements, each presenting in their way separate but related issues, and each requiring immediate attention.

Notes

1   The clear-up rate is more than those offences leading to a successful prosecution. An offence recorded as known to the police is said to be cleared up if a person is arrested, summoned or cautioned

for the offence; if the committing of an offence is attributed to a child below the prosecutable age; if the offence is taken into consideration by the court in sentencing an offender found guilty of another charge; or if the person known or suspected to be guilty of the offence cannot be prosecuted or cautioned, e.g. because he has died. See HMSO, *Criminal Statistics 1976*, Cmnd 6909.

2   This feature is now built into the 1969 Children and Young Persons Act, where the police and social workers have a duty to consult before deciding to prosecute, and the decisions to prosecute have to be based on the possibility of providing help for the offender. Those not needing help will therefore not be prosecuted.

3   The influence of the Director of Public Prosecutions should not be discounted for it is he and he alone who decides to prosecute, particularly for serious offences. His decision is based on the public interest.

4   They may also be cautioned. There are two types of caution, the informal and formal, the latter occur where the police advise the offender that an offence has been committed and the offender is usually warned about the consequences of further offences.

5   All magistrates' courts have full-time salaried clerks who are lawyers and who advise magistrates on legal matters as well as administer the courts.

6   High courts are divided into bands, the upper band taking the most serious offences such as murder, the lower bands, which are not presided over by a high court judge, but by a recorder, take the least serious.

7   Community service orders are an alternative and they to some extent remain in the probation system although they are technically speaking more a method of 'repaying the debts to society' than would exist within a usual probation order.

8   Local prisons are those prisons which take all newly sentenced prisoners, together with many serving short sentences and those remanded awaiting trial or sentence. Other types of prisons, i.e. the training prisons, have much less pressure on facilities because they tend to avoid the short-sentenced prisoner.

9   The point was taken from the American Friends Service Committee who call the uncertainty of the indeterminate sentence 'one of the more exquisite forms of torture' (Hill & Wang (1971) p. 29).

References

American Friends Service Committee (1971), *Struggle for Justice*, Hill & Wang.

Babst, D. V., and Mannering, J. W. (1965), 'Probation vs imprisonment for similar types of offenders – a comparison by subsequent violations', *Journal of Research in Crime and Delinquency*, vol. II.

Bean, P. T. (1975), 'Social enquiry reports: a recommendation for disposal', *Justice of the Peace*, 11 and 18 October, pp. 568–9 and 585–6.

Bean, P. T. (1976), *Rehabilitation and Deviance*, Routledge & Kegan Paul.

Bean, P. T. (1977), 'Rehabilitation: some issues and implications', *Justice of the Peace*, 16 July, pp. 413–15.

Bean, V. W. (1975), 'The juvenile court in transition', M.Phil. thesis, University of Nottingham.

Bean, V. W. (1976), 'In whose best interests?' *Family Law*, vol. vi, no. 4.

Bottomley, A. K. (1973), *Decisions in the Penal Process*, Martin Robertson.

Bottoms, A. E. (1974), 'On the decriminalization of the English juvenile court', in R. G. Hood (ed.) *Crime, Criminology and Public Policy*, Heinemann, pp. 319–46.

Devlin, Sir P. (1966), *Trial by Jury*, University Paperbacks.

Durkheim, E. (1964), *The Rules of Sociological Method*, Free Press.

Fox, S. (1974), 'The reform of juvenile justice: the child's right to punishment', *Juvenile Justice*, August.

Giller, H. and Morris, A. (1977), 'Juvenile courts or children's hearings?' *Legal Action Group Bulletin*, October.

Handler, J. (1973), *The Coercive Social Worker*, Rand McNally.

Hardiker, P. (1977), 'Social work ideologies in the probation service', *British Journal of Social Work*, vol. VII, no. 2.

Hardiker, P. (1978), 'The role of the probation officer in sentencing', in H. Parker (ed.), *Social Work in the Courts*, Arnold.

HMSO (1968), *Children in Trouble*, Cmnd 3601.

HMSO (1969), *People in Prison*, Cmnd 4214.

HMSO (1974), *Report of the Advisory Council of the Treatment of Offenders; The Young Adult Offender.*

HMSO (1975), *Criminal Statistics*, Cmnd 6566.

HMSO (1976a), *Criminal Statistics*, Cmnd 6909.

HMSO (1976b), *Report of the Work of the Prison Department*, Cmnd 6884.

Hogarth, J. (1971), *Sentencing as a Human Process*, Toronto University Press.

Hood, R. G. (1975), 'The case against executive control over time in custody: a rejoinder to Professor Walker's criticisms', *Criminal Law Review*, October, pp. 545–52.

Hood, R. G. and Sparks, R. F. (1970), *Key issues in criminology*, Weidenfeld & Nicolson.

Jones, H. (1965), *Crime in a Changing Society*, Penguin.

Lemert, E. (1967), *Human Deviance, Social Problems and Social Control*, Prentice-Hall.

Matza, D. (1964), *Delinquency and Drift*, Wiley.

May, D. (1971), 'Delinquency control and the treatment model', *British Journal of Criminology*, vol. xi, pp. 359–70.

Perry, F. (1974), *Information for the Court*, Institute of Criminology, Cambridge.

Radzinowicz, L. (1964), 'The criminal in society', *Journal of the Royal Society of Arts*, vol. cxii, pp. 916–29.

Radzinowicz, L. and Wolfgang, M. (1977), *Crime and Justice*, 2nd edn, vol. III, Basic Books.

Ryall, R. (1974), 'Delinquency: the problem for treatment', *Social Work Today*, vol., no. 4, 16 May.

Schur, E. M. (1965), *Crimes without Victims*, Prentice-Hall.

Schur, E. M. (1973), *Radical Non-intervention*, Prentice-Hall.

Sparks, R. F. (1969), 'The depraved are not just deprived', *New Society*, 24 July.

Taylor, I., Walton, P. and Young, J. (1973), *The New Criminology*, Routledge & Kegan Paul.

Taylor, I., Walton, P. and Young, J. (1975), *Critical Criminology*, Routledge & Kegan Paul.

Wheeler, S. *et al.* (1968), 'Agents of delinquent control', in S. Wheeler (ed.) *Controlling Delinquents*, Wiley, pp. 31–60.

Wilkins, L. T. (1958), 'A small comparative study of the results of probation', *British Journal of Delinquency*, vol. VIII, pp. 201–9.

10

An Overview – Retrospect and Glimpse of the Future

David C. Marsh

There is no need to recount even in summary the fundamental changes in social policy and administration which have taken place in this country in modern times, but it is important to recognize how and why such changes came to be made. Clearly they were not brought about by the words or deeds of any one particular person or any single set of circumstances, but undoubtedly social reformers, leaders of pressure groups, public servants, and politicians all had their part to play. In the eighteenth century one thinks of John Howard and his efforts to reform the prisons; of Captain Coram and his hospital for foundlings; of Jonas Hanway and his concern for fallen women and pauper children; and of others with similar humanitarian motives who inspired the ideas of social reform.

The nineteenth century was to witness even more widespread attempts and not only through the activities of reformers who were also in some cases politicians, like Lord Shaftesbury, and William Wilberforce, but also through the activities of mutual aid organizations such as co-operative societies, friendly societies, and trade unions; voluntary charitable organizations such as the Charity Organisation Society; and, of course, through political organizations such as the Fabian Society. Novelists too, played their part in awakening the social conscience, and the extension of the suffrage made the main political parties respond to the varied demands for reform. By the end of the century the role of government – central and local – was very different from what it had been in the past and especially in the field of social policy. We were now clearly on the path leading towards a welfare state, and in the twentieth century that path was to be widened and extended.

The first decade of the twentieth century was full of excitement for those who campaigned for a new kind of society in which injustice and inequality would be reduced. The mood of the times and of the ideas of some of the political leaders in that period is summed up by Thomas Jones who, in his biography of Lloyd George, said of him

> His early speeches had been those of a young and fiery
> Welsh radical who could not but be moved by the violent
> social contrasts of incalculable wealth and indescribable
> poverty found side by side. Speaking in Bangor in January,
> 1906, he observed: 'I believe there is a new order coming for
> the people of this country. It is a quiet but certain
> revolution.' This was his belief in early manhood; and as
> Cabinet Minister his policies were to reflect this belief.

Lloyd George's name has ever since been associated with the Liberal reforms of that period, his role has perhaps been over-praised, but nevertheless, despite grave defects in principles and cumbersome administration, the fact that ordinary men and to a lesser extent women could become contributors to a national insurance scheme aimed (as Lloyd George once said) 'to provide as far as may be for every worker some kind of shelter against the slings and arrows of fortune' was a major step forward on the road to the welfare state.

The First World War and then the great depression of the inter-war period were to prove the ineffectiveness of many of the measures of reform introduced in earlier years. The national insurance schemes were not successful in combating unemployment or abolishing poverty; educational inequalities remained despite the introduction and extension of compulsory education; there were still very wide variations in the incidence of disease among the different social classes and wide discrepancies in the rates of infant mortality; housing conditions were still far from satisfactory for too many people; and though working conditions were less inhuman and subject to greater statutory control than in the past there were still very marked differences in, for example, pay and other conditions of employment between those who worked with their hands and those who wore 'clean clothes'.

The inter-war years, though they were miserable for many people, especially those in the depressed areas of the country, were reasonably good for those who were in full-time employment and already there were signs of 'a slowly advancing prosperity' (as Maurice Bruce has written) for those who lived in areas of growing population and new industries. For the people who lived in these more prosperous areas centred on the Midlands and the south east of England, real wages were rising and signs of affluence in the form of new houses, cars and facilities for comfort and enjoyment were becoming apparent. The social services, however, were still relatively ineffective, and though the Poor Law had been drastically affected by the introduction of unemployment assistance on a national scale in 1934, the five giants of want, ignorance, disease, idleness and squalor were by no means conquered.

The threat of, and then the outbreak of, war were to provide the stimulus to the economy which led to a radical reduction in unemployment, the setting up of new industries and to a revival of the basic industries such as iron and steel, coal, shipbuilding and textiles, which had suffered heavily during the depression. The war also led to quite dramatic changes in the attitudes of the political parties towards social reform which were summarized so well by R. M. Titmuss in his *Problems of Social Policy*. The coalition government during the war, despite the enormous problems with which it had to contend, was sufficiently far-sighted to make plans for post-war social reconstruction. The plans made between the Beveridge Report of 1942 and the election of a Labour government in 1945 have by now been well documented. The legislation passed by the Labour government of 1945–51 and the services which came into being appeared at first sight to be revolutionary, but, as Maurice Bruce has so cogently argued, the nationalization of the mines and the railways was far from revolutionary in that 'nationalisation of the mines had been urged by Winston Churchill as Liberal Policy in 1906 and that of the railways recommended by the Sankey Commission in 1919'. In an admirably succinct passage, Maurice Bruce has stated in his *The Coming of the Welfare State* that

The greatest achievement of the 1945–51 Government lies less in its samples of nationalisation than in the firm rounding-off of half a century's constructive work of welfare, and the final shaping of the Welfare State on the lines first laid early in the century on the basis of nineteenth-century experience and investigation.

The Conservative government of 1951–64 did not substantially alter the basic framework of the welfare state, despite the avowed aims of the Conservative Party to set the people free of State controls, to reduce the role of the State over the whole field of social policy, and to make a deliberate move towards the creation of a 'self-help' State in which the individual is more and more encouraged to provide for himself and his family. Indeed it cannot be rationally argued that either of the two major political parties, when in office, have remotely fulfilled the aims of their party manifesto and there would seem to be very little to choose between them in their achievement of their avowed aims. Labour governments cannot claim to have greatly reduced inequality, any more than Conservative governments can claim to have set us free and from the point of view of dramatic changes for the better in social policy and its implementation a non-partisan observer would be forced to the conclusion that our welfare state in 1978 is not so very different from what it was in, say, 1958.

There have of course been visible manifestations of changes in our social and economic life. To maintain our welfare state we have a larger bureaucracy than ever before in our history, many hundreds of thousands upon hundreds of thousands of civil servants, local government officers and social workers – and this despite the continual promises of successive governments to reduce manpower in the public services. The material resources, especially paper, consumed by the social services are enormous, and the proliferation of advisory bodies, tribunals and other quasi-judicial organizations has reached staggering proportions.

In recent years there have been massive re-organization schemes for local government, and the health services, the creation of supervisory bodies such as the Central Council for Education and Training in Social Work which employs large numbers of trained social workers and has at present a budget of well over a million pounds per annum; of advisory bodies such as the Personal Social Services Council; of a 'think tank' to advise recent prime ministers and hosts of expert advisers to departmental ministers.

It used to be said that even before the Second World War the organization of the social services was so complex that not many people understood the whole field and in 1959 in a letter to *The Times*, the present writer complained that the provision of social security services was 'a hotchpotch of administrative units, a tangle of legislative complexity and a jungle of vested interests'. Those same words apply today not only to social security but to the whole field of social provision in our welfare state.

What then of the future? Already demographic changes have brought about the need to revise our plans for social provision. The decline in the birth rate since the middle 1960s has resulted in the need to reconsider the number of new schools to be built and in the number of teachers to be trained. Some colleges of education have already been closed down in order to reduce the supply of teachers; some schools will no doubt have to be closed because there will be no pupils for the primary stage of education and in due course for secondary and higher education. There will be a higher proportion of elderly people than was planned for even a few years ago and changes of these kinds will clearly bring about alterations in the services demanded from a welfare state.

One wonders, however, whether the variations in manpower (or should one now say personpower?) will respond rationally to the changing needs. Thus in the field of education we have so far been told only of a reduction in the number of teachers, but ought there not equally to be a reduction in the number of administrators? On past experience the administrators will safeguard their employment and there will again be seen the operation of Parkinson's Law which when first propounded applied to the fact that after the Second World War, when the number of ships in the navy was reduced the number of administrators in the Admiralty was increased. If this were to apply to the fields of social service described in this book then the future would be frightening in that the absurd position could be reached where the number of doctors and nurses in the hospitals was less than the number of hospital administrators, and that in the penal services the number of prison and borstal officials was larger than the number of prisoners and that there were more probation officers than offenders on probation!

Predicting the future in this field is a hopeless task since the past in the field of social policy and administration is not a reliable pointer to the future. It may perhaps be said with a reasonable degree of conviction that the welfare state is here to stay, but it is to be hoped that it will not be quite the same in its aims and methods of achievement as it is and has been in the recent past.

Further Reading

Chapter 1
Social Policy and Administration

Butterworth, E. and Holman, R. (eds) (1975), *Social Welfare in Modern Britain*, Fontana/Collins.

Donnison, D. V. *et al*. (1975), *Social Policy and Administration Revisited*, Allen & Unwin.

Eyden, J. L. M. (1969), *Social Policy in Action*, Routledge & Kegan Paul.

Fraser, D. (1973), *The Evolution of the British Welfare State*, Macmillan.

Gilbert, B. (1966), *The Evolution of National Insurance in Great Britain, the Origins of the Welfare State*, Joseph.

Gilbert, B. (1970), *British Social Policy. 1914–1939*, Batsford.

Jones, K. *et al*. (1978), *Issues in Social Policy*, Routledge & Kegan Paul.

Marsh, D. C. (1964), *The Future of the Welfare State*, Penguin.

Pinker, R. (1971), *Social Theory and Social Policy*, Heinemann.

Rein, M. (1970), *Social Policy: Issues of Choice and Change*, Random House.

Reisman, D. A. (1977), *Richard Titmuss: Welfare and Society*, Heinemann.

Robson, W. (1976), *Welfare State and Welfare Society: Illusion and Reality*, Allen & Unwin, 1976.

Rowbottom, R. (1974), *Social Services Developments: Developing Patterns of Work and Organisation*, Heinemann.

Timms, N. and Watson, D. (eds) (1976), *Talking about Welfare: Readings in Philosophy and Social Policy,* Routledge & Kegan Paul.

Titmuss, R. M. (1970), *The Gift Relationship*, Allen & Unwin.

Townsend, P. (1976), *Sociology and Social Policy*, Penguin.

Journals

Journal of Social Policy – the journal of the Social Administration
    Association, quarterly, Cambridge University Press.
Social and Economic Administration, Edutext Publications Ltd, in
    association with Exeter University, quarterly.

Chapter 2
Social Policy in Relation to Industry

Florence, P. S. (1957), *Industry and the State*, Hutchinson.
Freund, K. (1977), *Labour and the Law*, Stevens.
Hobsbaum, E. J. (1968), *Industry and Empire*, Weidenfeld & Nicolson.
Pelling, H. (1963), *A History of Trade Unionism*, Penguin.
Wedderburn, K. W. (1965), *The Worker and the Law*, Penguin.
Young, A. F. (1968), *Social Services in British Industry*, Routledge &
    Kegan Paul.
In addition see also the *Annual Report of the Manpower Services
    Commission*, the *Employment Gazette* (Department of
    Employment), and descriptive leaflets on legislation, published by
    the Department of Employment, the Health and Safety Commission,
    Equal Opportunities Commission, etc, in lists published monthly by
    HMSO – *Government Publications*.

Chapter 3
Urban Planning and Social Policy

Aldridge, M. (1979), *The British New Towns Programme*, Routledge &
    Kegan Paul.
Ashworth, G. (1954), *The Genesis of Modern British Town Planning*,
    Routledge & Kegan Paul.
Benevolo, L. (1967), *The Origins of Modern Town Planning*,
    Routledge & Kegan Paul.
Cherry, G. (1972), *Urban Change and Planning*, Foulis.
Cullingworth, J. B. (1976), *Town and Country Planning in Britain* (6th
    edn), Allen & Unwin.
Hall, P. *et al.* (1973), *The Containment of Urban England, vols I & II*,
    Allen & Unwin.
Howard, E. (1965), *Garden Cities of Tomorrow*, Faber.
Lambert, C. and Weir, D. *Cities in Modern Britain*, Fontana.
Pahl, R. (1970), *Patterns of Urban Life*, Longmans.
Stewart, M. (ed.) (1972), *The City: Problems of Planning*, Penguin.

Chapter 4
Social Policy and Housing Need

Berry, F. (1974), *Housing: the Great British Failure*, Charles Knight.
Community Development Project (1976), *Profits Against Housing*,

(available from Urban Deprivation Unit, Home Office, London).
HMSO (1977), *Housing Policy: a Consultative Document & technical* vol. I–III, Cmnd 6851.
Murie, A., Niner, P. and Watson, C. (1976), *Housing Policy and the Housing System*, Allen & Unwin.

Journals

Roof (Shelter's housing magazine) – published 6 times a year.
Housing Review (Housing Centre Trust journal) – 6 times a year.

Chapter 5
Education

Bernstein, B. (1975), *Class, Codes and Control*, vol. 3, London, Routledge & Kegan Paul.
Fowler, G *et al.* (eds) (1973), *Decision Making in British Education*, London, Heinemann.
Halsey, A. H. (1972), *Educational Priority*, vol. 1, Dept of Education and Science, London, HMSO.
Karabel, J. and Halsey, A. H. (1977), *Power and Ideology in Education*, New York, Oxford University Press.
Kogan, M. (1975), *Educational Policy Making: A Study of Interest Groups and Parliament*, London, Allen & Unwin.
Lawton, D. (1977), *Education and Social Justice*, London, Sage Publications.
Musgrave, P. W. (1968), *Society and Education in England since 1800*, London, Methuen.
Rubinstein, D. and Simon, B. (1969), *The Evolution of the Comprehensive School*, London, Routledge & Kegan Paul.
Silver, H. (ed) (1973), *Equal Opportunity in Education*, London, Methuen.
Tyler, W. (1977), *The Sociology of Educational Inequality*, London, Methuen.

Chapter 6
Health

Brown, R. G. S. (1973), *The Changing National Health Service*, Routledge & Kegan Paul.
Cochrane, A. L. (1972), *Effectiveness and Efficiency: Random Reflections on Health Services*, NPHT.
De Kadt, E. (1976), 'Wrong priorities in health', *New Society*, 3 June, pp. 525–6.
Heller, T. (1978), *Restructuring the Health Service*, Croom Helm.
McKeown, T. (1976), *The Role of Medicine: Dream, Mirage or Nemesis?*, NPHT.

Townsend, P. (1974),'Inequality and the health service', *Lancet*, vol. 1, pp. 1179–90.

Watkin, B. (1978), *The National Health Service: The First Phase*, Allen & Unwin.

Chapter 7
'Social Security'

Atkinson, A. B. (1970), *Poverty in Britain and the Reform of Social Security*, Cambridge University Press.

Atkinson, A. B. (1973), *Wealth, Income and Inequality*, Penguin.

Atkinson, A. B. (1974), 'Poverty and income inequality in Britain', *in* D. Wedderburn (ed.) *Poverty, Inequality and Class Structure*, Cambridge University Press.

Bull, D. (ed.) (1971), *Family Poverty*, Duckworth.

Child Poverty Action Group (1975), *Unemployment: the Facts*.

Coates, K. and Silburn, R. (1970), *Poverty: the Forgotten Englishmen*, Penguin.

Field, F., Meacher, M. and Pond, C. (1977), *To Him Who Hath: a Study of Poverty and Taxation*, Penguin.

George, V. (1968), *Social Security: Beveridge and After*, Routledge & Kegan Paul.

Goldthorpe, J. H. (1974), 'Social inequality and social integration in modern Britain', in D. Wedderburn (ed.) *Poverty, Inequality and the Class Structure*, Cambridge University Press.

Hill, M. J. (1973), *Men out of Work*, Cambridge University Press.

Hill, M. J. (1974), *Policies for the Unemployed*, CPAG.

HMSO (1974), *Better Pensions*, Cmnd 5713.

Kincaid, J. (1973), *Poverty and Equality in Britain*, Penguin.

Lister, R. (1975), *Reform of Social Security*, CPAG.

Lynes, T. (1974), 'Policy on social security', in M. Young (ed.), *Poverty Report*, Temple Smith.

Miliband, R. (1974), 'Politics and poverty', in D. Wedderburn (ed.) *Poverty, Inequality and the Class Structure*, Cambridge University Press.

Parker, J. (1975), *Social Policy and Citizenship*, Macmillan.

Piven, F. F. and Cloward, R. A. (1972), *Regulating the Poor*, Tavistock.

Rutter, M. and Madge, N. (1976), *Cycles of Disadvantage*, HEB.

Sinfield, A. (1970), 'Poor and out of work in South Shields', in P. Townsend (ed.), *The Concept of Poverty*, Heinemann.

Townsend, P. (ed.) (1970), *The Concept of Poverty*, Heinemann.

Townsend, P. (1974), 'Poverty as relative deprivation; resources and style of living' in D. Wedderburn (ed.) *Poverty, Inequality and Class Structure*, Cambridge University Press.

Wedderburn, D. (1965), 'Facts and theories of the welfare State', in *The Socialist Register*, reprinted in (1973), *Social Administration*, Birrell *et al.* (eds), Penguin.

Westergaard, J. and Resler, H. (1975), *Class in a Capitalist Society*, Heinemann.

Department of Health and Social Security, annual reports, especially those dealing with national insurance and supplementary benefits. Leaflets published regularly by the department, e.g. on family benefits, pensions, and allowances, etc. Annual social security statistics, Child Poverty Action Group publications, especially the quarterly journal *Poverty*.

Chapter 8
The Personal Social Services

Butterworth, E. and Holman, R. (eds) (1975), *Social Welfare in Modern Britain*, Fontana/Collins.

Cheeseman, D. *et al.* (1972), *Neighbourhood Care and Old People*, NCSS.

Cooper, M. H. (1973), *Social Policy: A Survey of Recent Developments*, Basil Blackwell.

DHSS (1976), *Priorities for the Health and Personal Social Services in England*, HMSO.

DHSS (1977), *The Day Forward: Priorities in the Health and Social Services*, HMSO.

DHSS (1975), *Better Services for the Mentally Ill*.

DHSS (1978), *The Elderly at Home*, HMSO.

Hall, P. (1977), *Reforming the Welfare: the Politics of Change in the Personal Social Services*, Heinemann.

Jones, K. (1972), *A History of the Mental Health Services*, Routledge & Kegan Paul.

Lees, D. (ed.) (1974), *Impairment, Disability and Handicap*, Heinemann.

McKay, A. *et al.* (1973), 'Consumers and social services departments' *Social Work Today*, vol. IV, no. 16.

Neill, J. E. *et al.* (1973), 'Reactions to integration', *Social Work Today*, vol. IV, no. 15.

Shanas, E. *et al.* (1968), *Old People in Three Industrial Societies*, Routledge & Kegan Paul.

Taylor, D. (1977), *Physical Impairment: Social Handicap*, Office of Health Economics.

Tizard, J. *et al.* (1975), *Varieties of Residential Experience*, Routledge & Kegan Paul.

Chapter 9
Social Policy in Relation to Crime

American Friends Service Committee (1971), *Struggle for Justice*, Hill & Wang.

Bean, P. T. (1976), *Rehabilitation and Deviance*, Routledge & Kegan Paul.

Bottomley, A. K. (1973), *Decisions in the Penal Process*, Martin Robertson.

Carson, W. G. and Wiles, P. N. (eds) (1973), *Crime and Delinquency in Britain*, Martin Robertson.

Hood, R. G. and Sparks, R. (1970), *Key Issues in Criminology*, Weidenfeld & Nicolson.

King, R. D. and Elliott, K. W. (1977), *Albany: Birth of a Prison — End of an Era*, Routledge & Kegan Paul.

Prins, H. (1973), *Criminal Behaviour*, Pitman.

Radzinowicz, Sir L. and Wolfgang, M. (1971), *Crime and Justice*, (revised edition), 3 vols, Basic Books.

Bibliography

Abel-Smith, B. (1964), *The Hospitals 1800–1948*, Heinemann.

Abel-Smith, B. and Townsend, P. (1965), *The Poor and the Poorest*, G. Bell & Sons.

Aldridge, M. (1979), *The British New Towns*, Routledge & Kegan Paul.

Ambrose, P. and Colenutt, B. (1975), *The Property Machine*, Penguin.

American Friends Service Committee (1971), *Struggle for Justice*, Hill & Wang.

Anderson, M. (1971), *Family Structure in 19th Century Lancashire*, Cambridge University Press.

Arnstein, S. (1969), 'A ladder of citizen participation in planning', *Journal of American Institute of Planners*.

Ashworth, G. (1954), *The Genesis of Modern British Town Planning*, Routledge & Kegan Paul.

Atkinson, A. B. (1970), *Poverty in Britain and the Reform of Social Security*, Cambridge University Press.

Atkinson, A. B. (1973), *Wealth, Income and Inequality*, Penguin.

Atkinson, A. B. (1974), 'Poverty and Income Inequality in Britain' in D. Wedderburn (ed.), *Poverty, Inequality and the Class Structure*, Cambridge University Press.

Babst, D. W. and Mannering, J. W. (1965), 'Probation vs. imprisonment for similar types of offenders – a comparison by subsequent violations', *Journal of Research in Crime and Delinquency*, vol. II.

Batley, R. *et al.* (1970), *Going Comprehensive*, Routledge & Kegan Paul.

Bean, P. T. (1975), 'Social enquiry Reports: a recommendation for disposal', *Justice of the Peace*, 11 and 18 October.

Bean, P. T. (1976), *Rehabilitation and Deviance*, Routledge & Kegan Paul.

Bean, P. T. (1977), 'Rehabilitation, some issues and implications', *Justice of the Peace*, 16 July.

Bean, V. (1975), 'The juvenile court in transition', M.Phil. thesis, University of Nottingham (unpublished).

Bean, V. (1976), 'In whose best interests?' *Family Law*, vol. VI, no. 4.

Bellaby, P. (1977), *The Sociology of Comprehensive Schooling*, Methuen.

Bellamy, E. (1951), *Looking Backward 2000–1887*, Random House.

Benevelo, L. (1967), *The Origins of Modern Town Planning*, Routledge & Kegan Paul.

Bernstein, B. (1975), *Class Codes and Control*, vols I and III, Routledge & Kegan Paul.

Bernstein, B. and Davies, B. (1969), 'Some sociological comments on Plowden', in R. S. Peters (ed.), *Perspectives on Plowden*, Routledge & Kegan Paul.

Berry, F. (1974), *Housing – the Great British Failure*, Charles Knight.

Beveridge, W. H. (1944), *Full Employment in a Free Society*, Allen & Unwin.

Blackstone, T. (1971), *A Fair Start*, Allen Lane.

Booth, C. (1892), *Life and Labour of the People of London*, Macmillan.

Bottomley, A. K. (1973), *Decisions in the Penal Process*, Martin Robertson.

Bottoms, A. E. (1974), 'On the decriminalization of the English juvenile court', in R. G. Hood (ed.), *Crime, Criminology and Public Policy*, Heinemann.

Bourdillon, F. C. (ed.) (1945), *Voluntary Social Services*, Methuen.

Bowlby, J. and Fry, M. (1955), *Child Care and the Growth of Love*, Penguin.

Bradley, I. (1978), 'The centre of Tory thinking', *The Times*, 13 February.

Briggs, A. (1964), *The Listener*, 27 February.

Brown, R. G. S. (1973), *The Changing National Health Service*, Routledge & Kegan Paul.

Bruce, M. (1961), *The Coming of the Welfare State*, Batsford.

Bull, D. (ed.) (1971), *Family Poverty*, Duckworth.

Butler, J. R. (1973), *Family Doctors and Public Policy*, Routledge & Kegan Paul

Butterworth, E. and Holman, R. (eds) (1975), *Social Welfare in Modern Britain*, Fontana/Collins.

Buxton, R. (1970), *Local Government*, Penguin.

Byrne, D. *et al.* (1975), *The Poverty of Education*, Martin Robertson.

Carson, W. G. and Wiles, P. N. (eds) (1973), *Crime and Delinquency in Britain*, Martin Robertson.

Central Advisory Council on Education (1963), *Half our Future*.

Central Housing Advisory Committee (1969), *Council Houses, Purposes, Priorities and Procedures*, Ministry of Housing and Local Government.

Chambers, D. C. (1961), *The Workshop of the World*, Oxford University Press.

Cheeseman, D. *et al.* (1972), *Neighbourhood Care and Old People*, National Council for Social Service.

Cherry, G. (1972), *Urban Change and Planning*, Foulis.

Child Poverty Action Group (1975), *Unemployment: the Facts*.

Coates, K. and Silburn, R. L. (1970), 'Education in Poverty', in D. Rubinstein and C. Stoneman, *Education for Democracy*, Penguin.

Cochrane, A. L. (1972), *Effectiveness and Efficiency*, Nuffield Provincial Hospitals Trust.

Community Development Project (1977), *The Costs of Industrial Change*, CDP.

Community Development Project (1977a), *Gilding the Ghetto – the State and the Poverty Experiments*, CDP.

Cooper, M. H. (1973), *Social Policy: A Survey of Recent Developments*, Basil Blackwell.

Cox, C. B. and Dyson, A. E. (eds) (1969), *Black Paper One*, Critical Quarterly Society.

Crosland, C. A. R. (1956), *The Future of Socialism*, Cape.

Crosland, C. A. R. (1974), *Socialism Now*, Cape.

Cullingworth, J. B. (1976), *Town and Country Planning in Britain*, 6th edn, Allen & Unwin.

Davidoff, P. (1965), 'Advocacy and pluralism in planning', *Journal of American Institute of Planners*, November.

de Kadt, E. (1976), 'Wrong priorities in health', *New Society*, 3 June.

DHSS (1975), *Better Services for the Mentally Ill*.

DHSS (1976), *Priorities for Health and Personal Social Services in England*.

DHSS (1976), *Sharing Resources for Health in England*.

DHSS (1977), *The Way Forward: Priorities in Health and Social Services*.

DHSS (1978), *The Elderly at Home*.

DOE (1977), *Unequal City*, HMSO.

DOE (1977), *Inner London, Policies for Dispersal and Balance*, HMSO.

DOE (1977), *Change and Decay*, HMSO.

Devlin, Sir P. (1966), *Trial by Jury*, University Paperbacks.

Doll, R. (1967), *Prevention of Cancer: Pointers for Epidemiology*, Nuffield Provincial Hospitals Trust.

Donnison, D. V. (1967), *The Government of Housing*, Penguin.

Donnison, D. V. and Eversley, D. (eds) (1975), *London: Patterns, Problems and Policies*, Heinemann.

Donnison, D. V. *et al.* (1975), *Social Policy and Administration Revisited*, Allen & Unwin.

Dubos, R. (1968), *Man, Medicine and Environment*, Pall Mall Press.

Durant, E. (1939), *Watling*, P. S. King & Sons.

Durkheim, E. (1956), *Education and Sociology*, Free Press.

Durkheim, E. (1964), *The Rules of Sociological Method*, Free Press.

Eckstein, H. H. (1959), *The English Health Service*, Oxford University Press.

Eckstein, H. H. (1960), *Pressure Group Politics*, Allen & Unwin.

Eggleston, J. (1973), 'Decision making in the school curriculum: a conflict model', *Sociology*, vol. VII, 1973.

Eggleston, J. (1977), *The Sociology of the School Curriculum*, Routledge & Kegan Paul.

Environmental Studies, Centre for, *Annual Report*, 1975–6.

Environmental Studies, Centre for (1976), *Demographic Change and Social Policy, The Uncertain Future*, June.

Expenditure Committee, thirteenth report (1974), *New Towns*, HMSO.

Expert Committee on Compensation and Betterment (1942), Cmd 6386, HMSO.

Eyden, J. L. M. (1969), *Social Policy in Action*, Routledge & Kegan Paul.

Fallidi, A. (1973), *A Reader in Planning Theory*, Pergamon.

Fay, C. R. (1962), *Great Britain from Adam Smith to the Present Day*, 5th edn, Longmans.

Field, F. *et al.* (1977), *To Him who hath. A Study of Poverty and Taxation*, Penguin.

Florence, P. S. (1957), *Industry and the State*, Hutchinson.

Foley, D. (1960), 'British town planning, one ideology or three?', *British Journal of Sociology*, vol. II, no. 3.

Ford, J. (1975), 'The role of the building society manager in the urban stratification system', *Urban Studies*, vol. XII.

Fowler, G. *et al.* (eds) (1973), *Decision Making in British Education*, Heinemann.

Fox, S. (1974), 'The reform of juvenile justice: the child's right to punishment', *Juvenile Justice*, August.

Fraser, D. (1973), *The Evolution of the British Welfare State*, Macmillan.

Freund, K. (1977), *Labour and the Law*, Stevens.

Gauldie, E. (1974), *Cruel Habitations: a History of Working Class Housing, 1780–1818*, Allen & Unwin.

George, V. N. (1968), *Social Security, Beveridge and After*, Routledge & Kegan Paul.

George, V. N. (1973), *Social Security and Society*, Routledge & Kegan Paul.

George, V. N. and Wilding, P. (1976), *Ideology and Social Welfare*, Routledge & Kegan Paul.

Gilbert, B. (1966), *The Evolution of National Insurance in Great Britain, the Origins of the Welfare State*, Michael Joseph.

Gilbert, B. (1970), *British Social Policy, 1914–1939*, Batsford.

Giller, H. and Morris, A. (1977), 'Juvenile courts or children's hearings?' *LAG Bulletin*, October.

Glass, R. (1973), 'The evolution of planning', *International Social Science Journal*, vol. II, No. 3.

Goldthorpe, J. H. (1970), 'Social inequality and social integration in modern Britain', in D. Wedderburn (ed.), *Poverty, Inequality and the Class Structure*, Cambridge University Press.

Gostin, L. O. (1977), *A Human Condition*, MIND.

Hall, P. (1977), *Reforming the Welfare; the Politics of Change in the Personal Social Services*, Heinemann.

Hall, P. *et al.* (1973), *The Containment of Urban England*, vols I and II, Allen & Unwin.

Halsey, A. H. (1972), *Educational Priority*, vol. I, Department of Education and Science.

Handler, J. (1973), *The Coercive Social Worker*, Rand McNally.

Hardiker, P. (1977), 'Social work ideologies in the probation service', *British Journal of Social Work*, vol. VII, no. 2.

Hardiker, P. (1978), 'The role of the probation officer in sentencing', in H. Parker, *Social Work in the Courts*, Arnold.

Hargreaves, D. H. (1967), *Social Relations in a Secondary School*, Routledge & Kegan Paul.

Harloe, M. (1975), *Swindon: a Town in Transition*, Heinemann.

Harloe, M. *et al.* (1974), *The Organization of Housing*, Heinemann.

Harris, A. (1971), *The Handicapped and Impaired in Britain*, Social Survey Division of the Office of Population Census and Surveys.

Hayward, J. and Watson, M. (eds) (1975), *Planning, Politics and Public Policy: the British, French, and Italian Experience*, Cambridge University Press.

HMSO (1940), *Royal Commission on the Distribution of the Industrial Population*, Cmd 6153 (Barlow Commission).

HMSO (1942), *Committee on Land Utilisation in Rural Areas*, Cmd 6378 (Scott Report).

HMSO (1942), *Rehabilitation and Resettlement of Disabled Persons*, Cmd 6415 (Tomlinson Committee).

HMSO (1942), *Social Insurance and Allied Services*, Cmd 6404 (Beveridge Report).

HMSO (1942/3), House of Commons Select Committee on National Expenditure, 19, *Health and Welfare of Women in War Factories*, Third Report.

HMSO (1945), Ministry of Labour and National Service, *Juvenile Employment Service* (Ince Committee).

HMSO (1946), *The New Towns Committee Final Report* Cmd 6876, (Reith Report).

HMSO (1946), *Report of the Care of Children Committee*, Cmd 6922.

HMSO (1944–6), *Royal Commission on Equal Pay*, Cmd 6937.

HMSO (1952), *Training for Skill. Recruitment and Training for Young Workers in Industry*, report by a subcommittee of the National Joint Advisory Council (Carr Committee).

HMSO (1957), *Report of the Royal Commission on the Law relating to Mental Illness and Mental Deficiency*, Cmnd 169.

HMSO (1959), *Report of the Working Party on Social Workers in the Local Authority Health and Welfare Services*.

HMSO (1960), *Report of the Committee on Children and Young Persons*, Cmnd 1191.

HMSO (1961), *Homes for Today and Tomorrow*, report of the sub-committee of the Central Housing Advisory Committee.

HMSO (1963), *The North East*, Cmnd 2206.

HMSO (1964), *Ministry of Housing and Local Government, The South East Study*.

HMSO (1965), *The Future Development of the Youth Employment Service*, report of a working party of the National Youth Employment Council.

HMSO (1965), *The Child, the Family and the Young Offender*, Cmnd 2742.

HMSO (1967), *Children and their Primary Schools*, Central Advisory Council for Education (Plowden Report).

HMSO (1968), *Report of the Committee on Local Authority and Allied Personal Social Services*, Cmnd 3703 (Seebohm Report).

HMSO (1968), *Children in Trouble*, Cmnd 3601.

HMSO (1969), Ministry of Housing and Local Government, *People and Planning* (Skeffington Report).

HMSO (1969), *Digest of Health Statistics*.

HMSO (1969), *People in Prison*, Cmnd 4214.

HMSO (1971), Hospital Advisory Service, *Annual Report for 1969/70*.

HMSO (1971), *Better Services for the Mentally Handicapped*, Cmnd 4683.

HMSO (1972), *Report of the Committee of Enquiry into Whittingham Hospital*, Cmnd 4861.

HMSO (1972), *Report of the Departmental Committee on the Adoption of Children*, Cmnd 5107.

HMSO (1973), *Widening the Choice – the Next Steps in Housing*, Cmnd 5280.

HMSO (1974), *Report of the Committee of Enquiry into South Ockendon Hospital*.

HMSO (1974), *Report of the Advisory Council on the Treatment of Offenders; The Young Adult Offender* (Younger Committee).

HMSO (1974), *Better Pensions*, Cmnd 5713.

HMSO (1975), *Criminal Statistics*, Cmnd 6566.

HMSO (1976), *A Review of the Mental Health Act (1959)*.

HMSO (1976), *Social Trends*.

HMSO (1976), *Criminal Statistics*, Cmnd 6909.

HMSO (1976), *Report on the Work of the Prison Department*, Cmnd 6884.

HMSO (1976/7), *Fit for the Future, Report of the Committee on Child Health Services*, Cmnd 6684.

HMSO (1977), *Report of the Committee of Enquiry on Industrial Democracy*, Cmnd 6706 (Bullock Committee).

HMSO (1977), *Housing Policy, A Consultative Document*, Cmnd 6851.

HMSO (1977), *Policy for the Inner Cities*, Cmnd 6845.

HMSO (1977), *Health and Personal Social Services Statistics for England*.

HMSO (1977), *General Household Survey (1974)*.

Heywood, J. S. (1959), *Children in Care*, Routledge & Kegan Paul.

Hill, M. J. (1973), *Men out of Work*, Cambridge University Press.

Hill, M. J. (1974), *Policies for the Unemployed*, CPAG.

Hobsbaum. E. J. (1968), *Industry and Empire*, Weidenfeld & Nicolson.

Hogarth, J. (1971), *Sentencing as a Human Process*, Toronto University Press.

Home Office (1976), *Community Development Projects, Profits against Housing*, The Urban Deprivation Unit.

Hood, R. G. (1975), 'The case against executive control over time in custody', *Criminal Law Review*, October.

Hood, R. G. and Sparks, R. F. (1970), *Key Issues in Criminology*, Weidenfeld & Nicolson.

Howard, E. (1965), *Garden Cities of Tomorrow*, Faber.

Hutchins, B. L. (1912), *Robert Owen*, Fabian Society (Biographical Series no. 2).

Illich, I. (1975), *Medical Nemesis*, Calder & Boyars.

Jacobs, J. (1964), *The Death and Life of Great American Cities*, Penguin.

Jencks, C. *et al.*(1972), *Inequality: A Reassessment of the Effect of Family and Schooling in America*, Basic Books.

Jones, H. (1965), *Crime in a Changing Society*, Penguin.

Jones, K. (1960), *Mental Health and Social Policy*, Routledge & Kegan Paul.

Jones, K. (1975), *A History of the Mental Health Services*, Routledge & Kegan Paul.

Karabel, J. and Halsey, A. H. (1977), *Power and Ideology in Education*, Oxford University Press.

Keddie, N. (ed.) (1973), *Tinker, Tailor . . . the Myth of Cultural Deprivation*, Penguin.

Kincaid, J. (1973), *Poverty and Equality in Britain*, Penguin.

King, R. (1970), 'The head teacher and his authority', in B. Allen (ed.), *Headship in the 1970s*, Blackwell.

King, R. D. and Elliott, K. W. (1977), *Albany, Birth of a Prison – End of an Era*, Routledge & Kegan Paul.

Kirkham, G. B. (1908), *Philanthropy and the State*, P. S. King & Son.

Kogan, M. (1973), 'The function of the Central Advisory Council in educational change', in G. Fowler (ed.) *Decision Making in British Education*, Heinemann.

Kogan, M. (1975), *Educational Policy Making : A Study of Interest Groups and Parliament*, Allen & Unwin.

Kogan, M. and van der Eyken, W. (1973), *County Hall*, Penguin.

Lacey, C. (1970), *Hightown Grammar*, Manchester University Press.

Lafitte, F. (1962), inaugural lecture, University of Birmingham.

Lambert, J. *et al.* (1975), *Neighbourhood Politics and Housing Opportunities*, Centre for Environmental Studies.

Lambert, C. and Weir, D. (eds) (1975), *Cities in Modern Britain*, Fontana.

Lawton, D. (1977), *Education and Social Justice*, Sage Publications.

Lees, D. (ed.) (1974), *Impairment, Disability and Handicap*, Heinemann.

Lemert, E. (1967), *Human Deviance, Social Problems and Social Control*, Prentice-Hall.

Levin, P. (1976), *Government and the Planning Process*, Allen & Unwin.

Lister, R. (1975), *Reform of Social Security*, CPAG.

Little, A. and Westergaard, J. (1964), 'The trend of class differences in educational opportunity in England and Wales', *British Journal of Sociology*, December.

Lynes, T. (1974), 'Policy on social security', in M. Young (ed.) *Poverty Report*, Temple Smith.

MacDonagh, O. (1958), 'The 19th century revolution in government: a reappraisal', *Historical Journal*, vol. I.

McGregor, O. R. (1961), *Sociology and Welfare*, Sociological Review Monograph No. 4, July.

McKay, A. *et al.* (1973), 'Consumers and social services departments', *Social Work Today*, vol. IV, no. 16.

McKeown, T. (1976), *The Modern Rise in Population*, Arnold.

McKeown, T. (1976), *The Role of Medicine. Dream, Mirage or Nemesis?*, Nuffield Provincial Hospitals Trust.

McLoughlin, B. (1973), *Control and Urban Planning*, Faber.

MacLure, J. S. (1965), *Educational Documents, England and Wales*, Methuen.

Marriott, O. (1967), *The Property Boom*, Hamish Hamilton.

Marris P. and Rein, M. (1974), *Dilemmas of Social Reform*, Penguin.

Marsh, D. C. (1950), *National Insurance and Assistance in Great Britain*, Pitman.

Marsh, D. C. (1964), *The Future of the Welfare State*, Penguin.

Marsh, D. C. (1965), *An Introduction to the Study of Social Administration*, Routledge & Kegan Paul.

Marshall, T. H. (1963), *Sociology at the Crossroads*, Heinemann.

Marshall, T. H. (1965), *Social Policy*, Hutchinson.

Marshall, T. H. (1972), 'Value problems of welfare capitalism', *Journal of Social Policy*, vol. I, no. 1.

Martin, F. M. (1975), 'Social factors in the aetiology of mental illness', in *Aspects of the Social Care of the Mentally Ill*, BASW.

Matza, D. (1964), *Delinquency and Drift*, Wiley.

May, D. (1971), 'Delinquency control and the treatment model', *British Journal of Criminology*, vol. XI.

Miliband, R. (1974), 'Politics and poverty' in D. Wedderburn (ed.) *Poverty, Inequality and the Class Structure*, Cambridge University Press.

More, H. (1925), *Selected Letters Reprinted*, John Lane, The Bodley Head.

Morris, W. (1891), *News from Nowhere, or an Epoch of Rest*, London.

Morrison, A. and McIntyre, D. (1971), *Schools and Socialization*, Penguin.

Murie, A. *et al*. (1976), *Housing Policy and the Housing System*, Allen & Unwin.

Musgrave, P. W. (1968), *Society and Education in England since 1800*, Methuen.

Nash, R. (1973), *Classrooms Observed*, Routledge & Kegan Paul.

National Community Development Project (1974), *Interproject Report*, CDP.

Navarro, V. (1976), *Medicine under Capitalism*, Croom Helm.

Neill, J. E. *et al*. (1973), 'Reactions to integration', *Social Work Today*, vol. IV, no. 15.

Nevitt, A. A. (1966), *Housing, Taxation and Subsidies*, Nelson.

Packman, J. (1975), *The Child's Generation*, Basil Blackwell & Martin Robertson.

Pahl, R. (1970), *Patterns of Urban Life*, Longmans.

Pahl, R. (1976), *Whose City?*, Penguin.

Parker, J. (1975), *Social Policy and Citizenship*, Macmillan.

Pelling, H. (1963), *A History of Trade Unionism*, Penguin.

Perry, F. (1974), *Information for the Court*, Institute of Criminology, Cambridge.

Peterson, W. (1968), 'The ideological origins of Britain's new towns', *Journal of American Institute of Planners*, May.

Pickvance, C. (ed.) (1976), *Urban Sociology*, Tavistock.

Pinker, R. (1971), *Social Theory and Social Policy*, Heinemann.

Piven, F. F. and Cloward, R. A. (1972), *Regulating the Poor*, Tavistock.

Planning Advisory Group (1976), *The Future of Development Plans*, HMSO (Page Report).

Powles, J. (1973), 'On the limitations of modern medicine', *Science, Medicine and Man*, vol. I.

Prins, H. (1973), *Criminal Behaviour*, Pitman.

Purdom, C. B. (1949), *The Building of Satellite Towns*, Dent.

Radzinowicz, L. (1964), 'The criminal in society', *Journal of the Royal Society of Arts*, vol. cxii.

Radzinowicz, L. and Wolfgang, M. (1977), *Crime and Justice*, (3 vols), revised edn, Basic Books.

Ratcliffe, J. (1976), *Land Policy*, Hutchinson.

Rein, M. (1970), *Social Policy, Issues of Choice and Change*, Random House.

Reisman, D. A. (1977), *Richard Titmuss: Welfare and Society*, Heinemann.

Robb, B. (1967), *Aid for the Elderly in Government Institutions. Sans Everything: a Case to Answer*, Nelson.

Roberts, D. (1968), *Victorian Origins of the British Welfare State*, New Haven.

Robinson, P. (1976), *Education and Poverty*, Methuen.

Robson, W. A. (1976), *Welfare State and Welfare Society: Illusion and Reality*, Allen & Unwin.

Rowbottom, R. (1974), *Social Services Departments, Developing Patterns of Work and Organization*, Heinemann.

Rowntree, S. (1901), *Poverty: a Study of Town Life*, Macmillan.

Royal Town Planning Institute (1971), *Town Planners and their Future: a Discussion Paper*, RTPI.

Rubinstein, D. and Simon, B. (1969), *The Evolution of the Comprehensive School*, Routledge & Kegan Paul.

Rutter, M. and Madge, N. (1976), *Cycles of Disadvantage*, Heinemann.

Ryall, R. (1974), 'Delinquency: the problem for treatment', *Social Work Today*, vol. V, no. 4, May.

Sainsbury, S. (1968), *Registered Disabled*, G. Bell & Sons.

Saville, J. (1975), 'The Welfare State: An historical approach', in E. Butterworth and R. Holman (eds), *Social Welfare in Modern Britain*, Fontana.

Schur, E. M. (1965), *Crimes without Victims*, Prentice-Hall.

Schur, E. M. (1973), *Radical Non-Intervention*, Prentice-Hall.

Shanas, E. *et al.* (1968), *Old people in Three Industrial Societies*, Routledge & Kegan Paul.

Sharpe, L. I. (1975), 'Innovation and change in British land-use planning', in J. Haywood and M. Watson (eds) *Planning, Politics and Public Policy; The British, French and Italian Experience*, Cambridge University Press.

Silver, H. (ed.) (1973), *Equal Opportunity in Education*, Methuen.

Simon, B. (1965), *Education and the Labour Movement, 1870–1920*, Lawrence & Wishart.

Simon, B. (1974), *The Politics of Educational Reform, 1920–1940*, Lawrence & Wishart.

Sinfield, A. (1970), 'Poor and out of work in South Shields', in P. Townsend, *The Concept of Poverty*, Heinemann.

Smith, D. (1977), *The Facts of Racial Disadvantage*, Penguin.

Social Policy, Centre for Studies in (1974), Publications list.

Social Policy, Centre for Studies (1977), *What the Centre is and does*, September.

Sparks, R. F. (1969), 'The depraved are not just deprived', *New Society*, July.

Stewart, M. (ed.) (1972), *The City: Problems of Planning*, Penguin.

Swift, D. F. (1968), 'Social class and educational adaptation', in H. J. Butcher and H. B. Pont (eds) *Educational Research in Britain*, London University Press.

Tawney, R. H. (1926), *Religion and the Rise of Capitalism*, John Murray.

Tawney, R. H. (1961), *The Acquisitive Society*, Fontana.

Taylor, D. (1977), *Physical Impairment: Social Handicap*, OHE.
Taylor, I., Walton, P. and Young, J. (1973), *The New Criminology*,
   Routledge & Kegan Paul.
Taylor, I., Walton, P., and Young, J. (1975), *Critical Criminology*,
   Routledge & Kegan Paul.
Timms, N. and Watson, D. (eds) (1976), *Talking about Welfare:
   Readings in Philosophy and Social Policy*, Routledge & Kegan Paul.
Titmuss, R. M. (1950), *Problems of Social Policy*, HMSO and
   Longmans.
Titmuss, R. M. (1968), *Commitment to Welfare*, Allen & Unwin.
Titmuss, R. M. (1970), *The Gift Relationship*, Allen & Unwin.
Titmuss, R. M. (1974), *Social Policy: an Introduction*, Allen & Unwin.
Tizard, J. *et al.* (1975), *Varieties of Residential Experience*, Routledge &
   Kegan Paul.
Townsend, P. (ed.) (1970), *The Concept of Poverty*, Heinemann.
Townsend, P. (1974), 'Inequality and the health service', *Lancet*, vol. I.
Townsend, P. (1974), 'Poverty as relative deprivation, resources and
   style of living', in D. Wedderburn (ed.) *Poverty, Inequality and Class
   Structure*, Cambridge University Press.
Townsend, P. (1976), *Sociology and Social Policy*, Penguin.
Tudor Hart, J. (1971), 'The inverse care law', *Lancet*, vol. I.
Turner, J. F. and Fitcher, R. (1972), *Freedom To build*, Macmillan.
Tyler, W. (1977), *The Sociology of Educational Inequality*, Methuen.
Wedderburn, K. W. (1965), *The Worker and the Law*, Penguin.
Wedderburn, D. (1965), 'Facts and theories in the welfare state',
   Socialist Register.
Weir, S. (1976), *Roof* (Shelter's housing magazine), vol. I, no. 4, July.
Westergaard, J. and Resler, H. (1975), *Class in a Capitalist Society*,
   Heinemann.
Wheeler, S. *et al.* (1968), 'Agents of delinquent control', in S. Wheeler
   (ed.), *Controlling Delinquents*, Wiley.
Wigham, E. (1976), *Department of Employment Gazette*, March.
Wilkins, L. T. (1958), 'A small comparative study of the results of
   probation', *British Journal of Delinquency*, vol. VIII.
Willcocks, A. J. (1967), *The Creation of the National Health Service*,
   Routledge & Kegan Paul.
Women's Group on Public Welfare (1948), *The Neglected Child and his
   Family*, Oxford University Press.
Young, A. F. (1968), *Social Services in British Industry*, Routledge &
   Kegan Paul.
Young, M. F. D. (1971), *Knowledge and Control*, Collier-Macmillan.
Young, T. (1934), *Becontree and Dagenham*, the Pilgrim Trust.

Index

Abercrombie, Patrick, 67, 68
Advisory Conciliation and Arbitration Service, 32, 55
Age Concern, 209
Albemarle, Lady, 39
American Friends Service Committee, 247
Anglo-American Council on Productivity, 44
Area Health Authorities, 155
Attendance Allowance, 171, 196

Babst, D. W. and Mannering, J. W., 238
Barlow Commission, *see* Royal Commission on the Distribution of the Industrial Population
Bean, Philip, T., 243, 244, 248
Bean, Valerie W., 248, 253
Beggars and Vagabonds, Act Concerning Punishment of (1531), 8, 194
Bellamy, Edward, 64
Bentham, Jeremy, 11, 14
Bernstein, Basil, 132, 133, 136, 138
Bevan, Aneurin, 111, 142, 143, 152, 157
Beveridge Report, 167, 259
Beveridge, William, 33, 51, 142, 168
Bevin, Ernest, 33, 34, 36
Blind Persons Act 1920, 195
Blind, Royal Commission on, 195

Board, Race Relations, 47
Board of Trade, 33, 37, 38
Booth, Charles, 19, 23, 177
Bottomley, A. Keith, 230
Bottoms, A. E., 250
Boyle, Edward, 117, 127
Bruce, Maurice, 2, 10, 259, 315
Building societies, 99, 101, 103, 104
Bullock, Lord, 56

Cadbury, 31
Careers Advisory Service, 37, 38
Carr, Sir Robert, 45
CBI, 45
Central Advisory Councils for Education, 123, 127, 130, 137
Central Council for Education and Training in Social Work, 260
Central government, 117, 121, 122, 123, 128
Chadwick, E., 14, 16, 91
Charity Organisation Society, 3
Child Benefits, 175, 182
Child Poverty Action Group, 182, 183
Children's Act (1948), 213
Children's Act (1975), 217
Children and Young Persons Acts: (1933), 212, 249; (1963), 215; (1969), 216, 218, 249, 250
Children's Charter, 212
Children in Trouble, 249, 250, 252
Chronic sick, 146, 149, 156, 161

Chronically Sick and Disabled Persons Act (1970), 197
Churchill, Winston, 33, 259
Cities: Birmingham, 94; Glasgow, 71; Health in, 61, 66; Inner city policies, 83–5; Liverpool, 84; London, 71–3, 77, 83–4, 85; Manchester, 61, 84; Newcastle, 85; nineteenth-century cities, 61–2, 66; provincial cities, 83; urban research, 85–6
Classicism, 240–1
Combination Acts (1799 and 1800), 29
Committee on Land Utilisation in Rural Areas (1942), 68
Commission for Racial Equality, 48
Community Care, 148
Community Development Project, 81–2, 97
Community Health Councils, 155
Community Relations Commission, 47, 48
Community Work, 39
Conciliation Act (1896), 32
Conservative Party, 127
Consolidated Factories Act (1901), 31
Consultative Document on Priorities, 148
Contracts of Employment Acts (1963 and 1972), 52
Coram, Capt. P., 257
Council housing, 93–4, 105–10
Council for Preservation of Rural England, 67
Courts (and juvenile), 230–1, 249
Crime: as bad timing, 227–8; damage, 225–6; extent of, 225–30; hidden, 228–9; juvenile, 248–53; living with, 229; responses to, 224; and Social Policy, 223–4; as a social problem, 223; see also offences
Crosland, A., 6, 117
Curriculum, 117, 119, 122, 123, 125, 133, 156, 157
Curtis, Myra, 212

Darwin, Charles, 16
Devlin, Sir, P., 231
Designated employment, 40
Disabled Persons (Employment) Act (1944), 40, 51, 196
Disablement Resettlement Officer, 40

Disablement, 39
Discrimination, 46, 47, 48
Distribution of Industry Act 1945, 69
Doctors, 145, 147, 148, 155; see also General Practitioners
Domiciliary services, 146, 147, 153, 156
Donnison, David, 110, 111
Donovan, Lord, 54
Durkheim, Emile, 223, 224

Education: adult, 135; aims of, 115–16, 135, 137; Choice of Employment Act (1910), 37, 38; content of, 136; cost of, 115; elementary, 118; functions of, 115–17; further, 125; higher, 123, 125, 136; nursery, 135; policy, 117, 119, 120, 133, 135; post-elementary, 118; primary, 119; secondary, 117, 118, 119, 122, 125, 126, 128, 136; social implications of, 128–35; social justice and, 136; state system of, 115, 118, 119, 137, 138; system of, 121, 123, 124, 128, 131, 132, 134, 135, 137
Education Acts: (1902), 118; (1944), 117, 118, 119; (1976), 122
Education and Science, Department of, 123
Educational Priority Areas, 133–35
Elderly, 149
Employment, Department of, 32, 38
Employment Exchanges, 37
Employment Medical Advisory Services Act (1972), 43
Employment and Productivity, Department of, 34
Employment, Secretary of State for, 34
Employment Service Agency, 34, 35, 39
Employment and Training Act (1973), 34, 38, 39
Environment, 157, 158
Environmental Studies, Centre for, 1
Equality: 136; of opportunities, 35
Ergonomists, 31
Essential work orders, 36
Expert Committee on Compensation and Betterment (Uthwatt Committee), 68–9

Factory Act (1802), 28, 29; (1833), 29; (1961), 32, 34, 41, 42, 48, 51
Factory Inspectors, 29, 34, 42
Fair Deal at Work, 54
Families, one-parent, 181
Family income supplement, 175, 176, 182
Fatigue, industrial, 36
Fox, Sandford, 252, 253

Garden cities: 63–4, 67; Letchworth, 64; Welwyn, 64
Garden City and Town Planning Association, 64
Gauldie, E., 92
General Household Survey, 146, 160
General practitioners, 144–7, 153, 154; *see also* Doctors
General Strike, 32
George, Victor, and Wilding, Paul, 57
Giller, H., and Morris, A., 249, 251
Graduated contribution, 172

Halsey, A. H., 134, 135, 136
Handicapped, Survey of (1971), 193
Handler, Joel, 242
Hanway, Jonas, 10, 257
Hardiker, Pauline, 241
Harloe, M., 93, 98
Head teacher, 123, 124
Health, 145, 148, 157, 158, 159, 161, 162
Health centre, 146
Health, Department of, and Social Security, 152, 155
Health, Medical Officer of, 144
Health, Ministry of, 195
Health and Morals of Apprentices Act (1802), 29
Health and Munition Workers Committee, 35, 37
Health and Safety, 41
Health and Safety Commission, 43
Health and Safety Expenditure, 43
Health and Safety at Work Act (1974), 42, 52
Health services, 145–6, 154, 158
Hill, Octavia, 91
Hogarth, John, 246
Home Office, 34
Hood, Roger, 238, 245
Hospital Advisory Service, 152
Hospitals, 144–56

Houghton Committee, 217
Housing, access for, 97–8, 102–4, 108–10
Housing Acts: general, 65; Cross, 63; Torrens (1868), 63
Housing finance, 94–7, 98–101, 105–7
Housing need, 89–92
Housing standards, 97, 101–2, 107–8
Howard, Ebenezer, 63–5
Howard, John, 10, 257

Ince, Sir Godfrey, 38
Incrementalism, 123, 127
Industrial Council, 32
Industrial democracy, 55, 56
Industrial Disablement Benefits, 174–5
Industrial Health Research Board, 36
Industrial Injuries Act (1946), 30, 51
Industrial Injuries Scheme, 173
Industrial Organisation and Development Act (1947), 44
Industrial Psychology, 36
Industrial Rehabilitation Units, 41
Industrial Relations Act (1947), 53, 54
Industrial Revolution, 28
Industrial Training Act, 43, 45, 52
Industrial Tribunals, 50, 53, 55
Industrial welfare, 31
Industry Bill, 55
Inequality, 129, 137
Inner city, *see under* City
Inner Urban Areas Act (1978), 84–5
In Place of Strife, 54
International Labour Organisation, 34, 49
Invalid Care Allowance, 171, 196
Invalidity benefit, 170

Job Centre, 35
Job creation, 39
Joint consultation, 33
Joint Production Committee, 33
Jones, Howard, 228
Justice, juvenile, 248–53
Juvenile courts, *see* Courts

Kilbrandon Report, 215
Kingsley, Charles, 63
Kogan, Maurice, 117, 121, 122, 123, 126, 128, 135

Labour Exchanges, 33
Labour Exchanges Act (1909), 19, 32, 37
Labour government, 119, 127
Labour, Ministry of, 33, 34, 37, 38, 40
Labour movement, 31, 116, 118, 126
Lafitte, François, 4
Lambert, J., 109
Land: betterment, 68–9, 70; compensation, 68–9, 70; compulsory purchase, 70; legislation, 69
Learner in education, 117, 136
Leicestershire, 126
Legal rules, 224
Lemert, Edwin, 247
Less eligibility, 12
Llewelyn-Smith, Herbert, 33
Lloyd George, David, 258
Local Authority, 118, 121, 122, 123, 128, 155
Local Authority (Social Services) Act (1970), 191, 219
Local Government Act (1972), 221
Local plans, 73–7
London School of Sociology and Economics, 3
London School of Economics and Political Science, 3

Malthus, T. R., 11
Manpower Services Commission, 34, 35, 39, 41, 45, 46
Marshall, T. H., 4, 6, 20
Maternity benefit, 171
Matza, D. 227, 252, 253
May, D. 241, 242
Means tests, 143
Medical technology, 156, 158
Medicine, 149, 150, 157, 158
Mental Health Act (1959), 204
Mental Illness, 150, 151, 152
Mentally sick, 149
Mental Treatment Act (1930), 202
Middle class, 118
Midwifery, 147
Mines and Quarries Acts (1954, 1969), 42
Ministry of Labour, 33, 34, 37, 38–40
Mobility allowance, 196
Mond-Turner talks, 32
More, Hannah, 11

Morris, William, 86

National Advisory Council for the Employment of Disabled People, 41
National Assistance, 168
National Assistance Act (1948), 8, 196
National Corporation for the Care of Old People, 209
National Economic Development Council, 33
National Health Insurance, 143
National Health Service, 30, 141–8, 152–62
National Health Service Act (1946), 141, 142, 154, 203
National Health Service (Reorganisation) Act (1973), 221
National Industrial Conference, 32
National Insurance Acts: (1911), 40; (1946), 196
National Insurance (Industrial Injuries) Act (1946), 196
National Service, 34
Nevitt, A. A., 95
New Towns, see Towns
Niner, Pat, 109
Norwood Report, 119, 136
Nurses, 145

Oastler, Richard, 30
Offences: 226; cleared up, 225, 226, 229; indictable, 225, 230, 237; non-indictable, 230
Offices, Shops and Railway Premises Act (1963), 42
Owen, Robert, 2, 30, 37, 62, 86
Owner-occupation, 98–104

Pahl, Ray, 85, 102
Parkinson's Law, 261
Parliamentary Debates, 53
Participation, 56, 77–81
Participation (Skeffington Report), 80–1
Partnership scheme, see Cities
Peel, Robert, 30
Penal system, 231–8, 239–48
Pensions, Ministry of, 40
Perry, Fred, 244
Personal Social Services Council, 221, 260
Personnel Management, 30, 31, 36, 37

Planning Advisory Group, 72
Planning blight, 80
Planning Institute, Royal Town, 79
Planning profession, 78–9
Plowden Report, 123, 130, 133, 134
Pluralism, 121, 122, 127
Poor Laws, 2, 38, 168, 194, 259
Population, 60–2, 71–2, 83
Positive discrimination, 81–2, 84–5, 120, 134
Poverty, relative, 159, 178
Preventive health services, see Health services
Prison: 231, 235, 236–7; population, 237, 238–9; rules, 234–5
Private practice, 143
Private renting, 94–8
Private and Urban Development, 66, 71, 72, 83
Probation and after-care, 231
Public Health, 91, 92
Public Health Act (1848), 15, 62
Psychology, industrial, 36

Queen Elizabeth's Training College, 40
Quota scheme, 40–1

Race, discrimination, 46, 98, 110
Race Relations Acts: (1965), 46–7; (1968), 47–8; (1976), 48, 50
Race Relations Board, 47, 48, 50
Radzinowicz, Sir, L., 228, 247
Redundancy Payments Act (1965), 52
Regional Health Authorities, 155
Regional policies: general, 67, 82; Industrial Development certificates, 69, 83, 84; see also Barlow Commission
Register of Disabled Persons, 40
Rehabilitation, 40, 41
Remploy, 41
Reith, Lord, 68, 70
Relief of the Poor Act (1601), 8
Resources Allocation Working Party, 153
Revolution, Industrial, 28
Robbins Report, 130, 137
Rowntree, Seebohm. 3, 31
Royal Commission on the Distribution of the Industrial Population (1940), (Barlow Commission), 67–8
Royal Commission on Equal Pay, 49

Royal Commission on Labour, 32
Royal Commission on Trade Unions and Employers Associations, 54
Ruskin, J., 63
Ryall, R., 251

Safety representatives, 43
Saville, John, 7
Schools: 119, 130, 132, 134, 136, 137; comprehensive, 126, 127, 133, 135; council, 122, 123, 136; grammar, 118, 126, 127; public, 116, 118; secondary modern, 126
Schur, E., 229, 248
Scott, Committee, see Committee on Land Utilisation in Rural Areas (1942)
Seebohm, Frederick (Report), 219, 220
Select Committee on National Expenditure 36
Sentencing, 230–9
Sentences, in the penal system, 232–3, 234–5
Sex Discrimination Act (1975), 48–50
Shaftesbury, Lord, 30, 257
Shelter, 104
Sickness benefit, 170
Simon, J., 170
Skill Centres, 46
Smith, Adam, 11
Smith, Daniel J., 98, 110
Social administration, definition of study, 3
Social class, 159, 160, 162
Social Policy, Centre for Studies in, 1
Social policy, definition of, 4
Social Security Act (1975), 169
Social Security Benefits Act (1975), 170
Social Security (Pensions) Act (1975), 172
Social services, 4
Social structure, 120, 125, 131, 135
Social Work (Scotland) Act (1968), 220
Social Work Training, see Central Council for Education and Training in Social Work
Speenhamland system, 11
Standardised mortality ratios, 153, 160
Statute of Artificers (1563), 28, 43

Structure plans, 73–77, 82
Suburbs: garden, 65, 67; Dagenham, 66; ribbon development, 66; Watling, 66
Supplementary Benefit, 196

Tawney, R. H., 9
Taylor, Ian (and Walton, P., and Young, J.) 239, 248
Taxation, 141–4, 152
Teaching hospitals, 148, 150, 153
Thatcher, Margaret, 127
Titmuss, Richard, 4, 6, 141, 142, 193, 259
Tomlinson Committee, 40
Town Development Act (1952), 71
Town planning, 92, 104, 105
Town Planning Acts: (1909), 65; (1919), 65; (1932), 62; (1947), 69–70, 72–3, 78; (1968), 73–7, 79, 82; (1969), 73; (1971), 73
Towns: Act (1946), 69, 70; Cumbernauld, 71; development corporation, 70–1, New, 70–1; Northampton, 72; Peterborough, 72; Stevenage, 70; see also Garden cities
Trade Board Act (1909), 32
Trade, Board of, 38
Trade Union Act (1871), 29, 53
Trade Union Council, 45
Training, 43
Training Boards, 45
Training Services Agency, 34, 35, 46
Training for skill, 45
Treatment model, 241–8
Truck Acts (1831, 1887, 1896 and 1940), 30
Turner, J. F. C., 90

Unemployed, 181

Unemployed Workmen Act (1905), 19, 33
Unemployment Assistance, 259
Unemployment Assistance Act (1934), 19
Unemployment Insurance Act (1911), 19
Universalism, 143, 153
Universities, 116, 117, 136
Uthwatt Committee, see Expert Committee on Compensation and Betterment

Vocational guidance, 38, 39

Wages Councils, 32, 50
War: First World, 35, 37, 40, 44, 49; Second World, 33, 34, 36, 37, 38, 40, 44, 49, 51
Way Forward, The, 148
Webb, Sidney and Beatrice, 3, 33
Welfare State, 2, 19, 20, 21, 51, 141
Wells, H. G., 64
Wheatley, John, 111
Wheeler, S., 246
Whitley Committees, 33
Widow's benefit, 172
Wigham, Eric, 32
Wilberforce, William, 257
Wilkins, L. T., 238
Wilson, Harold, 126
Women, 35, 46, 49
'Work experience', 39
Workhouses, 150
Working class, 116, 118, 130
Workmen's Compensation Acts (1897 and 1925), 30, 39

Young adult offenders, 245
Younghusband Report, 197
Youth Employment Executive, 38
Youth Employment Service, 38, 39